Blackness Visible

Also by Charles W. Mills:
The Racial Contract

Blackness Visible

Essays on Philosophy and Race

Charles W. Mills

Cornell University Press   Ithaca and London

First published 1998 by Cornell University
Press.

First printing, Cornell Paperbacks, 1998.

Printed in the United States of America.

Cornell University Press strives to utilize
environmentally responsible suppliers and
materials to the fullest extent possible in the
publishing of its books. Such materials
include vegetable-based, low-VOC inks and
acid-free papers that are also either recycled,
totally chlorine-free, or partly composed of
nonwood fibers.

Cloth printing 10 9 8 7 6 5 4 3 2 1
Paperback printing 10 9 8 7 6 5 4 3 2 1

Library of Congress Cataloging-in-
Publication Data

Mills, Charles W. (Charles Wade)
    Blackness visible : essays on philosophy
and race / Charles W. Mills.
        p.   cm.
    Includes index.
    ISBN 0-8014-3467-X (cloth : alk. paper).
— ISBN 0-8014-8471-5 (pbk. : alk paper)
    1. United States—Race Relations—
Philosophy. 2. Afro-American
philosophy. 3. Racism—United States—
Philosophy. 4. Afro-Americans—Race
identity. 5. Afrocentrism.   I. Title.
E185.615.M54   1998
305.8'00973—dc21   97-45768

Toward a better vision for the world

I am invisible, understand, simply because people refuse to see me ... because of a peculiar disposition of the eyes of those with whom I come in contact. A matter of the construction of their inner eyes.

—RALPH ELLISON, *INVISIBLE MAN*

Contents

Preface

Philosophy, like any other subject, has its own distinctive set of images, standard tropes, and classic scenes that help to define both what it is and, by implication, what it is not. These figures act as intellectual signposts, pointing us toward certain areas of investigation and away from others, shaping our conceptions of what counts as a respectable and legitimate topic of philosophical inquiry, indeed of what should be regarded as *philosophy* in the first place. One thinks of Plato's cave dwellers, blithely ignorant of the world above; Descartes in his study wondering whether other people exist; Locke's cobbler's soul passing into the body of the prince and so changing its personal identity; Kant's ideal Enlightenment contractarianism, in which raceless persons give each other equal respect; Hegel's triumphantly expanding World-Spirit; the lifeboat dilemma of having to choose between saving one's wife and saving the brilliant cancer researcher, between a morality of personal commitment and a morality of abstract welfare; the cognitive possibility that one is actually a brain in a vat being electronically fed a false picture of one's history and reality. And one gets a template, accordingly, of what the proper concerns of philosophy should be, an iconography of the acceptable and the unacceptable.

In many cases this directing of attention will be perfectly reasonable, indicating the existence of genuine disciplinary boundaries. But sometimes what purport to be objective definitions of the appropriate limits of the world of philosophical inquiry and authoritative pronouncements about what is conceptually interesting in that world have a more questionable provenance. Sometimes they arise out of the specific life-world and local interests of particular populations. Thus the seemingly universal view from nowhere may well be a view from somewhere; the magisterial voice from the heavens turns out to be broadcast from earth. And sometimes it is only through the emergence of alternative views and voices that one begins to appreciate how much of what had seemed genuinely universalistic was really particular. In the dazzle of their official illumination, the canonical images blind us to different possibilities.

The clearest example of this phenomenon is seen in new work on gender. One of the most exciting developments in philosophy over the second half of the twentieth century has been the growth of a feminist theory stimulated by the mass entry of women into the profession. New conceptual and theoretical philosophical horizons have been opened up, revealing realities that in a sense were always there but that were either not seen or not deemed worth mapping. The "maleness" of orthodox philosophy is now visible in a way that it was not before. Heterodox conceptualizations have thrown conventional assumptions into relief and raised questions about what previously seemed like unchallengeable verities.

There are welcome signs that parallel possibilities may be opening up around the question of race. We have witnessed a remarkable upsurge of interest in matters to do with race and African-American philosophy. Numerous books and anthologies (numerous by comparison with the past, that is) are forthcoming, and a new journal, the *Journal of Africana Philosophy*, is in the works. We are beginning to see how many old questions can be given a twist and how many new questions can be posed once the color line in Western philosophy is breached. There has always been an alternative, oppositional intellectual tradition in the West centered on the shaping reality of race, but for the most part it has been excluded from the academy in general and from philosophy in particular. (Lewis Gordon chides me here for an analytic chauvinism that makes generalizations about "philosophy" that are actually untrue, or at least far less true, of the Continental tradition.) Now, however, the situation may be on the verge of changing.

Such a change is certainly overdue. The "whiteness" of academic philosophy has long been a source of wonder and complaint to minorities. Among the humanities, it has been one of the most resistant to what have come to be called "multiculturalist" revisions. The very nature of the discipline seems to some practitioners to preclude such innovation: by virtue of its abstractness, philosophy supposedly *already* generally encompasses the human condition. As almost any introductory textbook can confirm, mainstream philosophy has no room for race as a reality that significantly affects in any way such traditional divisions of the field as metaphysics, epistemology, ethics, social and political philosophy, philosophy of law, history of philosophy. The writings of the classic Euro-American authors are treated simultaneously as canonical and as raceless and universal. To the extent that race is discussed, if it is discussed at all, it is usually within the severely restricted category of debates about affirmative action, in a subsection on applied ethics. It is taken for granted that the main debates—about personal identity, existential situations, criteria for epistemic justification, moral topographies, conceptions of the polity, theories of social explanation, jurisprudential disputes, and the evolution of Western philosophy itself—are not affected by race, that race has no implications for the characteristic framings, standard scenarios, and conventional theoretical mappings of these debates. Colorless and universal, they will be able to continue in the same way whether there is a significant nonwhite presence or not; indeed, a significant nonwhite presence is not really necessary, since such concerns are supposedly *already* subsumed within these seemingly abstract and all-encompassing categories.

For feminists, this line of argument is familiar. In the case of gender, it has famously come to be identified as the "just add women and stir" approach. The assumption is that it is merely a matter of equal semantic representation, an introduction of a few "she's" where previously there were only "he's" and a linguistic purging of openly sexist statements. There is little or no appreciation of the fact that, since gender exclusion has shaped these discourses, gender egalitarianism may require that they be rethought from the ground up. The case that those working on race need to make is that a recognition of the centrality of race in the encounter between Europe and the non-European world, and its social, economic, political, moral, and intellectual ramifications for both, may be similarly revolutionary in its implications for rethinking.

But making this case requires the overcoming of major conceptual obstacles. Why is race—in some respects so obvious—so hard for white philosophers to "see" theoretically? What is there about its patent visibility that makes it philosophically invisible? For an answer, I think we need to look both to the negative associations that "race" has developed in recent, more enlightened years and to the peculiar features of the discipline itself, above all the abstraction that seems to legitimate ignoring such characteristics as irrelevant.

Since its emergence as a major social category several hundred years ago, race has paradigmatically been thought of as "natural," a biological fact about human beings, and the foundation of putatively ineluctable hierarchies of intelligence and moral character. The discrediting of old-fashioned racism of this sort has made a truism in liberal intellectual circles of a claim that would once have seemed quite revolutionary: that race does not really exist. But if this is true, if indeed it is a mark of one's liberalism and sophistication to proclaim that it is true, one then naturally wonders as a white philosopher why blacks should think that developing a theory of race could be anything but a foredoomed enterprise. And an enterprise that is not pointless yet harmless, but rather one that seems to run the risk of becoming an inverted black version of traditional white-supremacist theory. So almost overnight race goes from being in the body to being in the head, and one shows one's liberal commitment to bringing about a color-blind society by acting as if it already exists, not seeing race at all, and congratulating oneself on one's lack of vision.

The response must be, then, that if this foundation for public policy is misguided, it is arguably little better as an aid to philosophical understanding. What needs to be shown — and what I try to show in this book — is that room has to be made for race as both real and unreal: that race can be ontological without being biological, metaphysical without being physical, existential without being essential, shaping one's being without being in one's shape.

But a discipline that conceives of itself as seeking out the most general truths about human beings may find it difficult to see any significance in issues centered on race. For philosophers in particular, a major conceptual barrier is that neither mainstream nor radical Western philosophy has much space for such a notion. On the one hand, in dealing with questions of being and the person, mainstream analytic philosophers tend to assume the isolated Cartesian individual, the presocial figure of contractarian theory. They abstract away from history and social process to get at ostensibly necessary and universal truths about people qua people, the deep eternalities of the human condition. On the other hand, in circles sympathetic to the notion of a *social* ontology, one that is contingent and relative, as in the Continental tradition, this intellectual space has been dominated by the class-based account of Marxist theory. So in neither case is there conceptual room for the notion of race as "deep" and "metaphysical." Since the idea of race as biology, race as destiny, has been discredited, it can't be an innate part of the human being. And since it's not class — part of a larger theory about class society (which is at least a familiar and, via Marxism, a well-explored category in Western theory) — it can't be part of a social ontology, either.

So the task of those working on race is to put race in quotes, "race," while still insisting that *nevertheless, it exists* (and moves people). This is part of the significance of the "critical" in contemporary critical race theory: to make plausible a social ontology neither essentialist, innate, nor transhistorical, but real enough for all that. And (as I argue in *The Racial Contract*) the most illuminating framework for defending this claim is, literally, a global one: the thesis that European expansionism in its various forms — expropriation, slavery, colonialism, settlement — brings race into existence as a global social reality, with the single most important conceptual division historically being that between "whites" and "nonwhites." Those termed *white* have generally had a civil, moral, and juridical standing that has lifted them above the other "races." They have been the expropriators; others have been the expropriated. They have been the slave owners; others have been the slaves. They have been the colonizers; others have been the colonized. They have been the settlers; others have been the displaced. So one gets a formal ontological partitioning in the population of the planet, signified by "race."

Now this is not, to say the least, a standard framework within which to approach Western philosophy. Such matters, it will be felt, are better left to history or sociology. What does this have to do with the standard concerns of the subject, with those classic, timeless images and tropes cited at the beginning? But the claim is that even the seemingly rarefied and remote realm of philosophy has reflected its embeddedness in this binary universe, manifested in conceptions of the person, the existential plight of human beings, the appropriate epistemic norms for cognizers, the descriptions of and prescriptions for the polity. Within this social and historical framework, "race" becomes significant. Indeed, Westerners *created* race in the first place, by demarcating themselves from other "races," bringing into existence a world with two poles, so it is doubly ironic that they should feign a hands-washing ignorance of these realities. Once the sociality and historicity of the term is recognized, the claim that philosophy, along with other, less lofty varieties of intellectual labor, is going to be influenced by race should seem less provocative and controversial. This claim does not imply any kind of biological determinism; rather, it entails a pervasive social construction, a set of positions in a global structure, for which race will be an assigned category that influences the socialization one receives, the life-world in which one moves, the experiences one has, the worldview one develops — in short, in an eminently recognizable and philosophically respectable phrase, one's *being and consciousness.*

And this recognition, I suggest, enables us to answer the argument that the very abstractness of philosophy is proof of its immunity to cultural or racial bias, that philosophy could not possibly have a color when we are simply talking about abstract persons investigating and prescribing for the world. For insofar as these persons are conceived of as having their personhood uncontested, insofar as their culture and cognitions are unhesitatingly respected, insofar as their moral prescriptions take for granted an already achieved full citizenship and a history of freedom — insofar, that is, as race is *not* an issue for them, then they are already tacitly positioned as white persons, culturally and cognitively European, racially privileged members of the West.

These essays represent my exploration of the possibilities generated when race is taken seriously in some of the standard areas of the field: metaphysics, epistemology, ethics, applied ethics, social and political philosophy. With one exception, all were written within the span of four years and show the development of my thinking.

"Non-Cartesian *Sums*" is a reflection on my experience in teaching my first course in African-American philosophy and having to work out the distinctive features of such a philosophy. By drawing a comparison between the Cartesian *sum*, that classic statement of European modernism, and the radically different *sum* of Ralph Ellison's classic novel of the black experience, *Invisible Man*, I try to get at some of these differences. This essay first started me thinking systematically about the subject and introduced many of the topics and themes that I later developed in other essays. Appropriately enough, the novel also provided my title, dedication, and epigraph: this is a book about making the black experience philosophically visible, in part through attempting to remove the conceptual and theoretical cataracts on the white eye.

The chapter that focuses specifically on epistemological issues is "Alternative Epistemologies." Though it is now somewhat dated in its references (I have added a few sources), the concerns it addresses are still very much with us: the notion that subordinated groups have a privileged epistemic position, and the attempts to defend this claim and adjudicate competing claims of privilege. Written in a period less thoroughly post-Marxist than our own, it compares different varieties of "standpoint theory"—the original Marxist model and feminist and black variants—and argues, against postmodernism, for a situated objectivism. I still endorse this position, my sympathies being generally realist. And in light of the obvious divergence between black and white perspectives on the world, it remains true that the task of constructing and defending a "black" epistemology is an important one that has yet to be seriously tackled by black philosophers.

Issues of personal identity have been around at least since John Locke. In "But What Are You *Really?*" I examine the "metaphysics" of race, explaining the ways in which race is "real" and showing how conflicting criteria may generate interesting issues of *racial* identity. The point in part is to make plausible the idea of race as "ontological" and to sketch, correspondingly, a set of background realities that needs to be taken more seriously by mainstream social and political philosophy. (My title was inspired by Anthony Appiah's *Journal of Philosophy* article "'But Would That Still Be Me?'" [1990].)

In 1994 I was invited to Toronto to participate in a public symposium and lecture series on black-Jewish relations in the city. The lecture I gave there, "Dark Ontologies," introduces the idea of white supremacy as a system both local and global. I argue that this idea should play in critical race theory the same role that class society and patriarchy play in Marxist and feminist theory, respectively. In other words, one should look at race as systemic and objective rather than primarily in terms of attitudes and values. "Revisionist Ontologies" explores this idea in greater detail, from what is more of a Third World perspective. (The original paper was presented in Mexico to the Caribbean Studies Association.) I focus on the idea of a "subperson," first raised in "Non-Cartesian *Sums*," and make some suggestions about the re-thinking of political philosophy that are further developed in "The Racial Polity." The point of all three essays is that racial domination should be seen as a kind of political system, whose workings need to be recognized and theorized if normative political theory is to be guided properly.

Some interesting work has been done on the idea of "naturalizing" ethics, in line with the older project of naturalizing epistemology. In "White Right" I examine a naturalized ethic of a *Herrenvolk* variety; that is, the moral code one would get in a social order explicitly or implicitly predicated on white supremacy. This type of analysis may yield insights into the typical structuring of white moral consciousness that are not so readily available from the perspective of conventional ethical theory. Since progressive social change in respect to race will require the understanding and transformation of this consciousness, the failure of mainstream ethics to pay more attention to its characteristic features is an important omission, one that reflects a broader failure to appreciate the centrality of race in our society.

Finally, the last chapter, "Whose Fourth of July?," brings these issues together by considering the question raised by the great Frederick Douglass in his famous 1852 speech, a question that still reverberates in the United States and elsewhere these many years later—whether blacks will ever be included on fully equal terms in the polities created by the West in the "New World." If we are to hope that one day this question will be answered in the affirmative, the issue of race must be honestly faced rather than evaded, and philosophy can play a key role in this enterprise.

This book is my own small contribution to the project of expanding that set of paradigmatic philosophical images cited at the start, so that one will also think of W. E. B. Du Bois's black cave dwellers, trying desperately to make contact with the white world above; Ellison's invisible man in his basement wondering whether he exists; James Weldon Johnson's ex-colored man passing into the white body politic and so changing his racial identity; Kant's actual racial contractarianism, in which white persons give disrespect to nonwhite subpersons; Frantz Fanon's wretched of the earth and Du Bois's global color line as the unhappy outcome of European expansionism; Huck Finn's dilemma of having to choose between turning Jim over to his mistress and helping him to escape, between a *Herrenvolk* ethics and race treachery; the cognitive possibility that as a slave, as an aborigine, as one of the colonized, one may actually have been ideologically fed a false picture of one's history and reality....

Blackness Visible can be seen as a companion volume to *The Racial Contract,* published by Cornell University Press in 1997. It covers some of the same territory but explores it in greater depth and detail. *The Racial Contract* is a high-flying overview; *Blackness Visible* is closer to the ground. The two complement each other as different perspectives, long distance and close up, on philosophy and race.

I gratefully express my appreciation to Alison Shonkwiler of Cornell University Press for coming up with the idea of an essay collection in the first place and for guiding it carefully through its various phases, from conception to completion. The conscientious comments, criticisms, and suggestions of the two readers for Cornell have assisted me greatly in improving the original manuscript.

My thanks to the University of Oklahoma for a junior faculty summer research fellowship in 1989, when I first tentatively began to think about the issue of philosophy and race. Some of these essays were written or revised in my year as a Fellow of the Institute for the Humanities, University of Illinois at Chicago (UIC), and the whole manuscript was put into its final shape during a semester's sabbatical here. As before, I am indebted to John Biro and Kenneth Merrill of the University of Oklahoma and to Richard Kraut, Dorothy Grover, and Bill Hart of UIC, department chairs, for their support of my research, and to Bernard Boxill, Dave Schweickart, and Robert Paul Wolff for their referees' recommendations for the UIC fellowship. Charlotte Jackson and Valerie McQuay, the UIC Philosophy Department's administrative assistants, have continued to provide invaluable service, and without Charlotte's electronic expertise I would doubtless still be trying to format the manuscript to Cornell's satisfaction. (Her photographic talents with an unprepossessing subject are on display on the jacket of *The Racial Contract.*)

Feedback and criticisms on various of these chapters have come from Linda Alcoff, Susan Babbitt, Bernard Boxill, Susan Campbell, Barry Chevannes, Frank Cunningham, Norman Girvan, Lewis Gordon, Roger Gottlieb, Sandra Harding, Leonard Harris, Nancy Holmstrom, Patricia Huntington, Frank Kirkland, Jane Kneller, Hugh LaFollette, Bill Lawson, Horace Levy, Rupert Lewis, Andrew Light, Louis Lindsay, Grace Livingston, Steve Martinot, Bill McBride, Howard McGary Jr., Brian Meeks, Carlos Moore, Lucius Outlaw Jr., John Pittman, the PCDGC/Politically Correct Discussion Group of Chicago (Sandra Bartky, Holly Graff, David Ingram, David Schweickart, Olufemi Taiwo), Reuel Rogers, Laurence Thomas, and Robert Paul Wolff. I thank Lewis Gordon in particular for his thorough, thoughtful, and systematic engagement with the material, and I tip my hat in respect to one who has shown us all, as black philosophers, what is possible.

As always, my father, Gladstone Mills, and my wife, Elle Mills, have been indefatigable supporters of my work. My special appreciation to both of them for the encouragement they have given me in bad times as well as good.

Some of the chapters in this book were originally presented at conferences and invited talks. I thank the organizers for their invitations and the audiences for their criticisms and comments. A paper titled "Non-Cartesian *Sums*" (the inspiration for rather than the ancestor of my first chapter) was presented in 1992 at a University of Toronto Philosophy Department conference, "Philosophy and Non-European Cultures," and in 1993 on a York University panel, "Rethinking the Curriculum": thanks to André Gombay and David Trotman, respectively. In 1996 Susan Babbitt and Susan Campbell jointly organized the Queen's University Philosophy Department's symposium "Philosophy and Racism," where " 'But What Are You *Really?*' The Metaphysics of Race" was presented, and it was also read later the same year at the second national conference of the Radical Philosophy Association, held at Purdue University. The University of Toronto Philosophy Department and Toronto's Holy Blossom Temple cosponsored the 1994 two-day symposium "Race and the City," where "Dark Ontologies: Blacks, Jews, and White Supremacy" was given as a public lecture. My appreciation to Frank Cunningham and Wayne Sumner, in particular. Brian Meeks, Folke Lindahl, and Rupert Lewis were the main forces behind the political theory panel at the 1994 Caribbean Studies Association meeting in Mérida, Mexico, where "Revisionist Ontologies: Theorizing White Supremacy" was read. Finally, "White Right: The Idea of a *Herrenvolk* Ethics" was presented at the University of Western Ontario Philosophy Department's 1995 conference, "Pluralism and Conflict," organized by Samantha Brennan, Tracy Isaacs, and Michael Milde, and was also read later that year as an invited talk at the Philosophy Department of Purdue University. Hugh LaFollette and Bill McBride provided detailed comments, for which I am much obliged.

Finally, I gratefully acknowledge permission to reprint the following chapters:

"Non-Cartesian *Sums*: Philosophy and the African-American Experience" first appeared in *Teaching Philosophy* 17 (September 1994).
"Alternative Epistemologies" first appeared in *Social Theory and Practice* 14 (Fall 1988).
" 'But What Are You *Really?*' The Metaphysics of Race" is scheduled to appear in a forthcoming volume of selected essays from the second national conference of the Radical Philosophy Association (Humanities Press).

"Dark Ontologies: Blacks, Jews, and White Supremacy" first appeared as a chapter in *Autonomy and Community: Readings in Contemporary Kantian Social Philosophy*, edited by Jane Kneller and Sidney Axinn (Albany: SUNY Press, 1998).

"Revisionist Ontologies: Theorizing White Supremacy" first appeared in *Social and Economic Studies* 43 (September 1994).

"The Racial Polity" is scheduled to appear as a chapter in *Philosophy and Racism*, edited by Susan Babbitt and Susan Campbell (Ithaca: Cornell University Press, in press).

"Whose Fourth of July? Frederick Douglass and 'Original Intent'" is scheduled to appear as a chapter in *Frederick Douglass: Philosopher*, edited by Frank Kirkland and Bill Lawson (Cambridge, Mass.: Blackwell, in press).

CHARLES W. MILLS

Chicago, Illinois

Blackness Visible

1 Non-Cartesian *Sums*

Philosophy and the

African-American Experience

Some years ago, I taught, for the first time, an introductory course in African-American philosophy. In a sense, that course led to the present book, of which this is, appropriately, the first chapter. The course forced me to think more systematically about the issue of philosophy and race than I had ever done before. Though my general area of specialization is ethics and social and political philosophy, and I am African-American (at least in the extended sense that the Caribbean is part of the Americas), my main research interests and publication focus had not been in this particular area. So I had to do more preparatory work than usual to come up with a course structure, since at that time, because of the relatively undeveloped state of African-American philosophy, I found nothing appropriate in my search for a suitable introductory text, with articles that would cover a broad range of philosophical topics from an African-American perspective and that would be accessible to undergraduates with little or no background in the subject. Often the structure of a textbook provides an organizing narrative and an expository framework for a course. Here, by contrast, I had to think the course out and locate and assign readings from a variety of sources.[1] And in order to put them all together, of course, I had to work out what African-American philosophy really was, how it was related to mainstream (Western? European/ Euro-American? Dead White Guys'?) philosophy—where it challenged and contradicted it, where it supplemented it, and where it was in a theoretical space of its own.

1

Blacks and White Philosophy

The natural starting point of my reflections was blacks and philosophy itself. There are as yet so few recognized black philosophers that the term still has something of an oxymoronic ring to it, causing double takes and occasional quickly suppressed reactions of surprise when one is introduced.[2] As a result, I would imagine that most black philosophers think about philosophy and race to some extent, even if they don't actually write or publish in the area. What exactly is it about philosophy that so many black people find alienating, which would explain the fact, a subject of ongoing discussion in the *APA Proceedings and Addresses,* that blacks continue to be far more underrepresented here than in most other humanities and that black graduate students generally steer away from philosophy?[3]

I reject explanations that attribute this pattern entirely to present-day (as against past) racist exclusion. Rather, I suggest that a major contributory cause is the self-sustaining dynamic of the "whiteness" of philosophy, not the uncontroversial whiteness of skin of most of its practitioners but what could be called, more contestably, the *conceptual* or *theoretical* whiteness of the discipline. This alone would be sufficient to discourage black graduate students contemplating a career in the academy, so that, through mechanisms familiar to those who study the reproduction of dynamic systems, certain defining traits are perpetuated unchallenged or only weakly challenged, and the socialization and credentialing of newcomers proceeds in a way that maintains the "persistently monochromatic" character of the profession.[4]

This notion is hard to tease out; it is a pretheoretical intuition, and as with all intuitions, it can be hard to convey to those who do not, in this case because of their color, spontaneously feel it in the first place. But I will make the attempt, using gender as a comparison, because of the interesting similarities and interesting differences, and because the line of argument here is far better known, even by those who do not accept it.

In an enlightening paper in *Teaching Philosophy,* Thomas Wartenberg described the experience, from the perspective of a white male instructor, of trying to see his assigned texts from the viewpoint of his female students and gradually developing a revelatory sense of the "schizophrenic relationship" they would be bound to have to works characterized by "a systematic denigration of the nature of women."[5] There is no mystery, then, about why women are likely to feel at least some initial discomfort with classic philosophy. But the response of blacks poses more of a challenge, because for the most part blacks are simply not mentioned in classic philosophy texts. Whole anthologies could be and have been filled by the misogynistic statements of various famous philosophers, and entire books could be and have been written on the inconsistencies between the ostensibly general moral and political prescriptions of famous philosophers and their proclaimed views on the status of women.[6] But in Western philosophy there is no rationale for black subordination in particular (as against arguments for slavery in general) that can compare in detail and in theoretical centrality to the rationale for female subordination.[7] A collection of explicitly racist statements about blacks from the major works of the central figures in the Anglo-American canon would not be a particularly thick document.[8] It is more that issues of race do not even arise than that blacks are continually being put down.

What, then, is the source for blacks of a likely feeling of alienness, strangeness, of not being entirely at home in this conceptual world? The answer has to be sought at another level, in a taxonomy of different kinds of silences and invisibility. The position of women in society had to be theoretically confronted by Western thinkers (after all, they were right *there* as mothers, sisters, wives) in a way that the position of enslaved blacks did not. The embarrassing moral and political problems posed by the fate of slaves could more readily be ignored, dealt with by not saying anything about them. As David Brion Davis observes in his book on slavery in Western culture: "[N]o protest against the traditional theory [of slavery] emerged from the great seventeenth-century authorities on law, or from such philosophers and men-of-letters as Descartes, Malebranche, Spinoza, Pascal, Bayle, or Fontenelle.... The inherent contradiction of human slavery had always generated dualisms in thought, but by the sixteenth and seventeenth centuries Europeans had arrived at the greatest dualism of all—the momentous division between an increasing devotion to liberty in Europe and an expanding mercantile system based on Negro [slave] labor in America. For a time most jurists and philosophers met this discrepancy simply by ignoring it."[9]

So the result is a silence—a silence not of tacit inclusion but rather of exclusion: the black experience is not subsumed under these philosophical abstractions, despite their putative generality. An enlightening metaphor might be the notion of a parallel universe that partially overlaps with the familiar (to whites) one but then, because of crucial variations in the initial parameters, goes radically askew. For the inhabitants of this universe, the standard geometries are of limited cartographic use, conceptual apparatuses predicated on assumptions that do not hold true. It is not a question of minor deviations, which, with a bit of bending and twisting here and there, can be accommodated within the framework. Rather, so to speak, some of the Euclidean axioms have to be rejected; a reconceptualization is necessary because the structuring logic is different. The peculiar features of the African-American experience — racial slavery, which linked biological phenotype to social subordination, and which is chronologically located in the modern epoch, ironically coincident with the emergence of liberalism's proclamation of universal human equality — are not part of the experience represented in the abstractions of European or Euro-American philosophers. And those who have grown up in such a universe, asked to pretend that they are living in the other, will be cynically knowing, exchanging glances that signify "There the white folks go again." They know that what is in the books is largely mythical as a *general* statement of principles, that it was never intended to be applicable to them in the first place, but that within the structure of power relations, as part of the routine, one has to pretend that it does.

Thus there is a feeling, not to put too fine a point on it, that when you get right down to it, a lot of philosophy is just white guys jerking off. Either philosophy is not about real issues in the first place but about pseudo-problems; or when it is about real problems, the emphases are in the wrong places; or crucial facts are omitted, making the whole discussion pointless; or the abstractness is really a sham for what we all know but are not allowed to say out loud. The impatience or indifference that I have sometimes detected in black students seems to derive in part from their sense that there is something strange in spending a whole course describing the logic of different moral ideals, for example, without ever mentioning that *all of them* were systematically violated for blacks. So it is not merely that the ideal was not always attained but that, more fundamentally, *this was never actually the ideal in the first place.* A lot of moral philosophy will then seem to be based on pretense, the claim that these were the principles that people strove to uphold, when in fact the real principles were the racially exclusivist ones.

The example of Locke here is paradigmatic of the kind of guilty silence I am talking about: the pillar of constitutionalist liberal democracy; the defender of the natural equality of all men; and the opponent of patriarchalism, of enslavement resulting from a war of aggression, of *all* hereditary slavery, who nevertheless had no difficulty reconciling his principles with investments in the Atlantic slave trade and a part in writing the Carolina slave constitution. Women are, of course, also unequal in the Lockean polity, but their subordination is at least addressed, explained (inconsistently) on the basis of natural disadvantage.[10] But nothing at all is formally said in the *Second Treatise of Government* about justifying *black* subordination: blacks are just outside the scope of these principles. Similarly, in the two most widely used contemporary political texts, John Rawls's *A Theory of Justice* and Robert Nozick's *Anarchy, State, and Utopia,* it will certainly be noticed by blacks, if not commented on, that U.S. slavery and its aftermath barely appear.[11] The only slavery Rawls mentions is that of antiquity, while Nozick's thoughts on the possible need for rectificatory reparations occupy a few sentences and an endnote reference. So the focus on "ideal theory" (Rawls) here will seem in part ideological, a steering away from disquieting questions and unresolved issues. It is a generalism, an abstractness, which is covertly particularistic and concrete, in that it is really based on a white experience for which these realities were not central, not that important.

And it is because of this *interconnection* between "white" principles and black philosophy that it is not really accurate, at least for African-Americans, to characterize the issue purely in terms of promoting "multiculturalism" and "cultural diversity."[12] This description would be fair enough in the case of geographically and historically discrete communities, with different cultures and worldviews, coming into contact through voluntary immigration. But in the case of the African-American experience, what is involved is a subject population simultaneously linked to and excluded from the dominant group — the "sixty percent solution" of the Constitution, the 1857 *Dred Scott* v. *Sanford* decision that blacks in America had no rights that whites were bound to respect — whose culture and worldview are, as a consequence, deeply motivated by the necessity of doing a critique *of* the dominant view. A lot of black thought has simply revolved around the insistent demand that whites *live up to their own (ostensibly universalist) principles,* so that African-Americans such as David Walker could challenge American slavery and white supremacy in the name of the Declaration of Independence, and the Saint-Domingue (Haitian) revolutionaries who triumphed over French colonial slavery could be described as "black Jacobins" acting in the name of the "Rights of Man."[13] Thus African retentions in the "New World" and the elements of a syncretic new culture growing out of slavery were necessarily intellectually shaped in their development by the experience of resistance to white oppression in a way that African thought developing on the home continent in the precolonial period was not. *African-*Americans, as such writers as James Baldwin and Ralph Ellison have always pointed out, are also African-*Americans,* with the result that a relationship simultaneously of influence by and opposition to white theory and practice imprints their cognition from the start. What is involved, then, is not so much a purely externalist collision of different cultures as a (partially) internalist critique of the dominant culture by those who accept many of the culture's principles but are excluded by them. In large measure, this critique has involved telling white people things that they do not know and do not want to know, the main one being that this alternative (nonideal) universe *is* the actual one and that the local reality in which whites are at home is only a nonrepresentative part of the larger whole.

The Personal Experience of Subpersonhood

Back to the course and the problem of finding an organizing principle for it. Obviously, African-American philosophy comprises not just the philosophical writings of black people, because then any article—on the Gettier problem, on counterfactuals, on bivalence, on the French Enlightenment—would count, and of course there are such articles. The unifying theme had to be something like the struggles of people of African descent in the Americas against the different manifestations of white racism (cf. Leonard Harris's title [note 1]: *Philosophy Born of Struggle*). The political, economic, social, and legal dimensions of this struggle were clear enough and well documented. But how exactly was the philosophical aspect of this struggle to be characterized?

I decided that "personhood," or the lack of it, could provide an ingress to this universe, and that I would work with the concept of a "subperson" as my central organizing notion. This strategy arguably captures the defining feature of the African-American experience under conditions of white supremacy (both slavery and its aftermath): that white racism so structured the world as to have negative ramifications for every sphere of black life—juridical standing, moral status, personal/racial identity, epistemic reliability, existential plight, political inclusion, social metaphysics, sexual relations, aesthetic worth.

What is a (racial) "subperson"? (The term, of course, is a translation of the useful German *Untermensch.*) What are its specific differentiae? A subperson is not an inanimate object, like a stone, which has (except perhaps for some green theorists) zero moral status. Nor is it simply a nonhuman animal, which (again, before recent movements to defend "animal rights") would have been regarded, depending on one's Kantian or Benthamite sympathies, as outside the moral community altogether, or at best as a member with a significantly lower utility-consuming coefficient. Rather, the peculiar status of a subperson is that it is an entity which, because of phenotype, seems (from, of course, the perspective of the categorizer) human in some respects but not in others. It is a human (or, if this word already seems normatively loaded, a humanoid) who, though adult, is not fully a person. And the tensions and internal contradictions in this concept capture the tensions and internal contradictions of the black experience in a white-supremacist society. To be an African-American was to be, in Aristotle's conceptualization, a living tool, property with a soul, whose moral status was tugged in different directions by the dehumanizing requirements of slavery on the one hand and the (grudging and sporadic) white recognition of the objective properties blacks possessed on the other, generating an insidious array of cognitive and moral splits in both black and white consciousness. As Davis points out, "the concept of man as a material possession has always led to contradictions in law and custom ... laws that attempted to define the slave's peculiar position as conveyable property, subject to rules respecting debt, descent, and taxation; and as a man who might be protected, punished, or prevented from exercising human capacities.... Everywhere [in the Americas these laws] embodied ambiguities and compromises that arose from the impossibility of acting consistently on the premise that men were things."[14] This, then, is a more illuminating starting point than the assumption that in general all humans have been recognized as persons (the "default mode," so to speak). In other words, one would be taking the historical reality of a partitioned social ontology as the starting point rather than the ideal abstraction of universal equality, qualified with an embarrassed marginal asterisk or an endnote to say that there were some exceptions.

If this is your foundation, then the nature of your perspective on the world and the philosophy that grows organically out of it are bound to be radically different. Even after emancipation, you are categorized on the basis of your color as an inferior being, since modern racial slavery (unlike the slavery of antiquity) ties phenotype to subordination. So you are seen as having less mental capacity, with rights on a sliding scale from zero to a ceiling well below that of your white co-humans, a creature deemed to have no real history, who has made no global contribution to civilization, and who in general can be encroached upon with impunity. Once you have faced this social ontology without evasion and circumlocution, then the kind of problems with which you must grapple, the existential plight, the array of concepts found useful, the set of paradigmatic dilemmas, the range of concerns, is going to be significantly different from that of the mainstream white philosopher. And this means that many of the crucial episodes and foundational texts (The Great Moments in Western Philosophy) that make up the canon and the iconography of the Western tradition will have little or no resonance.

As an illustration, let me contrast two kinds of paradigmatic philosophical situations and two kinds of selves or *sums*, the Cartesian self with which we are all familiar and an Ellisonian one that will be unfamiliar to many readers. I think that these selves epitomize the different kind of problematic involved.

The enunciation of the Cartesian *sum* can be construed as a crucial episode in European modernity. Here we have vividly portrayed the plight of the individual knower torn free from the sustaining verities of the dissolving feudal world, which had provided authority and certainty, and entering tentatively into the cognitive universe of an (as yet unrecognized) revolutionizing individualist capitalism, where all that is solid melts into air. So the crucial question is posed: "What can I know?" And out of this question, of course, comes modern epistemology, with the standard moves we all know, the challenges of skepticism, the danger of degeneration into solipsism, the idea of being enclosed in our own possibly unreliable perceptions, the question whether we can be certain other minds exist, the scenario of brains in a vat, and so forth. The Cartesian plight, represented as an allegedly universal predicament, and the foundationalist solution of knowledge of one's own existence thus become emblematic, a kind of pivotal scene for a whole way of doing philosophy and one that involves a whole program of assumptions about the world and (taken-for-granted) normative claims about what is philosophically important.

Contrast this *sum* with a different kind, that of Ralph Ellison's classic novel of the black experience, *Invisible Man*.[15] What are the problems that this individual faces? Is the problem global doubt? Not at all; such a doubt would never be possible, because the whole point of subordinate black experience, or the general experience of oppressed groups, is that the subordinated are in no position to doubt the existence of the world and other people, especially that of their oppressors. It could be said that only those most solidly attached to the world have the luxury of doubting its reality, whereas those whose attachment is more precarious, whose existence is dependent on the goodwill or ill temper of others, are those compelled to recognize that it exists. The first is a function of power, the second of subjection. If your daily existence is largely defined by oppression, by *forced* intercourse with the world, it is not going to occur to you that doubt about your oppressor's existence could in any way be a serious or pressing philosophical problem; this idea will simply seem frivolous, a perk of social privilege.

The dilemmas of Ellison's black narrator, the philosophical predicament, are therefore quite different. His problem is his "invisibility," the fact that whites do not see him, take no notice of him, not because of physiological deficiency but because of the psychological "construction of their *inner* eyes," which conceptually erases his existence. He is not a full person in their eyes, and so he either is not taken into account at all in their moral calculations or is accorded only diminished standing. If they did not have power over him, this white moral derangement would not matter, but they do. So his problem is to convince them that he exists, not as a physical object, a lower life form, a thing to be instrumentally treated, but as a person in the same sense that they are, and not as a means to their ends. Moreover, because of the intellectual domination these beings have over his world, he may also be frequently assailed by self-doubts, doubts about whether he *is* a real person who deserves their respect or perhaps an inferior being who deserves the treatment he has received. The *sum* here, then—the *sum* of those seen as subpersons—will be quite different. From the beginning it will be relational, not monadic; dialogic, not monologic: one is a subperson precisely because *others*—persons—have categorized one as such and have the power to enforce their categorization. African-American philosophy is thus inherently, definitionally *oppositional*, the philosophy produced by property that does not remain silent but insists on speaking and contesting its status. So it will be a *sum* that is metaphysical not in the Cartesian sense but in the sense of challenging a *social* ontology; not the consequent of a proof but the beginning of an affirmation of one's self-worth, one's reality as a person, and one's militant insistence that others recognize it also. In the words of Ellison's nameless narrator: "[Y]ou often doubt if you really exist.... You ache with the need to convince yourself that you do exist in the real world, that you're a part of all the sound and anguish, and you strike out with your fists, you curse and you swear to make them recognize you. And, alas, it's seldom successful."[16]

The universalizing pretensions of Western philosophy, which by its very abstractness and distance from vulgar reality seemed to be all-inclusive of human experience, are thereby shown to be illusory. White (male) philosophy's confrontation of Man and Universe, or even Person and Universe, is really predicated on taking personhood for granted and thus excludes the differential experience of those who have ceaselessly had to fight to have their personhood recognized in the first place. Without even recognizing that it is doing so, Western philosophy abstracts *away* from what has been the central feature of the lives of Africans transported against their will to the Americas: the denial of black humanity and the reactive, defiant assertion of it. Secure in the uncontested *sum* of the leisurely Cartesian derivation, whites find it hard to understand the metaphysical rage and urgency permeating the *non*-Cartesian *sums* of those invisible native sons and daughters who, since nobody knows their name, have to be the men who cry "I am!" and the women who demand "And ain't I a woman?"[17] From the beginning, therefore, the problems faced by those categorized as persons and those categorized as subpersons will be radically different. One can no longer speak with quite such assurance of *the* problems of philosophy; rather, these are problems for *particular* groups of human beings, and for others there will be different kinds of problems that are far more urgent. A relativizing of the discipline's traditional hierarchies of importance and centrality thus becomes necessary.

Some Problems of (Black) Philosophy

Consider, then, how different the philosophical terrain looks, how divergently the traditional map of divisions (metaphysical, epistemological, existential, theological, ethical, aesthetic, political ...) unfolds from this angle, and consider also the many obstacles to conveying this radically variant perspective to white philosophy majors. Drawing on a different racial experience and guided by the orthodox cartographies, they must make a significant effort to appreciate that their philosophical vantage point is not universal. Indeed, their experience will not seem to them to be racial in the first place—it will simply seem to be the *human* experience, the experience that "we" all have as part of the human condition. White experience is embedded as normative, and the embedding is so deep that its normativity is not even identified as such. For this would imply that there was some other way that things could be, whereas it is obvious that this is just the way things are. A relationship to the world that is founded on racial privilege becomes simply *the* relationship to the world. And black philosophy, correspondingly, necessarily appears as a somewhat deviant and peculiar exercise, contrasted not with "white" philosophy but with philosophy unqualified, philosophy *simpliciter*.

So the starting point needs to challenge this metaphysical complacency, to show that the white existential condition, the Cartesian predicament, is "white" to begin with and is quite unrepresentative. Various attempts have been made to capture the peculiarities of what Lewis Gordon calls "existence in black" (to distinguish it from a "black existentialism," which might seem to be merely ringing the changes on the familiar Sartrean story).[18] We have Ellison's classic trope of invisibility and the related ocular metaphor of the "double-consciousness" of W. E. B. Du Bois: "It is a peculiar sensation, this double-consciousness, this sense of always looking at one's self through the eyes of others.... One ever feels his twoness,—an American, a Negro;

two souls, two thoughts, two unreconciled strivings; two warring ideals in one dark body."[19] In both cases, the relation to the white Other is crucial, an Other not on an equal plane but with the supervisory power to determine whether one appears to (public) view and how one (privately) appears in one's own eyes. What must be conveyed to white students in particular is the difference in the framework of philosophical investigation. Rather than being an isolated ego in a depopulated universe or a recognized member of a community of equals, one is from the start in an adversarial and asymmetrical relationship with those for whom one's full existence is in question. As Robert Birt points out, the essential characteristic of racial domination and of black enslavement in particular is that blacks are "relegated to the subhuman, the bestial (or the category of things)," that "blacks lose altogether the status of human beings."[20]

And the reaction to this dilemma, the characteristic moves, will necessarily be different. One famous solution is associated with the French colonial *negritude* movement: "I feel, therefore I am." But as critics have argued, this solution is problematic for a number of reasons, the most important being that it basically accepts and tries to put a positive face on what is essentially a nineteenth-century racist mental division of labor, in which male Europeans think, whereas others emote. What should be a protest and a proud affirmation of one's equal humanity become instead a tacit handing over of the cognitive realm to whites. If one is seeking a sentence paradigmatic of black existential assertion, a far better candidate is the African proverb formulated by John Mbiti: "I am because we are; and since we are, therefore I am."[21] This statement captures and expresses the crucial point that the denial of black existence is not individual, a refusal of recognition to one particular black for idiosyncratic reasons, but collective. It is not that blacks as a group do not exist because individual blacks do not exist, but rather that individual blacks do not exist because blacks as a group do not exist: the nonexistence is racial. Hence the defiant, reactive "non-Cartesian *sum*" has a collective dimension even when expressed by individuals, because it is as a result of this imputed collective property, this propensity to disappear in white eyes, that the *sum* is denied in the first place. The refusal of this ontological elimination is an affirmation simultaneously of individual and group existence.

What this points toward is the importance of understanding the world in which black philosophy (or, for that matter, white philosophy) is situated. Notions of the "metaphysical" are usually invoked only in connection with the deep structure of the Universe, and are associated, correspondingly, with the eternal and necessary. Insofar as (what is taken as) the human condition is interpreted as inscribed directly on these underlying pillars of Being, it is difficult to think of race as ontic, especially in the light of a nouveau sophistication that declares race to be, in fact, unreal. If race is not even real for science, then how—at what is supposed to be the more foundational level of ontology—could it be real for philosophy? And the reply would be that at the level of interpersonal interaction, human beings and human Being are so radically shaped by the "second nature" of social structure that it becomes meaningful to speak of a metaphysics that is contingent and variable, real but historical, fundamental but nonnecessary: the social ontology of a racial world. Within this context one needs to locate race, not merely the overtly raced nonwhites, particularly blacks, but the seemingly unraced whites, whose racial markers vanish into the apparent universality of the colorless normative.

In this spirit, Lewis Gordon argues that for a leading black philosopher such as Frantz Fanon, "classical ontological descriptions" of the black condition are to be rejected in favor of a "sociogenic" approach that locates the anthropological in the socially existential. In other words, ontology must be historicized, so that we recognize a world that has been created "according to the expectations of a racist ontology," a world in which "reality is racialized"—what is, in Gordon's phrase, "an antiblack world."[22] These realities will be familiar enough to blacks, but the racial structuring of experience and knowledge in a de facto segregated society means that white students will often, in good faith, be genuinely bewildered and incredulous. Thus, for pedagogical reasons, it may be necessary to provide more of a historical and sociological background than is customary in a philosophy course. (One of my most educational early experiences after coming to the United States to teach was facing a graduate philosophy class in a southern, predominantly white university and realizing, to my astonishment, that what I had taken to be an uncontroversial banality—the centrality of racism and the subordination of blacks in U.S. history—was something that I was going to have to argue for. As a double outsider, nonwhite and non-American, I understood for the first time the kinds of evasions of the past that must be routine in the high school curricula here.) What needs to be brought home to students is that racism was not the aberrant ideology of a few Klansmen but structural and routine, a systematic set of theories and legally sanctioned institutionalized practices deeply embedded in the American polity and endorsed at the highest levels in the land. Unless I made explicit such a background history, my students could not achieve a real appreciation of the way slavery and then Jim Crow shaped national consciousness.

Traditional notions of ontology and identity, of who and what the self is, can then be explored within this challengingly different and nontraditional framework. For example, one can look at the "metaphysical" significance in a racially structured society of being a member of the privileged race R1 as against the subordinated race R2. (Or, even more dramatically, one can speculate on the implications for one's self-concept of discovering one is "really" of race R2 rather than race R1.) Correspondingly, the difference between race as a biological concept (fictitious) and race as a social construct (real) can be made clear, for example, through bringing to light the principles that stand behind the "one-drop rule" for people of mixed race when black ancestry is involved. The subject of personal identity can be interestingly translated into discussions of racial identity and how it should be adjudicated in cases of criterial conflict, for instance, when somebody looks white but has black ancestry. There is a rich body of literature in the African-American tradition that deals with issues of "passing" and with the tensions between one's objective/intersubjective acceptance by the white world and one's subjective phenomenological awareness of one's role-playing.[23] Public selves and private selves, the self as socially constituted and the self as internally socially resistant, appearance and reality ... What could be more "metaphysical" than that?

Moreover, a recognition within philosophy of this actual social ontology opens up a panorama of moral questions. When one thinks of ethics and race, the subject of affirmative action is likely to spring most readily to mind, because of the numerous discussions in the 1970s and 1980s. But a far more extensive landscape of concerns is actually lying there to be mapped. Racial self-identification has a moral as well as a metaphysical aspect in that, rightly or wrongly, people have been taken to have an obligation to identify themselves one way rather than another. It is not—or it has not usually been seen to be —up to the individual's morally neutral taste, like choosing vanilla over chocolate ice cream. Prescriptive matters are at stake also, normative claims about one's duties. People of "mixed" race—scare quotes are necessary here, since of course no one qualifies for the contrastive category of "pure" race—have faced this imperative most directly, since the burden has been partly on them (insofar as they have the option) to choose whether to identify with the privileged race, R1; the subordinated race, R2; a hybrid biracial category; or, in the challenge of the philosopher Naomi Zack, no race at all.[24] The standard accusation has been that a refusal to identify with the R2s is morally culpable, motivated by the desire to avoid their stigmatized fate, and that whatever other reasons are offered will really always be disingenuous, in bad faith.

But Zack's challenge actually has much broader reverberations; it is a gauntlet thrown down to all who continue to use racial categories. If, as most in the scientific community would now agree, race does not (biologically) exist, why should anybody, least of all those subordinated by race, continue to hold on to it? Zack, deftly and ironically, turns the "bad faith" accusation around: "[I]f racial designations are based on 'fictions and myths,' it is wrong to accept them as part of one's identity.... Not only is racial identification itself a web of lies constructed to rationalize oppression —and endorsing a web of lies is an epitome of bad faith—but the nature of the lies one endorses as the racialized person who is their object will impede one's freedom as an agent."[25] Thus for her, the discovery that race is "constructed" should provide a justification for its abandonment, not a rationale for its perpetuation. Somewhat similarly, Kwame Anthony Appiah, in a series of essays, has been pursuing what is basically the deflationary project of discrediting past Pan-Africanist and present Afrocentrist use of "race" as a category.[26] Appiah is concerned about the rise of black essentialism and the corollary emergence of identities that "come with normative as well as descriptive expectations," stipulating "proper black modes of behavior," thereby raising the danger of new forms of "tyranny" that threaten individual freedom and choice.[27] By contrast, Lucius Outlaw, with whom Appiah has been conducting a long-running dialogue over several years, insists on the need for a redemptive black nationalism for which a (suitably refurbished) notion of race is crucial.[28]

My sympathies, as should have become evident, are with a cautious and appropriately glossed employment of "race." As I argued earlier, the notion of subpersonhood is crucial for an appreciation of the black philosophical universe, and subpersonhood is tied to race. Thus to map the moral topography generated by this ontology of persons and subpersons, and to theorize the resistance to it, "race" is indispensable. Once one concedes that the history of the United States has been explicitly racially exclusionist, with personhood being assigned on racial lines, and that the abstract moral theory outlined in standard ethics texts was really intended only to apply to a subset of the human population, the conceptual apparatus one employs must necessarily register this difference. Even normative theory presupposes a certain factual background, and if this background is radically different from what it has been represented as being, the terms and relations in the normative theory arguably need to be modified. The moral concerns of African-Americans have centered on the assertion of their personhood, a personhood that could generally be taken for granted by whites, so that blacks have had to see these theories from a location outside their purview.

Simply proceeding as before, but now with the formalistic inclusion of blacks in the ahistorical world of the standard ethics text, will not capture these hidden moral realities.

In my course in African-American philosophy, I sought to convey this difference to white students. I began with a few pages from Kant's *Groundwork of the Metaphysic of Morals,* so that nonmajors could have a sense of the ideals of "personhood" and "respect" as crucial moral concepts.[29] I paired this excerpt with Mark Twain's famous exchange between Tom Sawyer's Aunt Sally and Huckleberry Finn (whom she mistakes for Tom). When she asks whether anybody was hurt in a (mythical) riverboat accident, Huck replies: "No'm. Killed a nigger." She relievedly comments, "Well, it's lucky; because sometimes people do get hurt."[30] Here, with the economy of a great artist, Twain gives us a vignette in which a whole social order is encapsulated, a world in which the moral community of full personhood terminates at the boundaries of white skin. I followed this passage with a long excerpt from William Faulkner's *Intruder in the Dust,* which tracks the maturation of the young white protagonist from his "insult" by the black Lucas Beauchamp's refusal to accept 70 cents for having saved the white boy's life to his eventual realization of the perniciousness of the moral code that tied his self-respect to the maintenance of black inequality.[31] Finally, I presented a chapter from Richard Wright's autobiography in which he tells of growing up in the South, titled, with an appositeness perfect for the course, "The Ethics of Living Jim Crow."[32]

The texts by Twain, Faulkner, and Wright provided my students a sense, from fiction and autobiography, of what could be called a "naturalized" ethics — in this case a *Herrenvolk* ethics — a look at the actual moral code of a white-supremacist system and its ramifications for dominant and subordinated groups. They give us moral knowledge of a universe of persons and subpersons, where disrespect for the latter from the former was not merely permissible but mandated in order to maintain the social hierarchy, and duties and rights were apportioned accordingly. They show us the behavioral contradictions in having to interact with "living tools," human insofar as they could be communicated with about their tasks but nonhuman in lacking any say about those tasks, with one attribute always threatening to affect the other. They describe the necessity for boundary patrolling, the intricate racial etiquette devised to police this hierarchy and ensure that subordinated blacks did not forget their place and become "uppity." Finally, they make it possible to understand the characteristic themes in the black experience: African-Americans' need to insist on their personhood, sometimes at the cost of death; the strategies for subverting the order when direct confrontation was judged futile; the importance of attaining self-respect; the tensions between the elusive dream of acquiring personhood on white terms, through the embrace of white culture (the mark of the "superior" being), and the insistence that one could be culturally black *and* a person. Thus they provide the raw material from which philosophers can extract the conceptual web of an alternative order, the structuring principles of a universe, giving us knowledge in a way that merely conceding that blacks were not always treated equally would not. This universe is, as I have emphasized, not some alternative cosmos of a science-fiction writer's imagination but *our world*. Yet if whites spontaneously generalize and universalize from their uncontested moral personhood, these moral realities will remain largely invisible to them.

For blacks, the body thus necessarily becomes central in a way it does not for whites, since this is the visible marker of black invisibility. With the exception of some phenomenological work in the Continental tradition (Sartre, Merleau-Ponty) and recent explorations in feminist philosophy, the body has not traditionally entered philosophical discourse. In the modern analytic tradition, it has been at best the "general" body of the mind/body debate, the body as the thinking brain, the scientific body. But since, in our world, it is precisely the body that has been the sign of inclusion within or exclusion from the moral community (the physical sign of the natural slave that Aristotle had sought in vain), the black body arguably deserves to become a philosophical object. Unlike the neutral white (male) body, normative ("flesh-colored," after all), unproblematic, vanishing from philosophical sight, invisibly visible, the black body is visibly invisible, deviant, nonneutral (unflesh-colored?), and problematic. So this is the "particular" body, the body for which the debate is whether it has a mind, the body as the unthinking black brain, the moral/political body. In a series of works drawing on Fanon and Sartre, Lewis Gordon has examined the existential and ontological dimensions of race from "the material standpoint of inquiry itself—the body": "The black body lives in an antiblack world as a form of absence of human presence.... [T]o see the black as a thing requires the invisibility of a black's perspective.... Rules that apply to white bodies ... change when applied to black bodies.... [T]o see that black is to see every black."[33] The body, then, is what incarnates one's differential positioning in the world.

There is also, in addition to existential and ontological dimensions, a specifically aesthetic dimension, particularly for women. Many black women have felt what could be termed a carnal or somatic alienation from their bodies because of the devastating interaction of the double hegemony of a sexist norm that values women primarily for their bodies and a racist norm that makes the Caucasoid somatotype the standard of beauty. These stereotypes of physical attractiveness necessarily influence sexual relations also, both intraracially and interracially. Moreover, black women feel the tugs of both sisterhood and blackness, and adjudicating between them in times of conflict can be a difficult task indeed. They have had, in effect, to fight on two fronts: against the frequent sexism of black men (and their accusation that feminism is just a white woman's thing, a diversion from black transgender unity against racism) and the frequent racism of white women (too often ignorant of and indifferent to the ways in which "universal" feminist theory needs to be inflected by race-specific concerns). Black feminism has been caught in what Joy James characterizes as the "limbo" of "suspension between two states"[34] and has thus needed to develop a conceptual apparatus that registers the realities of racial subordination without having race loyalty automatically trump gender.

Finally, it should be emphasized that for African-American philosophers, all these problems, and many others I have no space to address, are by no means scholastic riddles to occupy an idle hour but burningly *practical* issues, problems that really are deeply troubling. There are many conceptions of philosophy, arising in part from the existence of many different philosophies, but certainly African-American/black philosophy would see itself as antipodal to a philosophy that, in one famous formulation, "leaves everything as it is." Insofar as this is a philosophy that develops out of the resistance to oppression, it is a practical and politically oriented philosophy that, long before Marx was born, sought to interpret the world correctly so as better to change it. As Fred Hord and Jonathan Lee have suggested, "philosophy is here called upon to evaluate and counter the dehumanization to which people and ideas of African descent have been subjected through the history of colonialism and of European racism."[35] In a broad sense, virtually all African-American philosophy is "political," insofar as the insistence on one's black humanity in a racist world is itself a political act. But other writings that are more obviously political even by narrow mainstream conceptions are usually excluded from the standard texts and narratives of this subsection of philosophy. A history of Western political philosophy that runs from Plato to Rawls while ignoring the abolitionist, anti-imperialist, antisegregationist work of such figures as David Walker, Martin Delany, Frederick Douglass, W. E. B. Du Bois, Marcus Garvey, C. L. R. James, Frantz Fanon, and Martin Luther King Jr. is a history insidiously political in its amnesiac denial of the centrality of slavery, imperialism, and Jim Crow to the history of the West. From a black perspective, both now-triumphant mainstream liberalism and its radical Marxist challenger have provided inadequate conceptualizations of the polity, one that has left no conceptual room to accommodate its white-supremacist character. The political philosophical concerns of African-Americans, from the classic historical debates over slavery through the post-Emancipation conflicts between rival strategies (separatist, integrationist, revolutionary) for black liberation to current prescriptions for aiding the black "underclass," have generally been excluded from mainstream texts.[36] The eventual achievement of an end to black subordination will require, among other things, a redrawing of the conceptual political maps on which this subordination does not even appear.

I will conclude with a comment on philosophy courses and, more broadly, the revision of the curriculum. Seeking to placate black critics merely by adding a course or two in African-American philosophy and then continuing essentially as before cannot be a genuine answer to the long-term problem of canon reform. For when this is done, what happens, of course, is that these courses are simply ghettoized, considered peripheral to the core of the discipline, not to be taken seriously by real philosophers. Rather, what is desirable is a transformation of the mainstream curriculum so that even a general introductory course will include such material to make students realize the variety of human experiences and the corresponding multiplicity of philosophical perspectives. We need to look at the traditional main divisions of the field—metaphysics, epistemology, logic, value theory—and ask how their subject matter could be changed by the explicit incorporation of race, by writing "race" and seeing what difference it makes.[37]

In some cases, there seems to be little room for race to make a difference; it hardly makes sense to talk about developing a peculiarly African-American symbolic logic. In other areas, such as those I have indicated here, the possibilities are obviously far greater: philosophy of existence, social ontology and personal identity, ethics, feminism, political philosophy. But there is room for innovation elsewhere also, as more black philosophers enter the profession and more literature is produced. Epistemology courses with a subsection on standpoint theory could include material on race as well as gender; "naturalized" epistemology and cognitive psychology discussions could consider the pervasiveness, as a mental phenomenon, of white cognitive dysfunction and self-deception on matters of race and its necessitation by a situation of privilege based on systematic racial oppression. Debates from critical race theory could supplement standard presentations in philosophy of law and be used to trace the peculiar trajectory of blacks' status as rightsholders in the United States. Aesthetics courses could examine the historical challenge of articulating a black aesthetic. In philosophy of religion, specific problems of black theodicies could be added to the usual set of themes. The black tradition of "signifying" could be explored for its possible repercussions for mainstream philosophy of language. Philosophy of science courses could look at the history of "scientific racism" and what this development says about the social determinants of scientific investigation; analogously, philosophy of history courses could look at Aryanism and its impact on the fabrication of the historical record. Finally, in the standard narratives of the history of philosophy itself, quite apart from the currently contested and controversial claims about the influence of ancient Egypt on ancient Greece, the relation between modern European thought and modern European expansionism needs to be made explicit, so that the extent to which modernity involves interrelated conceptions of white personhood and nonwhite subpersonhood, white civilization and nonwhite "savagery" can be appreciated.

White students who take such courses would not only have an incentive to find out more about the black experience; they would be provided with better philosophical insight into their own reality, insofar as "whiteness" and "blackness" have reciprocally (though not equally or harmoniously) determined each other.[38] Black students would be given the recognition currently denied by illusorily general abstractions that pretend to a representativeness they do not in fact achieve. The aim would be to transform the discipline so that the eyes of the former are opened and the eyes of the latter do not glaze over, both visions converging in agreement about the real nature of the world we are living in and how its problems can be remedied so that black *sums* and white *sums* are no longer in a zero-sum game.

2 Alternative Epistemologies

The presumption that epistemology as it has traditionally been defined is a neutral and universalist theory of cognitive norms and standards has come under increasing attack by feminist philosophers. Though there are significant divergences in the diagnoses offered of the deficiencies of orthodox epistemology and corresponding variations in the positive proposals advanced for its improvement or supersession, a clear consensus has been established that some kind of "feminist epistemology" is called for.[1] A parallel critique has also come from some black philosophers, who have argued that philosophy has not been immune to the racism that has pervaded so much of Western thought about non-European peoples.[2] The literature here, however, is not remotely as extensive as that for the feminist case, reflecting the continuing underrepresentation of black scholars in the field.[3] Finally, there is, of course, the longstanding challenge of the Marxist political tradition, which some theorists, at least, have taken to be committed to the epistemic superiority of the proletarian over the bourgeois view of the world.[4]

In all three cases, then, we have the advocacy of what could be termed alternative epistemologies, in that the processes of cognizing validated by the dominant perspective are being characterized as somehow inadequate.

Here I will examine and elucidate some of the major arguments offered for and against the legitimacy of such epistemologies. But a preliminary clarification (and perhaps also a justification) is necessary for readers not acquainted with the literature. The proponents of such views do not, for the most part, see themselves as offering, within the conventional framework, alternative analyses of such traditional epistemological topics as memory, perception, and belief, or coming up with startling new solutions to the Gettier problem. Nor is their paradigmatic cognizer that familiar Cartesian figure, the abstract, disembodied individual knower, beset by skeptical and solipsistic hazards, trying to establish a reliable cognitive relationship with the basic furniture of the Universe.[5] Rather, the sentiment tends to be that this framework needs to be transcended and that the standard, hallowed array of "problems" in the field should itself be seen as problematic. Thus a destructive genealogical inquiry underpins part of their recommended reconceptualization, the suggestion being that certain issues have been seen as problems in the first place only because of the privileged universalization of the experience and outlook of a very limited (particularistic) sector of humanity—largely white, male, and propertied.

It can readily be appreciated, therefore, that such arguments or assertions would be unlikely to impress the average subscriber to *Mind*. They would be seen as question-begging, as presupposing that all the important issues have been settled. And it might be felt that such epistemologies—if the title is even conceded to them—do not therefore deal with the really serious, basic philosophical questions: the existence of the external world and of other minds, the reliability of perception, and the trustworthiness of memory.

But the following challenge could be mounted to orthodox dismissiveness: How serious is this seriousness really? If these alternative epistemologies admittedly focus on less fundamental beliefs, are they not redeemed by genuine rather than histrionic questioning? Hume pointed out long ago that whatever skeptical iconoclasm with respect to everyday beliefs philosophers may indulge in privately (or with their colleagues), "immediately upon leaving their closets, [they] mingle with the rest of mankind in those exploded opinions." Nor is this necessarily just a matter of expedient conformity with the unenlightened herd, for he admits that in his own case, when he tries to "return to these speculations" after a few hours at backgammon, "they appear so cold, and strain'd, and ridiculous, that I cannot find in my heart to enter into them any further."[6] So one could be forgiven for suggesting that much of mainstream epistemology's apparent intellectual radicalism and daring about foundational beliefs is purely ritualistic and (literally) academic, having no practical implications for the actual beliefs and behavior either of the nonphilosophical population at large or even of the philosophers themselves. But if this diagnosis is correct and mainstream epistemology is in fact just, or largely, a sterile conceptual game, then why should it be seen as intrinsically a more serious undertaking than the project of these alternative epistemologies: the genuine (not simulated) revolutionizing and reconstruction of our received, hegemonically commonsensical picture of social reality?

Such, at any rate, could be one possible line of defense for the validity of these epistemologies. Characteristically, then, their concerns will be not the problem of other minds but the problem of why women were not thought to have minds; not an investigation of the conditions under which individual memory is reliable but an investigation of the social conditions under which systematic historical amnesia about the achievements of African civilizations became possible; not puzzlement about whether physical objects exist but puzzlement about the cognitive mechanisms that make relational social properties appear under capitalism as reified intrinsic natural properties.

Arguments from Biological Causation

As Alan Soble has pointed out, two fundamentally different kinds of answers have been offered to the question why subordinate groups may have differential and superior insight into the structure of social reality: (1) There are biological differences in the cognizing equipment, or in the embodied interaction with the world, of the groups involved; and (2) there are significant, socially caused divergences in their situation that affect their perception.[7] My focus is on the latter, more prominent claim, but a few words on the biological answer are not inappropriate, if only to establish it as a foil.

The basic notion here is that traditionally subordinated groups, such as women and blacks, have an innately superior cognizing apparatus and so can better know the world than the dominant group of white males. (A democratized, "environmentalist" variation on this position would be that all humans have the potential for these capacities to develop, but the respective circumstances of subordination and domination have fostered their flourishing/atrophy.) What is involved, then, is a kind of "oppositional" biological determinism, which has been embraced both by radical feminists and by some sectors of the black nationalist movement.

Alison Jaggar, for example, cites the work of radical feminists who believe in female intuition, a female capacity to enter into a direct mystical connection with the world, and in specifically female parapsychological powers such as "lonth."[8] Similarly, Sandra Harding mentions the view that women's biological functions—menstruation, intercourse, pregnancy, nursing—afford them distinctive experiences that are physiologically based.[9] Along parallel lines, some adherents of the black philosophy of negritude, developed by Aimé Césaire and Léopold Senghor, have argued that there are characteristically black modes of cognition: "Senghor's theory of negritude ... contains within it a theory of knowledge, indeed an epistemology. The key notion in Senghor's theory is that of *emotion*, which he virtually erects into a function of knowledge and attributes to the African as a cardinal principle of his racial disposition."[10] And Harding cites more recent claims of the same kind, for example, that varying quantities of melanin, different sorts of amino acid, and divergent brain patterns "underlie cultural differences between Africans and Europeans."[11]

There are familiar, post-Kuhnian problems in evaluating these claims, since any reference to the meagerness or nonexistence of their scientific basis is likely to be met with the accusation of *petitio*. Yet if the usual distinction between belief and knowledge is not to be abandoned (and those who challenge traditional belief systems seem to have good reason for wanting to retain it), then claims to alternative and superior forms of noetic access would still have to be cashed out in fairly traditional ways to seem persuasive. It is not just a question here of convincing a white male audience (which might be dismissed as intellectually irredeemable anyway) but of winning over other women and blacks who do accept the standard paradigm and with whom dialogue would presumably be seen as important. (Though perhaps some kind of direct approach to the awakening in others of these putatively dormant cognitive powers could render discursive proof unnecessary, the deed superseding the word.) Finally, these positions have often been criticized by other women and blacks as implicitly endorsing the oppressors' theoretical framework. Thus Abiola Irele, summarizing some of the criticisms made of Senghor, comments: "Negritude is presented in these objections as not only too static to account for the diversified forms of concrete life in African societies but also, because of its 'biologism,' as a form of acquiescence in the ideological presuppositions of European racism."[12]

A more mundane basis than parapsychology for male/female cognitive distinctness would be sexual dimorphism in brain structure, since there is some indication that spatial and linguistic skills are not symmetrically distributed between the sexes.[13] Both feminists and antifeminists have taken these findings to establish innate cognitive differentiation, one side seeing female and the other male superiority in the data. As Lorraine Code has pointed out, though, the brain develops its functions by practice, so that even if these differences can be unequivocally substantiated, the ultimate causes may still be social rather than biological. Pending the transformation of patriarchal structures, widespread and continuing stereotyping of gender roles for children makes it very difficult to separate what is truly innate from what is merely socialized.[14]

Arguments from Social Causation

The major argument, that from social situation, is best developed within the Marxist tradition. The most influential version of "feminist epistemology" (feminist standpoint theories) explicitly invokes that tradition, so this is the place to begin.[15] Of course, there are multitudinous Marxisms, not to mention post-Marxisms, but the variety that lends itself best to this project is the relatively old-fashioned (some would probably say, more harshly, discredited), "scientific realist" interpretation of Marx. In this interpretation, Marx's appearance/reality dichotomy in *Capital* is a statement of the antipositivist, realist insistence on the necessity for distinguishing between naively spontaneous and methodologically adequate conceptualizations of empirical data.[16] Historical materialism would then be a theory of the workings of the capitalist system, which is — to cite some of the crucial scientific realist claims — objective, genuinely referential, and a better, more progressive approximation to truth than its predecessors.[17] It is within this framework that the most plausible defense can be given of the validity of "alternative epistemologies," a defense that avoids epistemological relativism.

The argument goes something like this. Marx's theorization of society includes a metatheoretical element, in that his general claims about the social determination of belief commit him to genetic explanations of other important competing theories and, reflexively, of the origins of Marxism itself. Thus, in this respect (though not, as I shall later contend, in others), he is in agreement with Barry Barnes and David Bloor when they insist on a "symmetry" of explanation schemes for theories deemed scientific and for those deemed unscientific.[18] The latter may, of course, have all kinds of causes, including idiosyncratic personal ones, but Marx's belief is that when it comes to the sociologically important patterns of long-term systematic error that affect significant sectors of the population, we should look for structurally generated misperceptions that arise out of the social system. In a brief but illuminating passage of *Capital*, Marx argues that Aristotle was hindered, despite his great intellect, from seeing human labor as the foundation of all value because Greek slavery presumed "the inequality of men and of their labor-powers."[19]

An implicit contrast with the later capitalist mode of production is involved here, for the suggestion seems to be that the low level of technological development and the economic and ideological centrality of slavery meant that there was no social group to whom the idea of human equality would "naturally" have occurred. So this particular societal illusion (innate human inequality) would have the whole society in its grip, with no countervailing ideational tendencies (or at least no materially based ones). By contrast, Marx believes that the illusory appearances of capitalism — though admittedly exerting a certain doxastic pull on everybody — can be at least partially "seen through" from a certain perspective—that of the working class, of course. The account Marx gives is of an ostensibly abstract, nongendered, and nonracialized capitalism, so that his theoretical focus is on class-related illusions. But feminists and black nationalists can argue that actually existing sexist and racist capitalism (which does include the capitalist systems Marx studied) also generates other illusory appearances, which are not reducible to class and are differentially penetrable cognitively by other social groups. So the key claim in all cases is that social causation can have both positive and negative epistemic effects.

This, then, is the central idea that has to be defended if the project of alternative epistemologies is to get off the ground: that social causation can be epistemologically beneficial. The next step is to clarify precisely what social characteristic is supposed to produce this superior insight. There are three main candidates, which are not always disentangled from one another: the oppression subordinate groups suffer, their potentially universal character, and their differential experience.

Let us begin with oppression. This term is broader than *exploitation* (in the technical Marxist sense) and, as such, can be extended to groups other than the working class. It is also harder to define. Alison Jaggar suggests the following analysis: "Oppression is the imposition of unjust constraints on the freedom of individuals or groups." She goes on to argue that the suffering of oppressed groups is epistemically beneficial: "Their pain provides them with a motivation for finding out what is wrong, for criticizing accepted interpretations of reality and for developing new and less distorted ways of understanding the world."[20]

But even if this tendency exists, there is also, as Jon Elster has pointed out, "the tendency of the oppressed and exploited classes in a society to believe in the justice of the social order that oppresses them."[21] So one has to be careful not to put too much weight on this explanation: suffering is not necessarily cognitively illuminating. It is significant that Marx did not seem to think that the (clearly oppressed) slaves of ancient Greece were likely to make the cognitive leap to the notion of universal human equality. And it is a familiar fact that although several subordinate classes could be regarded as oppressed under capitalism—the petty bourgeoisie, the peasantry, the lumpenproletariat, and the working class—only in the last of these did Marx think a revolutionary consciousness was likely to develop. (For the lumpenproletariat, whose condition could be regarded as most miserable, he had nothing but contempt, seeing them as most prone to sell out to capital.) Thus Alan Soble, who takes oppression to be the crucial factor in the feminist claim, argues against it on the grounds that "each oppressed group (women, workers, blacks, chicanos, the handicapped, etc.) can make a claim to epistemological superiority," so that "the result is that the Marx-based epistemological argument ... collapses into trivial pluralism."[22]

The mere fact of oppression, then, though possibly producing an openness to alternate views, is not enough. One must look at universality. In Marx's early writings, the proletariat are characterized as "an estate which is the dissolution of all estates ... which cannot emancipate itself without emancipating itself from all other spheres of society and thereby emancipating all other spheres of society."[23] Joseph McCarney draws on this vision of totality to argue that since the proletariat are the "universal class," "Marx was able to combine the necessity of social roots with the aspiration to the whole" because "the standpoint of the whole and that of the proletariat were identical in the historical circumstances of the time."[24]

But for a non-Hegelian Marxism, the seemingly teleological causality of this claim is not readily convincing. Why should the fact that a particular class will bring about a classless society in the future retroactively guarantee them a holistic perspective? Jon Elster has emphasized the necessity of providing "microfoundations," specific causal mechanisms, for teleological and functional claims.[25] The question then would be: What causal mechanisms could plausibly be suggested that would make this hypothetical causality operable? Moreover, even if it is conceded that the proletariat come closest of all the classes of capitalism to a genuinely universalist viewpoint, this certainly does not exhaust the taxonomy of important social groups. The experiences of blacks and women with working-class racism and sexism, the frequently sectarian practices of vanguard Marxist groupings in relation to nonclass struggles and issues, and the continuing underrepresentation of women in the upper echelons of the power structures of existing socialist states all cast doubt on the actual universality of the proletarian perspective. And if a good case cannot be made for the working class, then a fortiori it is hardly likely to be made for blacks or women.

What is left, then, is differential group experience, and it is on this foundation that the best case can be made for the cognitive superiority of alternative viewpoints. A metaphor that may be helpful is the idea of some kind of "experiential space," which is not homogeneous but is full of structured heterogeneities and discontinuities, so that a social dimension is built in to its architecture from the start. As Bhikhu Parekh puts it:

A society is not a collection of individuals, but a system of positions.... To be a member of a society is to occupy a prestructured social space and to find oneself already related to others in a certain manner.... Since [one's] relations with other positions are objectively structured in a determinate manner, so are [one's] social experiences.... Since [one's] social experiences are structured, [one's] forms of thought, the categories in terms of which [one] perceives and interprets the social world, are also structured.[26]

Far from its being the case, then, that an asocial Cartesian knower can move freely along all axes of this space, certain resistances linked specifically to one's social characteristics and group membership will determine, at least tendentially, the kinds of experiences one is likely to have and the kinds of concepts one is accordingly likely to develop. In virtue of our common humanity there is obviously a common ("universal") zone that makes the Cartesian project plausible in the first place; one must avoid the absurd kind of hyperbole that suggests there is no overlap at all between the experiences of different groups. But some areas of experience lie outside the normal trajectory through the world of members of hegemonic groups. The claim that defenders of alternative epistemologies must make is that subordinate groups' access to these areas gives them a more veridical picture of the dynamics of the social system. If it doesn't strain the metaphor too much, a rough distinction could probably be made between experiences that are outside the hegemonic framework in the sense of involving an external geography (a muckraking Frederick Engels brings details of British slum conditions to the shocked attention of a middle-class audience) and experiences that are outside because they redraw the map of what was thought to be already explored territory (feminists put forward the claim that most "seductions" have a coercive element that makes them more like rapes).

Thus in the latter situation the shock arises not merely from the simply alien but from the alienated familiar, the presentation of the old from a new angle. It is this kind of inversion of perspective that is most characteristic of alternative epistemologies. Given the initial scientific realist assumptions, the contention must be that these alternative sets of experiences are not epistemically indifferent vis-à-vis one another but that hegemonic groups characteristically have experiences that foster illusory perceptions about society's functioning, whereas subordinate groups characteristically have experiences that (at least potentially) give rise to more adequate conceptualizations. It is a question not so much of simple oppression, then, but rather of an oppression so structured that epistemically enlightening experiences result from it.

At this stage, though, it may be argued that I have overstated the degree of epistemic divergence between different perspectives. Granted that people have differing views, there is no reason why we cannot learn, through communication, to understand other viewpoints and so achieve a more balanced perspective; to exaggerate these admitted differences into alternative epistemologies is ridiculous.

One problem with this kind of liberal approach is that rival sets of experiences are often contradictory rather than complementary (as in perspective "inversion," for example), so a simple synthesis is not really possible. In addition, this approach underestimates the difficulty members of hegemonic groups have in accepting alternative descriptions of their experienced reality. Apart from the prima facie appearance of the situation, background hegemonic ideologies help to sustain a particular interpretation of what is happening and to denigrate other viewpoints. Thus conflicting reports generate skepticism. Sandra Harding points to "the struggle we have had to get women's testimony about rape, wife battering, sexual harassment, and incest experiences accepted as reliable by police, the courts, employers, psychiatrists, other men and women, etc."[27]

Moreover, many reports will not even be forthcoming, since members of subordinate groups may judge it imprudent, given the power relations involved, to give an honest account of how they feel about things. The oral and literary history of the black experience, for example, is full of stories and parables that emphasize the necessity of dissembling before even apparently sincere and concerned whites, the need to tell them what it is calculated they want to hear rather than the truth: the mask of the cheerful grin. Thus in a crucial episode at the beginning of Ralph Ellison's *Invisible Man,* the nameless narrator overhears (and is at the time bewildered by) his grandfather's deathbed advice to his father: "Son, after I'm gone I want you to keep up the good fight. I never told you, but our life is a war.... I want you to overcome 'em with yeses, undermine 'em with grins, agree 'em to death and destruction."[28]

Finally, psychological obstacles ("hot" mechanisms) stand in the way of acceptance of redescriptions that cast interpersonal transactions in terms of coercion and oppression, quite apart from the ("cold") skepticism that arises from the intrinsic incongruity of these reports with one's own hegemonic group experience.[29] It could be said that if there are things one needs to know, there are also things one needs not to know, and an interesting sociopsychological account could probably be constructed of mechanisms of societal blocking of unwanted information that would be the Marxist equivalent of the Freudian repression of unhappy memories. For all these reasons, then, members of hegemonic groups are in practice unlikely to be receptive to alternative viewpoints.

Some Criticisms

Jon Elster's basically positivist account of Marx is hostile to the idea that a "working-class perspective" has any merit, and his hostility would presumably extend, a fortiori, to any similar claims made by women and blacks. He sees as Marx's "most original contribution" to the theory of belief formation a particular version of the fallacy of composition, in this case the "idea that the economic agents tend to generalize locally valid views into invalid global statements." But he finds "no basis in [Marx's] work for suggesting different sorts of biases, or different frequency of bias, among the members of different classes."[30] Thus Elster's reading seems to suggest that all members of society, regardless of class position, are equally subject to cognitive distortion. Membership in the working class would not therefore confer any epistemic advantage.

This claim can fairly easily be demonstrated to be a misreading of Marx. As I indicated earlier, Marx does believe that capitalism produces general "illusions," and that all classes are subject to them. To take a frequently cited example from *Capital,* the voluntaristic character of the transaction between worker and capitalist is an "illusory appearance" produced at the market level ("the sphere of simple circulation"), since both parties to this transaction "are constrained only by their own free will." And this "phenomenal form," the wage form, constitutes, according to Marx, "the basis of all the juridical notions of both laborer and capitalist" and all the corresponding "illusions as to liberty."[31] Thus far, one can agree with Elster: transclass symmetry obtains. But the point is that this is only one doxastic tendency among others: Marx also delineates a countervailing, demystifying tendency that is class-specific rather than general. For in addition to the (common/"universal") experience of the deceptive equality of the market, workers also have the (class-determined/"particular") experience of economic constraint arising from the de facto capitalist monopoly of society's means of production and the *dis*illusioning experience of capitalist production. Thus workers have spontaneously and directly available to them a conflicting set of experiences that dramatically undercut the voluntaristic and egalitarian appearance of the transaction, and that would, if followed up conceptually, lead in quite a different theoretical direction.[32] Workers' divergent experiences, then, give them a cognitive advantage over capitalists in understanding the workings of the "hidden structure" of the system. Hence the experiential symmetry between them at the market level is absent at the deeper level of production.

But this account is not readily accommodated by Elster's reading of Marx. Capitalists may tend to globalize the locally valid by assuming (or, perhaps more accurately, not caring to think too much about the idea) that workers enjoy the same material freedom to enter or not enter the contractual relationship, but it would surely not be accurate to claim that workers are as prone (if at all) to make the same assumption. For workers feel the material constraints directly — no speculation is needed. And the point is, of course, equally cogent for many other differences in their respective situations. It is not romanticizing the capacities of the downtrodden to observe that throughout the history of the struggles of subordinate groups, those at the bottom of the social ladder have usually shown themselves to be quite well aware that the conditions of their social superiors differ from their own. Indeed, it is precisely the perception of this difference and its assessment as unjust that have often motivated such struggles in the first place.

Elster also offers a more general critique of the social causation of "epistemologies." He suggests that the epistemic norm for which we should strive is "rationally grounded beliefs." These beliefs will, of course, not necessarily be true, but they have a better chance of being true than nonrationally grounded beliefs, being evidentially based. The presumption is that to be rationally grounded, the beliefs must be rationally caused, which means "(i) the causes of the belief are reasons for holding it and (ii) the reasons cause the beliefs *qua* reasons, not in some accidental manner." One could, through nonrational causes, arrive at rationally grounded beliefs, but this outcome would be fortuitous. Material interest and social position, however, are nonrelevant causes; hence, Elster argues, "socially caused beliefs are not rationally caused."[33]

Why does Elster see this as so self-evidently true? I think it is because he has the following picture of social causation in mind. Someone comes to believe *p*, not through an objective investigation of the evidence for *p*, but because *p* "corresponds" to his or her class interests. For example, some capitalists may be receptive to libertarianism not because they have actually read Ayn Rand, Robert Nozick, Milton Friedman, and the rest of the crew and made some attempt to assess their arguments but because they oppose further expansion of the social welfare system and want a philosophy that supports such views. In this kind of case, the causes of the belief are independent of the state of affairs the belief is about, so that we have no reason to think the belief is rationally grounded.

But the category of socially caused beliefs is certainly not exhausted by such examples. If workers, on the basis of their experiences in the factory, at the bargaining table, or on the picket line, come to realize that the atomistic social ontology of liberalism is profoundly misleading and that society is really divided into opposing classes; if women, on the basis of their experiences at work, on dates, or on the streets at night, come to realize that the threat of rape by males is omnipresent and plays a major role in determining female behavior; if blacks, on the basis of their experiences with housing, the job market, and the police, come to realize how pervasive, despite official denials, white racism continues to be; then in all these cases their beliefs surely do have an evidential base. Yet the preceding causal chains can all meaningfully be described as "social," since these experiences are more likely to arise in one social group than in others. Elster's assumption seems to be that all social causal chains lack evidential links, but if this proposition is not demonstrated, it is merely a stipulative definition from which implications can be drawn only at the risk of circularity: social causation is causation that does not involve rational causation and so is unlikely to produce rationally grounded beliefs.

What is obviously called for, then, is the drawing of internal distinctions between different varieties of social causation, according to their likelihood of producing positive or negative epistemic consequences. Bloor and Barnes's "strong program" demands explanatory symmetry for both true and false beliefs, rejecting the notion that sociologists of belief should be restricted to the elucidation of genealogies of error. The conclusions they draw are epistemologically relativist, the ubiquity of social causation allegedly dissolving the pretensions of any belief set to epistemically privileged status. But as several critics have argued, one can accept symmetry about the *fact* of causation while still rejecting it with respect to the *nature* of causation and its probable differential consequences. W. H. Newton-Smith contrasts the cases of two people with particular beliefs about where they are sitting, only one of whom has operative perceptual faculties. In each case, belief is the result of causal processes, but this symmetry does not extend deeper: "In the case of a veridical perceptual belief the causal chain involved runs through the state of affairs that gives the belief its truth-value. With non-veridical perceptual beliefs the causal chain may have nothing to do with the state of affairs that gives the belief its truth-value."[34] In a parallel fashion, then, it can be argued that in the cases cited above, the actual state of affairs (differentially perceived) gives rise to the beliefs in particular social groups. Once we allow reasons to be causes, there is no contradiction in affirming that beliefs can be simultaneously socially and rationally caused.[35]

Naturalized Epistemology and Radical Theory

Work in so-called naturalized epistemology may be of value in establishing an empirical basis for the above claims about hegemonic and alternative belief systems. In his Introduction to *Naturalizing Epistemology,* Hilary Kornblith suggests that the interrelations among three questions can be said to generate the project of naturalizing epistemology: "(1) How ought we to arrive at our beliefs? (2) How do we arrive at our beliefs? (3) Are the processes by which we do arrive at our beliefs the ones by which we ought to arrive at our beliefs?"[36] The strong version of what Kornblith calls "the replacement thesis" would simply dissolve question 1 into question 2. Since the advocates of alternative epistemologies want to challenge hegemonic but mystifying ideologies and belief systems, they would obviously not want to give up the normative dimension of epistemology. A weaker version, however, in which psychological findings about belief acquisition are deemed to be relevant to the erection of normative standards, would not necessarily have this drawback, and indeed, could be valuable in several ways.

First of all, the explicit connecting of the epistemological project to the ways in which people actually do acquire beliefs about the world can only be a positive corrective to the solipsist figure of the Cartesian knower. As David-Hillel Ruben has emphasized in his book on the Marxist theory of knowledge, "knowledge is irreducibly *social.*"[37] Similarly, Lorraine Code has pointed out that the misleading image of the "autonomous epistemic agent" needs to be replaced by the idea of "a community of knowers":

> To a much greater extent than the examples commonly taken to illustrate epistemological points might lead one to believe, people are dependent, at a fundamental level, upon other people ... for what they, often rightly, claim to know.... Far from being autonomous in the senses discussed above, knowledge is an interpersonal product that requires communal standards of affirmation, correction, and denial for its very existence. So a study of the workings of epistemic community is as important a focus of epistemological inquiry as is an analysis of perception- and memory-based knowledge claims.[38]

And such a study could, of course, legitimately investigate subjects currently excluded from mainstream epistemology, such as the transmission of hegemonic ideologies to new members of the community. Similarly, the contextualization of the process of acquiring knowledge within a social matrix opens a theoretical space for the consideration of socially generated illusions, in contrast to the wearying parade of elliptical coins, apparently broken sticks, afterimages, color-varying objects, and all the other bric-à-brac of putatively problematic perceptual phenomena marched back and forth across the epistemological stage for the past few centuries.

Finally, and linked to the preceding point, the findings of cognitive psychology about specific mechanisms of inferential distortion may be useful for translating into twentieth-century terminology Marx's somewhat musty vocabulary of "appearance," "phenomenal form," and so on, as well as for detailing cognitive mechanisms he would not have had the theory to analyze himself. This would have the virtue of presenting Marx's claims in a framework more accessible to (and taken more seriously by) a mainstream philosophical audience—a point of obvious importance if these ideas are ever to achieve deghettoization.

Although there is no space here to follow this program up, I want to give at least one concrete illustration. Richard Nisbett and Lee Ross argue that "people's understanding of the rapid flow of continuing social events" depends less on formal "judgmental procedures" than on "general knowledge [and, one wants to insert here, what is wrongly taken to be knowledge] of objects, people, events, and their characteristic relationships," which may be articulated as explicit propositional theory and as subpropositional schematic cognitive structures, variously characterized as schemas, frames, scripts, nuclear scenes, and prototypes. These cognitive structures provide an "interpretative framework for the lay scientist" and "supplement" the information given with much "assumed" information.[39]

Work in the Marxist theory of ideology, particularly that resulting from the influence of Gramsci, has emphasized that perhaps even more important than ideologies at the explicit and articulated level (for example, libertarianism, biological determinism) are ideologies in the more primeval sense of underlying patterns and matrices of belief, or ideology as "common sense." The former are at least visible as ideologies, specific demarcated bodies of thought in contestation for people's belief, whereas the latter may seem to be mere neutral background, an ideational framework to be accepted by all, without political implications. Thus the latter may well be more influential and efficacious than the former simply by virtue of their ability to set the terms of the debate, to limit the options deemed worthy of consideration. (John McMurtry has argued that the "forms of social consciousness" Marx mentions in the 1859 Preface should be seen in this light, as the underpinnings of more explicit ideologies.)[40] What the left must obviously do, then, is to establish a link between Nisbett and Ross's "schemas" and hegemonic ideological patterns, showing that in oppressive societies these schemas are often so structured as to convey misinformation. Thus the British authors of a book on understanding racism and sexism emphasize that these ideas should not be viewed as "abstract concepts" but as "lived experience":

For the racist, beliefs are not only cognitive categories or stereotypes—they represent a way of making sense and reacting to a range of social experiences. Ideology, in this sense, is not simply imposed from the outside by some super-powerful socialization agency; on the contrary, it is used by people to define their own lives and to understand the struggles and conflicts of the world they live in. In encountering Blacks, Jews, and other groups, the white worker ... reproduces racism as a means of coping with the exigencies of the moment. It is easier to live with unemployment if you can account for it in terms of what appears to be an accessible explanation.[41]

Correspondingly, the argument would be that in such interactions, victims of racism and sexism have, because of their differential experience, a better chance of developing schemas that objectively reflect the situation.

Consider, in this light, one of the most important schemas cited by Nisbett and Ross:

The most general and encompassing lay theory of human behavior—so broadly applied that it might more aptly be termed a "metatheory"—is the assumption that behavior is caused primarily by the enduring and consistent dispositions of the actor, as opposed to the particular characteristics of the situation to which the actor responds.... [I]n large measure the error, we suspect, lies in a very broad proposition about human conduct, to wit, that people behave as they do because of a general disposition to behave in the way that they do.... The "dispositionalist" theory, in short, is thoroughly woven into the fabric of our culture.[42]

It may be argued that this general schema explains the propensity for what the left calls "blame the victim" theories.[43] Such theories come in conservative (naturalistic/biological) and liberal (culturalist/social) versions; in both cases, however, the focus is on the individual's alleged deficiencies, whether these are seen to be genetic or environmental (for example, the "culture of poverty") in origin. The importance of this kind of psychological research is that it demonstrates a plausible experiential base (Marx's "phenomenal forms") for such views, which can be established independently of any appeal to the role of hegemonic ideologies. On the one hand, oppressive social structures constrain people into certain roles, narrow their choices, and disable and restrict them in various ways, thereby creating apparent evidential support for negative dispositionalist accounts: low working-class IQ scores, the underrepresentation of women and blacks in intellectual fields, and the feminization and racialization of poverty. On the other hand, subordinated social groups that have actually tried to overcome the systemic roadblocks to their development will be (once again, as a result of social causation) in a better cognitive position to form true beliefs about the mechanisms of oppression and more receptive to "situationist" accounts than hegemonic groups, to whom these constraints will be less visible.

Objectivism and Alternative Epistemologies

For an older Marxism, of course, the problem of the interrelation of epistemologies simply would not have arisen. The presumed causal centrality of the capitalist system to all structures of oppression implied that the working-class vision, the proletarian perspective, was sufficiently comprehensive to encompass the viewpoints of all other oppressed groups. The term that has come to be used to describe these universalist pretensions is "class reductionism," in this particular case the implication that the phenomenological specificities of women's and blacks' oppression can be assimilated to the working-class's experience of exploitation.[44]

In response, socialist feminists have pointed to rape, wife-beating, sexual harassment, prostitution, objectification of female sexuality, domestic labor, and so on as phenomena that resist such assimilation and that are not readily theorizable in orthodox Marxist categories. They have argued that Marx's notion of alienation is impoverished and that the analysis of women's alienation would have to be extended to include alienation from one's sexuality and one's control of motherhood.[45] Obviously, then, many important experiences do not, in the normal course of events, enter the phenomenological world of the working-class male. Perhaps the strongest piece of evidence supporting the inadequacy of this perspective is the fact that, as Sandra Harding points out, only now, after the reemergence of the women's movement, has the "sex/gender system" become theoretically visible.[46]

Similarly, throughout most of the twentieth century the black liberation movement has been engaged in a debate about the relationship between race and class, and the ability of Marxist concepts to explain black oppression.[47] The challenge to orthodox Marxist theory may be even stronger in this case, since there is no equivalent to Engels's book on the family. Thus more than one theorist has concluded that "essentially, Marxism has no theory of nationalism."[48] Moreover, Marx and Engels were influenced by Hegel's distinction between "world-historic" and "non-world-historic" peoples, "civilized" and "barbarian" nations, and they display a clear Eurocentricity in their writings about nonwhite peoples.[49] Accordingly, Cedric

Robinson has argued that the racism that infects so much of Western thought is present in Marxist theory also, so it would be a fundamental error to see Marxism as "a *total* theory of liberation."[50] *Black Marxism,* the title of his book, is apparently cognate with "socialist feminism," but whereas socialist feminist critiques of orthodox Marxism (such as Jaggar's) use the (reconstructed) theory to criticize Marxism's conceptual lacunae, Robinson suggests that the African critique of Marxism would be a more external critique, challenging Marxism from a position outside Western thought. For the black experience in this case starts from an ontological status of official nonpersonhood, and as such the alienation is more fundamental and far-reaching than anything that can be spun out of Marxist concepts of estrangement. In this spirit, the Jamaican-American sociologist Orlando Patterson has proposed the notion of "natal alienation," that is, "the definition of the slave, however recruited, as a socially dead person": "[I]t goes directly to the heart of what is critical in the slave's forced alienation, the loss of ties of birth in both ascending and descending generations.... The slave was the ultimate human tool, as imprintable and as disposable as the master wished."[51] Even a reconstructed Marxism, then, may not have the theoretical resources to express this experience.

One reaction to the apparent failure of Marxism to live up to its promise of a genuinely unifying vision has been the post-Marxist embrace of a relativistic pluralism, the positing of multiple realities. This development is, of course, encouraged by a broader cultural trend toward a skeptical relativism. Thus in a discussion of Sandra Harding's book on feminist epistemology, Alison Wylie suggests that Harding displays a systematic ambivalence, vacillating between postmodernist pluralism and "a variant of the enlightenment ideal of producing a unitary, authoritative conception of reality."[52] That conception is seen in some quarters as politically dangerous, the "totalizing" vision necessarily leading (though this sometimes seems to be less argued for than derived by a kind of conceptual onomatopoeia) to "totalitarianism," the suppression of difference in the monofocal eye.[53]

An obvious problem with this apparently democratic relativism is that if all viewpoints are equally valid, then there seems to be no reason why currently hegemonic perspectives (classist, sexist, racist) should not be treated similarly, and if a choice is then going to be made on nonevidential grounds, these perspectives will have the advantages of tradition, widespread acceptance, privileged media dissemination, and so on. Moreover, alternative viewpoints are to a significant extent constructed out of phenomenological raw material by intellectuals: "Those who construct the standpoint of women must begin from women's experience as women describe it, but they must go beyond that experience theoretically and ultimately may require that women's experience be redescribed."[54] The decision to retain certain elements as theoretically significant while discarding others can be made only by appeal, implicit or explicit, to some set of normative criteria devised to guarantee objectivity and representativeness. Alternatively, if one wishes to invoke a democratic relativism here also, then what prevents the whole enterprise from degenerating into a multiplicity of individual viewpoints, so that the prized social dimension drops out, and we are left—as a *reductio* of the whole project—with those isolated Cartesian knowers again?

The temptations of relativism arise understandably out of the indubitable difficulty of assembling class, race, and gender perspectives into a coherent, syncretic outlook. Moreover, as is often pointed out, the positing of a "woman's perspective" (or a "working-class" or "black" perspective, for that matter) necessarily involves an artificial abstraction from other determinants: "[E]ven if one is always a man or a woman, one is never *just* a man or a woman. One is young or old, sick or healthy, married or unmarried, a parent or not a parent, employed or unemployed, middle class or working class, rich or poor, black or white, and so forth.... Experience does not come neatly in segments."[55] Thus some critics have suggested that the entire enterprise is doomed from the outset because of the fragmented and disjunctive character of what is being represented as unitary.[56] But even if a sufficient commonality of experience to justify the theoretical construction can be demonstrated, the daunting task remains of working out the epistemic implications of these overlaps and intersections of identity, for those who are oppressed in one context may be oppressors in another. Hence the retreat into a nonjudgmental epistemic neutrality.

But this differentiation makes the retention of normativity all the more necessary. Precisely because the working class Marx studied was not an abstraction but a group composed largely of white males, their subversive insight into the structure of social oppression (and the Marxist theory derived from it) was only partial. Women's perspective was required to uncover the significance of rape as a sustaining mechanism of patriarchal repression. But because the women who developed this analysis were themselves largely white, they in turn tended to miss the particular historical significance of rape accusations made against black men by white women. Again, therefore, a theoretical corrective was necessary, this time in the form of a critique of white, middle-class feminist theory by black women.[57] Putting all these analyses on the same epistemic plane, it seems to me, contradicts the evident truth that in each case a better approximation to the holistic reality of the situation is being achieved. An account of social subordination that does not draw on the experiences of women and blacks is simply theoretically weaker than one that does.

For the past century, Marxism has been the most powerful theory of the dialectic of social oppression. But it has become obvious that this oppression is multidimensional and that the historical forces that produced Marxism as a theory have now thrown up other perspectives, other visions, illuminating aspects of the structured darknesses of society that Marx failed to see. What is needed is a synthesis of these alternative epistemologies, which recognizes both the multiplicity and the unity, the experiential subjectivity and the causal objectivity, of hierarchical class-, gender-, and race-divided society.

3 "But What Are You *Really?*"

The Metaphysics of Race

Race has not traditionally been seen as an interesting or worthy subject of investigation for white Western philosophers, though it has, of course, been the central preoccupation of black intellectuals in the West.[1] Such sporadic discussions as have taken place in "white" Anglo-American philosophy have usually revolved around moral issues; for example, the debates from the 1970s onward about the rights and wrongs of affirmative action. But race raises interesting metaphysical issues as well, in terms of who and what we are, that can also properly be seen as philosophical and that deserve more analysis than they have usually received. The modern world has been profoundly affected by race for several centuries, not merely in the United States and the Americas, with their history of aboriginal expropriation and African slavery, but, more broadly, through the shaping of the planet as a whole by European colonialism. In a sense, then, this neglect by Western philosophy has been an evasion. That race *should* be irrelevant is certainly an attractive ideal, but when it has *not* been irrelevant, it is absurd to proceed as if it had been. There is a growing body of work — at this stage, largely by nonwhite philosophers — on such issues as slavery and colonialism, race and racism, culture and identity, bi- and no-racialism, Pan-Africanism and Afrocentrism,[2] and with the projected demographic shift in the United States over the next century to a majority nonwhite population, we can expect philosophical interest in these matters to increase. As a contribution to this emerging literature, I will try to elucidate what could be termed the "metaphysics of race" that underlie the question "But what are you *really?*"

Quace versus Race

Before talking about race, let me describe a hypothetical, contrasting system that could be termed *quace*. Imagine a nation in which at birth, or at naturalization, all citizens are assigned a code — Q1, or Q2, or Q3 — that indicates their "quacial" membership. This code is entered on birth certificates, naturalization papers, passports, state I.D.s, driver's licences, and the like. So all citizens have a quace. But the assignment is done randomly. There is no connection between quace and an individual's morphology (skin, hair, facial features) or genealogy. In other words, we could not tell a person's actual or likely quacial membership just by looking at him or her, and parents of a given quace would not automatically have children of the same quace. Nor is there any correlation between quace and historical patterns of exploitation and systemic discrimination. There are no Q1/Q2/Q3 ghettoes; no prohibitions, juridical or moral, on intermarriage between Q1s/Q2s/Q3s; no domination of the state or the corporate sector by representatives of a particular Q group; no embedded structural differentials in property ownership between the various Qs; no quacial division of labor; no trumpeting of the superiority of Qx culture; no calls to maintain Q1 purity or heart-wrenching accounts of the existential trauma of being a Q2. The designation comes down from some long-forgotten practice and is maintained by cultural momentum.

In such a society, if someone were to ask us what our quace was, we would, if we were truthful (and it means so little that we would have no motive to lie), just report the information on our passport, let us say, "Q3." But suppose the person persisted and asked, "No, but what are you *really?*" In such a society the question would barely be intelligible. "Really" contrasts with "apparently," but here there is no ontological depth, so to speak, to separate one from the other. We might wonder whether that person thought our code had originally been filled in incorrectly (the randomizing device actually generated "Q1," but the computer was on the blink, or the recording clerk was recovering from the previous night's debaucheries, so that "Q3" was entered instead). But the question would have no deeper significance, precisely because quace has no significance to the lives of the people in that society beyond bureaucratic irritation. "I am a Q1!" would have no metaphysical ring, no broader historical resonance to it, any more than our declaration of our passport number has any metaphysical ring or broader historical resonance to it. And this is, of course, in sharp contrast with declarations of racial membership, which in the United States and many other countries have historically had deeper reverberations and significances.

To get at the root of these differences, we could imagine an ideal racial system, a system of race rather than quace.[3] We could distinguish horizontal and vertical racial systems as contrasting types. In a horizontal system, race has no present or historical link with political power, economic wealth, cultural influence: the races are randomly distributed in the social order. So though race here is not like quace in that it is morphologically/genealogically grounded, it is like quace in being completely disconnected from patterns of discrimination. Whether such a society has ever actually existed seems unlikely, but the question need not engage us, since this abstract possibility has been mentioned only for the sake of the contrast with our real focus of interest: a vertical system. Here the polity and the economic order are expressly structured on a hierarchical axis in which $R_1 > R_2 > R_3$. The functional goal of the system is to privilege the R_1s and to subordinate the R_2s and R_3s. To this end, the R_1s are designated as the superior race. Different criteria are possible, but usually the most important dimensions of this metric of assessment will be intellectual/cognitive and characterological/moral; that is, the R_1s will be seen as more intelligent and of better moral character than the other races.[4] We could speak of this as an R_1-supremacist system, since the R_1s are systemically privileged over the other races.

An ideal vertical racial system would then have rules to regulate its internal structure and guarantee as far as possible its reproduction. Such a system should be complete. That is, every person in the system should have a racial designation, R_1, R_2, R_3 ..., and if there are people for whom that designation is R_0, this would be the outcome of the system's rules (rather than the result of confusion over where the person fits). The system should also be well formed; that is, clear-cut, unambiguous principles would determine to which race the products of intermarriage between Rs would belong. (And this system would have to be recursive to take account of what happens when those offspring intermarry.) Unless the system is closed (no immigration), it should also have rules for allocating new arrivals to the appropriate racial slots. The extent of the R_1 privileging (for example, in deciding public policy) should be determinate, whether through the stipulation of a strong "lexical" ordering of R_1 interests vis-à-vis R_2 and R_3 interests (R_1 interests as carrying infinite weight) or some weaker principle (R_1 interests as finitely weightier). Finally, it should be nationally uniform, in the sense that there should be no local variations in the rules according to state or region.

Obviously, in such a system, by contrast with a system of quace or the horizontal racial system, one's racial designation will have immense significance, since it will indicate one's social standing and profoundly affect one's life. And because the United States and many other nations have historically been vertical racial systems of this kind, race has significance. These systems have not been ideal because the rules have not usually been complete, well formed, determinate, or nationally uniform. Moreover, many of the privileged R1s have opposed the system ("race traitors"/"white renegades"), refused to abide by its prescriptions, and supported the efforts of R2s/R3s to change it. Nonetheless, the system has been sufficiently successful that, to take the United States as an example, more than two hundred years after its founding, people still think of themselves as raced; American cities are more segregated now than they were at the turn of the century; there is little intermarriage; blacks are still, by conventional economic measures, near the bottom of the ladder; and some leading black intellectuals are now speaking despairingly of "the permanence of racism."[5] So this, I suggest—as against the system of quace or the horizontal racial system—is the background against which the metaphysics of race needs to be examined and from which the question "But what are you *really?*" gains its ontological import.

Metaphysical Positions

The terms *social ontology* and *social metaphysics* (I will use them interchangeably) have a certain intuitive transparency, being obviously meant to refer to the basic struts and girders of social reality in a fashion analogous to the way "metaphysics" *simpliciter* refers to the deep structure of reality as a whole. So there are basic existents that constitute the social world, and that should be central to theorizing about it. Thus one readily understands what it means to say that the social ontology of the classic contractarians is an ontology of atomic individuals; that for Karl Marx, it was classes defined by their relation to the means of production; and that for radical feminists, it is the two sexes. In pre-postmodernist times, these categories would have been confidently put forward as part of foundationalist and theoretically exhaustive explanatory schemas—history as class or gender struggle. In the present, more cautious period, greater theoretical circumspection is wise. Note, then, that I am not claiming that race is the only principle of social hierarchy, or that racial struggle is the comprehensive key to understanding history, or that individuals' racial ontology is in all circumstances the most important thing about them. But systemic racial privilege has been an undeniable (though often denied) fact in recent global history, and exploring an ontology of race will contribute to (though not exhaust) our understanding of social dynamics. Other systems of domination besides race (class, gender) overlap and intersect with it. But in the United States (and

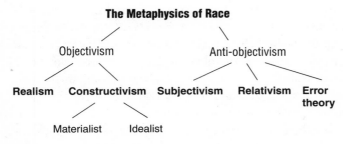

Figure 1. The metaphysics of race

elsewhere) race has correlated strongly with civic standing, culture, citizenship, privilege or subordination, and even designations of personhood. One's racial category has been taken as saying a great deal about what and who one is, more fundamentally. To what extent and in what ways, then, is race "real," and how deep is this reality?

Terminology developed elsewhere can illuminatingly be drawn upon to map representative positions on the ontology of race. As we know, philosophers of science and ethicists have an elaborate vocabulary for demarcating contrasting views on the reality of scientific entities and the metaphysics of moral value — realism, constructivism, conventionalism/relativism, instrumentalism, subjectivism, noncognitivism, nihilism/error theories, and so forth. Some of this vocabulary can usefully be appropriated to clarify debates on race. The correspondences are not exact and should not be pressed too far; moreover, some terms have no plausible "racial" equivalent at all. Too many qualifications and epicycles may so muddy the homology as to vitiate the whole exercise. Still, I expect the similarity that emerges to be sufficient to make the appropriation enlightening.

Let us distinguish, to begin with, between objectivism and anti-objectivism as umbrella categories of theories about the reality of race (see Figure 1). *Objectivism* is used in several ways, but usually it connotes the independence of what we choose, what we believe. There are two main objectivist positions: realist and constructivist.

In metaethics and the philosophy of science, the term *realism* usually denotes the view that acts have value or disvalue and that the entities postulated by natural science either exist or do not exist independently of human consensus or dissent. So, for example, killing the innocent is objectively wrong prima facie even if a certain community has no prohibitions against such actions, just as electrons objectively exist even if nobody knows about them.

What, by analogy, would be realism about race? A "racial realist" in the most minimal sense will be somebody who thinks it is objectively the case

—independent of human belief—that there are natural human races; in other words, that races are natural kinds. In the stronger, more interesting sense, a racial realist will also believe that the differences between races are not confined to the superficial morphological characteristics of skin color, hair type, and facial features, but extend to significant moral, intellectual, characterological, and spiritual characteristics also, that there are "racial essences."[6] Anthony Appiah argues that such a view (which he designates as "racialism") needs to be distinguished from racism proper, though racism presupposes it, since these traits may be thought to be distributed in such a way across the population that there is no clear-cut hierarchy among races.[7] Historically, however, not merely have all racists been realists but most realists have been racists. For the past few hundred years, realism has been the dominant position on race; that is, people have believed that there are natural biological differences among races and that these differences run deeper than mere phenotypical traits.

Such views of race are often hostilely characterized as *essentialist*, and this term coheres nicely with the "realist" categorization insofar as in the philosophy of science, realism is associated with a belief in natural kinds with defining essences. One way of making the theoretical commitments here vivid is to think of the issue in terms of transworld identity. For racial realists, people categorizable by their phenotype in our world, with its peculiar history, as belonging to a particular "race" will continue to have the same "racial" intellectual and characterological traits in another world with a radically different history. For racial realists who link culture to genotype, this view implies, for example, that black American culture would still be basically the same even if Africans had come here as voluntary immigrants and never been enslaved. And to the extent that relations between groups identified as races are also explained in these naturalistic terms, relations between white and black Americans would still be antagonistic.

Racial realism, whether in its racist or merely racialist versions, thus runs directly against the gathering consensus of anthropological and biological research. It is not merely that racism (the natural biological hierarchy of races) is false; it is not merely that culture, psychology, and intergroup relations are far more convincingly explained on the basis of contingent histories than of "natural" racial traits; it is that the very categories used to identify races are significantly transworld relative. Indeed, as commentators often point out, the U.S. one-drop rule for determining membership in the "black" race—that is, any "black" blood makes you black—is practically unique even in *this* world.[8] Many of those categorized as blacks in the United States would be categorized as browns/mulattoes or even whites in the Caribbean and Latin America. And one could easily imagine a parallel universe of the type beloved of science fiction writers, where—as a result, say, of the overrunning of Dark Ages Europe by an Islamic army of Moors and black Africans—an inverted racial order is established in which the one-drop rule is applied in reverse, and any discernible "white" blood relegates a person to membership in the conquered and despised tribe of native European "savages."

But from the fact that racial realism is false, it does not follow that race is not real in other senses; this is the point of developing objectivism as an umbrella category broader than realism. Many white liberals (and, indeed, historically many white Marxists also), aware of the verdict of science on race, are puzzled at black intellectuals' retention of race as a significant social category: they wish to move from the falsity of racial realism to global claims about the unreality of race in general and the corollary political mistakenness of race-centered political discourse such as one finds in black nationalism, Pan-Africanism, and Afrocentrism. But part of the point of my taxonomy of metaphysical positions is to show that there is conceptual room for a view of race as both real and unreal, not "realist" but still objectivist. This position is *racial constructivism*.

In metaethics and the philosophy of science, constructivism is a kind of epistemically idealized intersubjectivism; for example, the hypothetical moral agreement behind Rawls's veil of ignorance or in Habermas's ideal speech situation, or scientific consensus on what theory best explains the phenomena. Values and scientific existents are objective in the qualified sense of being independent of particular agents' *actual* judgments but not of their hypothetical *ideal* judgments. Thus constructivism contrasts with realism as a fellow objectivist view and with relativism and subjectivism as anti-objectivist views. For David Brink, nonrelativist constructivism "agrees with moral realism that there are moral facts and true moral propositions but disagrees with realism about the nature or status of these moral facts and truths.... [It] holds that there is a single set of moral facts that are constituted by some function of our beliefs, often by our moral beliefs in some favorable or idealized epistemic conditions."[9]

Now radicals, whether the depleted class of Marxists or the thriving tribe of postmodernists, often speak of the "social construction" of race, so that the term is already in use; I see this as more than a serendipitous homonymy.[10] What they mean, to begin with, is that there are no "natural" racial divisions between human groups but rather a continuous spectrum of varying morphological traits. That the lines of demarcation, the categorial boundaries, are drawn here rather than there is a social decision, and one that creates the (social) reality in question. So the resultingly racialized world is in part theory-dependent, constituted by these very beliefs. Under other circumstances, in other worlds, or even in our world at different times, different lines of demarcation could have been drawn. This view is not in itself particularly radical, since most anthropologists share it.[11] The additional claim that distinguishes the radical view is that the decision as to where to draw the line is politically motivated, to establish and maintain the privileges of particular groups. So, for example, the motivation for using the one-drop rule to determine black racial membership is to maintain the subordination of the products of "miscegenation."

There are obvious differences, however, between *constructivism* in this sense and the standard use of the term. The intersubjectivist agreement in moral and scientific constructivism is a hypothetical agreement of all under *epistemically* idealized conditions. Racial constructivism, by contrast, involves an actual agreement of some under conditions where the constraints are not epistemic (getting at the truth) but *political* (establishing and maintaining privilege); the "idealization" is pragmatic, instrumental to the best way of achieving this end. Nevertheless, the semantic virtue of retaining the same term (apart from the fact that it is already in use) is to highlight the crucial similarity: that an objective ontological status is involved which arises out of *intersubjectivity,* and which, though it is not naturally based, is real for all that. Race is not foundational: in different systems, race could have been constructed differently or indeed never have come into existence in the first place. Race is not essentialist: the same individuals would be differently raced in different systems. Race is not "metaphysical" in the deep sense of being eternal, unchanging, necessary, part of the basic furniture of the universe. But race is a *contingently* deep reality that structures our particular social universe, having a social objectivity and causal significance that arise out of *our* particular history. For racial realism, the social metaphysics is simply an outgrowth of a natural metaphysics; for racial constructivism, there is no natural metaphysics, and the social metaphysics arises directly out of the social history. Because people come to think of themselves *as* "raced," as black and white, for example, these categories, which correspond to no natural kinds, attain a social reality. Intersubjectivity creates a certain kind of objectivity.

Finally, it should be noted that constructivism comes in different varieties depending on the background theories of social dynamics presupposed. Materialist theories ("materialism" in the sense of patterns of social causality, not ontology), preeminently Marxism, will see this dynamic as economically driven, related to the structure of capitalism and the projects of the bourgeoisie, and embedded in (though not reducible to) class.[12] Nonmaterialist theories will either deny any causal preeminence at all (pluricausality with no dominant sector) or attribute it to culture/ideas/"discourses."[13]

Of the variety of anti-objectivist positions in metaethics and the philosophy of science, the ones relevant for our purposes are subjectivism, relativism, and nihilism/error theories. (Noncognitivism and instrumentalism have no plausible racial equivalents.)

Subjectivism in ethics is the view that what makes an action right or wrong is the agent's opinion. Subjectivism about race would be the view that since racial designations are arbitrary (as constructivists would agree), one can choose one's race. Subjectivism would therefore imply a kind of voluntarism about race, which is, of course, what makes it an anti-objectivist position. For constructivists, by contrast, the arbitrariness of racial designation is rooted in a particular social history and cannot be overturned by individual fiat.[14]

Ethical relativism and scientific conventionalism make the truth of moral and scientific claims dependent on actual (nonidealized) community agreement. An epicycle is required here, since racial constructivism does *itself* necessarily involve an element of relativism (the reality or objectivity of race is relative to the particular racial system concerned). So this would need to be distinguished from racial relativism proper. The latter would imply that within the (objective) constructed global racial system, which is, let us say, coextensive with the nation, it is possible to change race through the decisions of a subcommunity of like-minded people within the larger population.

Finally, error theories of ethics, such as, famously, John Mackie's, deny that moral terms refer to anything.[15] A corresponding error theory about race would deny not merely that races have no biological reality (as racial constructivism does) but also that they have no reality as *social* entities. As I noted earlier, many liberals, and those Marxists committed to an explanatory class reductionism, can be said to have an error theory about race in this sense. Traditional Marxist debates about race and class, or race versus class, can then be seen from this perspective as often being debates over whether racial error theories or racial objectivist theories (realist or constructivist) are correct.

It should be obvious by now that I am most sympathetic to a constructivist position on the metaphysics of race, a position that is objectivist but also antirealist and antiessentialist. This position is most congruent with the actual historical record, where race has not been an arbitrary social category, such as "quace" or an innocent designation, as in a horizontal system, but has functioned as a real marker, if imperfectly, of privilege and subordination in a *vertical* system. In such a system, racial subjectivism, racial relativism, and racial error theories seem to me to be mistaken; the metaphysics of race is an objectivist if antirealist metaphysics.

Criteria for Racial Identity

I want to turn now to the question of the possible criteria for determining racial identity and what happens when these criteria conflict. These are puzzle cases, what could be regarded as cases of racial transgression. I assume throughout a nonideal vertical racial system, where R1s are the privileged race.

Consider the more familiar philosophical debate on personal identity. In the literature on this subject, going back to Locke's classic discussion in *Essay Concerning Human Understanding*,[16] it has usually been assumed that there is an answer to the question "Who are you *really?*" that is not necessarily the same as the answer to the question who the person is *taken* to be. The whole point of the soul-transmigrating, brain-transplanting, and memory-loss examples is to get at this difference. The idea is that some kind of metaphysics is objectively there—who the person *is*—and that one may have intuitions that point at it, even if only fuzzily. Through problem cases one can draw on these intuitions, sometimes refining and reformulating them, sometimes giving them up altogether, in the attempt to capture the essence of personal identity, if not in terms of necessary and sufficient conditions, then perhaps in some looser formula that can at least cover most situations. Moreover, personal testimony, although it is given some weight, is not taken as indefeasible (e.g., cases of implanted memory); in some respects the individual has a privileged first-person perspective, but his or her self-identification may on occasion be mistaken. The question will be whether people's race, similarly, is an objective "metaphysical" fact about them, so that by considering puzzle cases in which the standard criteria conflict rather than agree, we can sharpen our intuitions as to what "race" really inheres in.

Seven possible candidates for racial self- and other-identification may be distinguished. They are not at all necessarily mutually exclusive, since they usually function in conjunction with one another. The interesting issue is what happens when this conjunction begins to disintegrate. The categories are bodily appearance, ancestry, self-awareness of ancestry, public awareness of ancestry, culture, experience, and self-identification.

When these categories all point to a specific racial designation, $R_1/R_2/R_3$, we do not hesitate to identify the person as a particular R, nor does the person. But since the United States has a nonideal racial system, with rules that are occasionally less than clear-cut, we may experience difficulty when the criteria conflict. Moreover, the problems in any decision procedure are compounded by the fuzziness of some of the criteria, which are not subject to precise stipulation. There is also the question whether R1/R2/R3-ness is a discrete, on-off affair, or whether on occasion allowance is made for degrees of R1/R2/R3-ness. This is separate from the question whether there is an *intermediate* category; the idea rather is that one could be seen as an R1 or an R2 or an R3 but in a somewhat qualified (sometimes grudging?) fashion, not wholeheartedly or full-bloodedly—to use biological metaphors, though the basis for the judgment need not be biological—an R1 or an R2 or an R3. It may also be that there is a partial gender asymmetry, so that what holds true for men in situations of criterial conflict does not always hold true for women. Finally, the fact of racial hierarchy (R1s being systemically privileged) may carry over into the criteria for racial identification; that is, in some circumstances the rules for adjudicating the racial identity of R1s may differ from the rules for R2s/R3s.

Bodily Appearance

Bodily appearance, the so-called eyeball test, is the criterion we all use to make summary judgments about race, since information about the other criteria is not usually immediately known to us. Historically, this has been true not merely for lay but for "scientific" judgments about race also, since before the advent of genetics earnest attempts were made to ascertain racial membership on the basis of such characteristics as skin color, skull measurements, and hair texture. In some racial systems, however, the appearance of R-ness is neither sufficient nor necessary for actual R-ness— though it will generally be a good evidential indicator—for some people may be able to "pass." Appearance is then the generally (but not always) reliable visible manifestation of a deeper essence that is taken to inhere in ancestry.

Ancestry

In the U.S. racial system, at least for whites and blacks, ancestry is usually taken as both necessary and sufficient for racial membership. (Elsewhere— in some Latin American countries, for example—appearance is more important, so that siblings of different colors may be assigned to different races despite their identical genealogy.) The rules for ancestral adjudication will, of course, be system-relative. A bipolar system, consisting exclusively of R1s and R2s, has no social and conceptual space for a third category, R3s, that would explode the binary opposition, so that the offspring of "miscegenation" are assimilated to either the R1s or the R2s. Where blacks and whites are concerned, U.S. policy has historically been to classify them with the R2s on the basis of the one-drop rule. This is what the anthropologist Marvin Harris calls the rule of "hypodescent," normative descent from the "lower" race.[17] So entrenched has this view been until recently in national folkways and popular consciousness that it seems obvious, "natural," when in fact it is simply the result of a conscious public policy decision.[18] The alternative policy of social *elevation* to R1 status not merely is an abstract possibility but was actually followed at certain times in the Dutch East Indies, where the children of Dutch men and Asian women were counted as Dutch.[19] Finally, in a tri- or multileveled racial system, such as obtains in the Caribbean and Latin America, there are formally recognized intermediate racial categories. (In the case of racial combinations, we may sometimes be satisfied with the less exact judgment "non-R1"; that is, even if the details of the racial mixture are not clear, we at least want to know whether the person counts as an R1, a member of the privileged race, or not.)

Self-Awareness of Ancestry

I have separated self-awareness (and public awareness) from ancestry in order to provide a conceptual entrée for some of the puzzle cases I will consider later. It might be thought that this is an epistemological rather than an ontological issue, that whether or not we *know*, or others know, if we are an R1 or an R2 is not relevant to the substantive metaphysical question whether we actually *are* an R1 or an R2. But since this is one of the very claims I will examine, it seems better to leave it open rather than conceptually foreclose it.

Public Awareness of Ancestry

"Public awareness" as a criterion is fuzzy because one may be officially classed as an R2 (e.g., on ancestral criteria) but, because of one's appearance, seem to be an R1, so that—unless one remains in a small community where one's genealogy is known to all—one's ancestral R status may be on the record but not generally known.

Culture

Traditional racial theory, committed to racial realism, sees culture as an emanation of biological race, so invoking it as an additional criterion would be otiose (except perhaps as confirmation in contested cases of "mixed" ancestry). If culture stems from genotype, then for R1s to adopt the cultural traits of R2s or vice versa either should be impossible (the strong version of the thesis) or should at least involve considerable psychological strain (the weaker version), so that one's "real" biological self is always immanent within the borrowed clothes of the alien culture, waiting to assert itself. For nonrealist theories, on the other hand, whether constructivist, relativist, or subjectivist, culture is seen as adoptable with greater or lesser degrees of fluidity and is detachable from biological race, so that it may play a role in racial identification. Sometimes a tacit or overt normative premise of a moral and political kind is presupposed, that those identifiable by other means as R1s/R2s should exclusively or predominantly embrace the culture associated with R1s/R2s. Failure to do so then makes one racially inauthentic. Note, though, that the use of culture as a criterion presumes relatively clear demarcating traits that differentiate R1 from R2 culture. But even if a clear genealogy of origins can be traced (not always the case), the constant intermingling of peoples means that patterns originally associated with one group can be adopted by others and, over time, transformed so as to be recognizably "theirs." Many Euro-American cultural practices have unacknowledged Native American and African roots, whereas the syncretism resulting from slavery makes dubious the dream of some Afrocentrists of recovering an uncontaminated African essence.

Experience

Like culture, "experience" has an unavoidable fuzziness, but it is important, for in the vertical racial systems we are considering it is part of the core of what it is to be (with all the metaphysical overtones of *be*) a member of a particular race. Thus in the United States, we naturally think of whiteness as being associated with the experience of racial privilege and of blackness as being associated with the experience of racial oppression. Since criterial divergence is possible, so that R2s who look like R1s and are not publicly identified as R2s will escape racism, it may then be alleged that these R2s are not "really" R2s, insofar as the essence of being an R2 is the experience of oppression *as* an R2.

Subjective Identification

Finally, subjective identification — what one *sees* oneself as — needs to be conceptually separated from self-awareness of ancestry, for one may refuse to recognize the validity of this criterion for racial membership; and from culture, for one could still identify oneself as an R1/R2 while embracing R2/R1 culture; and finally from experience, for one could have experiences characteristically taken to be definitive of the R1/R2 experience while denying that these experiences should be seen as definitive of who one is. As a further complication, self-awareness of ancestry is an either-or affair (either one knows or not), whereas subjective identification lends itself to degrees of variation, in that one can weakly or strongly identify oneself as an R1/R2, so that this identification is less or more significant to one's sense of oneself and one's life projects. Robert Gooding-Williams makes the useful distinction of "thin" and "thick" senses of "black" to differentiate these varying degrees of self-identification for African-Americans.

Racial Transgressives

What happens when these criteria conflict with one another? That is, what happens when, through naturally occurring or artificially devised problem cases, individuals are produced whose racial ontology is not immediately or maybe not even indefinitely clear? As in the parallel case of personal identity, the strategy simultaneously involves drawing on some intuitions and overturning others. At this point I will drop the abstract R1/R2 vocabulary and focus specifically on the U.S. situation, where R1s and R2s are whites (Ws) and blacks (Bs). The justification is that mobilizing our intuitions in any useful way requires us to contextualize them in a familiar situation.

Refer now to the "racial" criteria in Table 1. Standardly, we assume there is uniformity down the line: people who look respectively white/black are descended from ("pure") whites/(some) blacks, are aware of their descent, have public recognition of their descent, embrace the culture typically associated with whites/blacks, have experiences taken to be characteristic of the white/black experience, and identify themselves as white/black. These individuals are thus uncontroversially white/black. In Table 1, we alter some of the criteria to make them inconsistent with the others and then see what our intuitions say. We will consider both "natural" and "artificial" cases, where one expressly sets out to try to change one's race. (It may seem that this is an impossible dream, that race for an individual is permanent, but this is one of the intuitions I will try to undermine.)

Let us bracket the moral and political question whether one *should* try to change one's race, or at least one's apparent race. The motivation for such actions has often been seen as ignoble: the desire to enjoy the privileges of the dominant race while distancing oneself from the fate of the oppressed. But this is a separate issue, certainly of interest in its own right but distinct from the metaphysical one. So we should try to avoid the kind of cognitive interference that comes from thinking that because it is morally or politically *wrong* for black people to try to become white, they cannot succeed in doing so — that the (moral) "inauthenticity" of the decision somehow car-

Table 1. Types of racial transgressives, U.S. racial system

"Racial" criteria	I	II	III	IV	V	VI	VII
Bodily appearance	W	W	W	B	W*	W	W
Ancestry	B	B	B	B	B	W	W
Self-awareness of ancestry	Yes	Yes	No	Yes	Yes	No	Yes
Public awareness of ancestry	No	No	No	Yes	No	No	Yes
Culture	B	W	W	W	W	B	B
Experience	W/B	W	W	W/B	W	B	W/B
Self-identification	B	W	W	W	W	B	B
Person is:	?	?	?	?	?	?	?

Case I: Conscious episodic passing (natural whiteness) for strategic reasons
Case II: Conscious passing (natural whiteness) for ultimate assimilation
Case III: Unconscious passing (natural whiteness)
Case IV: Mr. Oreo
Case V: Mr. Oreo and the Schuyler Machine (artificial whiteness)
Case VI: Unconscious "passing" as black
Case VII: White renegade
Case VIII: ("Black") White renegade
Case IX: "Biracial" (self-identified)
Case X: "No-racial" (self-identified)

W = white; W* = artificially white; B = black.

Note: Case VIII involves variations of case VII. Case IX is open to multiple possibilities in several of the criteria. And racial details are unnecessary in case X, because one can subjectively identify oneself as no-racial independently of the other criteria—arguing, for example, that really nobody has a race.

ries over to infect the metaphysical status. (One would then be not a white person who is inauthentic but an inauthentic white person.) Unless, of course, a case can be made for such a connection.

Problem Case I

Consider first the case of someone whose body is naturally white because of the genetic lottery and who knows that he has at least one black ancestor but deliberately sets out to "pass." This is one of the most famous themes of the African-American experience and has been the subject of numerous stories, novels, and movies.[20] Let us begin with what I call "conscious episodic passing." This person leads a bifurcated life, passing for the purpose of taking advantage of differential economic opportunities in a segregated workplace or a better residential area or for whatever reason but continuing to think of himself as black and maintaining contact (cautiously, if necessary) with the black community. (The head of the NAACP from 1931 to 1955, the ironically named Walter White, had what was judged to be only one-sixty-fourth black ancestry. Socially categorized as black but with blond hair and blue eyes, he describes in his autobiography, *A Man Called White*, how he often posed as a white man—i.e., a man called white—so that he could investigate lynchings in the South.)[21] The public will not generally know such people are black, so that they will not have many of the negative encounters characteristic of the black experience. Nonetheless, we would generally conclude that these individuals, identifying with and acculturated by the black community, are indeed "really" black. We would not regard them as sometimes white and sometimes black; rather, we would say that they are always black but sometimes pretend to be white.

Problem Case II

Contrast this case with what I call "conscious permanent passing." Here the goal is not conjunctural advantage but ultimate assimilation: the person wants to be taken for white. Maintaining contact with black relatives, childhood friends, and neighborhood acquaintances will obviously jeopardize this endeavor, so it will be necessary to move away from them, sever all relationships, and give one's children a highly pruned version of the family tree. Similarly, to avoid betrayal by "black" cultural traits, such a person will consciously steep him- or herself in white culture. Suppose that this act of assimilation and acculturation is successful. (Historically, in fact, tens of thousands of U.S. blacks did take this step every year. One such person, exposed after his death, was the prominent New York literary critic Anatole Broyard.)[22] The person is accepted by his white neighbors as white, there is no public awareness in his social world of his black ancestry, he does not experience racism, and though he is naturally nervous for the first few years, he gradually comes to relax and feel confident that his deception will never be discovered.

Clearly, such an individual has changed his *apparent* race—that should not be controversial—so why shouldn't one go a step further and say he has changed his *actual* race? Racial realists rule this step out, since they identify race with biological criteria (ancestry, in the U.S. system). Perhaps they also imagine that biological race will continue tendentially to manifest itself—one will be sitting tuxedoed in the symphony hall listening to Schubert and suddenly get an uncontrollable ancestral urge to start boogeying. But even without these biocultural claims, racial realists may feel that the person is still *really* black. Once we accept a constructivist view of race, in what sense is this person still black? He looks white, is socially categorized as white, embraces white culture, has white experiences. Why can't we say that he has successfully changed his race and become white? (Acceptance of this description does not undermine commitment to an objectivist metaphysic. Constructivism about race implies that there are objective criteria to being a member of a race, and we have respected that objectivity by taking measures to meet those criteria. We cannot change our actual ancestry, but we can change awareness of it. And we can also change culture and experience. So a subjectivist view, according to which it would be a mere matter of will—one could just decide to be white without doing anything about it—is wrong, as is an error theory that denies the social reality of race.) The point of the example is to test the strength of our commitment to ancestry ("objective") as a definitive criterion. If our intuitions are somewhat tugged the other way, this indicates that intersubjective criteria (awareness of ancestry) are more important.

Nevertheless, it may still be insisted that there is a basis other than ancestry for applying the label "black," because the person (unless he has self-induced amnesia also) will be aware of his black ancestry and cannot avoid thinking of himself as a black person pretending, even if very successfully, to be white. Moreover, it may be argued, to describe the person's experience as "white" is question-begging, since by definition experience is a subjective, internal affair, not merely the third-person external description of events happening to an agent. Neither the average white person nor this particular individual will experience white racism, but the crucial difference, it will be argued, is that the average white person will never even think about this possibility (why should she?). The individual in question, however, will be ever watchful, always anticipating exposure as black, even if it never comes. Thus the phenomenological difference between the consciousness of the "real" white person and the "apparent" white person is alone sufficient to show that the person cannot *really* be white but is still black.

There is some merit to this argument. It could, of course, be replied that although this nervous consciousness is admittedly likely to be present at the beginning, it would quickly dissipate if, by hypothesis, the charade is successful, so that appearance would then become reality.[23] But let us grant this point of differentiation and move on to a case where it is no longer present.

Problem Case III

In both case I and case II, the person was aware of his nonwhite ancestry. Consider now a person who thinks her ancestry is white. If the first two cases come under the heading of conscious passing, this is a case of unconscious passing. This theme, too, has been treated often in American fiction. One classic treatment is Mark Twain's *Pudd'nhead Wilson* (1894), in which a slave mother switches her own light-skinned baby for the master's child at birth, so that her son grows up as her white master while the master's child is taken to be her slave son.[24] A real-life example is Gregory Williams's *Life on the Color Line*, subtitled *The True Story of a White Boy Who Discovered He Was Black.*[25] In case II, part of our hesitation to classify the person as white, even apart from realist sympathies, may be because we imagine a kind of psychic tension, an awareness that the presented persona is not the same as the internal one. The person is playing a role, performing an act, pretending to be something he is "really" not. But eliminating the condition of awareness of ancestry removes this feature of the situation: this person thinks of herself as white. So if this obstacle is no longer present, what is the objection to saying that the person is "really" white? Note, by the way, that demographers estimate that millions of officially "white" Americans actually fall into this category; that is, they have black ancestry unknown to them, so that by their nation's rules they are "really" black.

One way to think of the issue is as follows. In the determination of racial identity, an interesting combination of objective, subjective, and intersubjective factors is at work. For a constructivist as against a realist theory, ancestry is crucial not because it necessarily manifests itself in biological racial traits but simply, tautologously, because it is *taken* to be crucial, because there *is* an intersubjective agreement (originally in the dominant R1 population, later embraced by the R2s) to classify individuals in a certain way on the basis of known ancestry. As a result of this classification, one will typically think of oneself in a certain way, identify with a certain culture, and have certain kinds of experiences. But if the intersubjective classification is mistaken, then one will *not* think of oneself in that way, *not* identify with that culture, *not* have these experiences. The tendency is to see this as a case of mistaken racial attribution; thus Gregory Williams "discovers" he is black. His blackness is supposed to be a fact about him that continues to obtain even in the absence of the other features with which it is usually linked. But why not the alternative description: he was white, and then became black? (Indeed, one chapter title is "Learning to be Niggers.") If others say that he was really black all along, are they doing anything other than repeating the uncontested assertion that his ancestry was black? What other ontological freight does this judgment "really" carry?

Here's another way to think about it. The point of starting off with the story about the quace society was to create a foil for our actual society. In the quace society, there is never any difference in the answer to the questions "What are you?" (how are you classified?) and "What are you *really?*" because how you are classified, whether as a Q1/Q2/Q3, makes no difference to your life. The adverb "really" introduces a notion of ontological import, metaphysical depth, signifying something that *makes a difference* in some fairly profound way. But quace makes no difference, so there is no room for the added emphasis. It can be put in the sentence, but nothing answers to it. If one did find that one had been misclassified, one would barely give it a moment's thought. Race, however, can overturn a life, as it did for people in apartheid South Africa who found themselves reclassified to "Coloured," and as it did for Gregory Williams. Making the ancestral criterion the sole arbiter fails to capture this metaphysical dimension, because we are then reduced to saying that race is just how an individual is classified. Whereas the reality is that it is the *import* of this classification that, through subjective internalization and intersubjective recognition, is doing the metaphysical work. So once an example is set up in which this classification is made wrongly, it is possible for us to see what our intuitions are really responding to. People focus on ancestry because in this world ancestry and the other attributes usually go together, but separating them shows that ancestry is not really the important thing. What is important is the intersubjective/subjective criterion of what ancestry is *thought* to be.

But an objection may then arise. I began by distinguishing objectivist and anti-objectivist "metaphysical" positions on race and endorsing constructivism as an objective but nonrealist view of race. But it seems to be turning out that my view is not really that sharply distinguished from anti-objectivist positions. Realists about race may assert that race will continue to manifest itself in the same way through different possible histories, that it has an enduring transworld quality. But my position seems to be that race is just what one thinks it is. And how can this be a variety of objectivism? How is this different from the subjectivist and relativist positions on what is supposed to be the other side of the metaphysical fence?

The answer is complicated by the nonepistemic character of this "constructivism" and the relativist element it contains. But it *is* distinguished by the fact that the construction is intersubjectivist (not individual), state-backed, and usually crystallized both in law and custom. Subjectivism about race seems to imply a kind of voluntarism, that merely by being determined to deny race, or to think of oneself as raced differently than one is classified, one can change one's race.

Problem Case IV

Consider the case of someone I will call Mr. Oreo. Mr. Oreo cannot even think of passing, being quite dark with clearly black African features and with known black ancestry. But he is unhappy with his racial designation, so he fills in "white" on bureaucratic forms, identifies himself as white, and rejects black culture. Will these gestures make him white? The black community has a standard negative moral judgment of such people, which is of course signified by the name. Some notion of racial authenticity is presupposed, along with a normative judgment that this kind of repudiation is morally contemptible. It would be interesting to explore the values that underlie this judgment—after all, if race is constructed, what gives it moral significance?—but as I said at the start, my focus is on the metaphysics rather than the ethics. And the designation Oreo clearly has a metaphysical as well as a moral dimension, since it implies that the person is divided, black on the outside but white on the inside. Does this mean that for lay consciousness, the person *has* succeeded in changing his race, insofar as the spatial metaphors of inside and outside standardly correspond to essence and appearance? In some contexts, after all, it would critically be said of Mr. Oreo that "he's really white." But this is really a statement about values and identification; if pressed, people would deny that Mr. Oreo has actually become white. The sense would be that he is a black man pretending, or trying and failing, to be white, so that the moral opprobrium arises from the attempt, not the success or failure of the attempt.

Now, why do we not think the person has succeeded? For lay consciousness, which is typically realist, the simple answer is that race inheres in ancestry, appearance, and so on, so that it cannot be changed. But racial constructivists would also deny that race-changing in this fashion is possible, seeing this position as an untenable racial subjectivism or voluntarism. And a central reason for their claim will be that Mr. Oreo is still socially *categorized* as black, especially by the crucial population, the white one; he will still experience racism and so will still be black insofar as the experience of white racism is definitive of the black experience. When followed around in a department store, stopped by the police in a white neighborhood, or mistaken for the waiter in a restaurant, Mr. Oreo may protest, with a reassuring laugh, "No, no, you don't understand, I'm not one of *them*," but his protest is not likely to be effective. (Note, though, that this scenario opens the possibility of a more liberal, "cultural" racism, whereby people could be prima facie black but gain at least a virtual, courtesy whiteness by passing the appropriate cultural tests and thereby be distinguished from unreconstructed blacks.) So if racial subjectivism is a mistaken position on the metaphysics of race, Mr. Oreo will still be black.

Problem Case V

But suppose Mr. Oreo comes to understand this and is a sufficiently determined fellow. Let's give him the option of a technological fix, introducing to that end the Schuyler Machine. The well-publicized cosmetic transformation of Michael Jackson raises the possibility that advances in plastic surgery techniques or even genetic engineering may make it possible one day to transform one's skin, hair, and facial features so that one looks completely white. In George Schuyler's neglected satirical classic, *Black No More*, a black scientist invents a machine that can do just that, with the result that within a few months all the blacks in the United States vanish, having seized the opportunity to transform themselves into apparent whites.[26] Let us call this device the Schuyler Machine. (In the book it has no name.)

Suppose individuals such as Mr. Oreo whose bodies are *not* (as in the first three examples) naturally white make use of this device and then go on to assimilate as above. In these cases, does their artificially rather than naturally white bodily appearance support the doubts of those who question whether one can really change one's race? Why? What would the basis of this skepticism be? Compare another kind of physical transformation, that of bodily physique and strength. If a machine were invented (call this the Schwarzenegger Machine) that could transform 98-pound weaklings into massively muscled supermen capable of pressing hundreds of pounds without the tedium of years of special diets and weight training, would we say that the person only *looked* strong but had not really *become* strong? Obviously not: his new body, new physique, new strength are real. So what is the difference? (The question here is not the deep ontological one whether an apparently white body makes a person really racially white, since we have already seen that—at least by itself—it doesn't necessarily do so. Rather, the question is the shallow ontological one whether an apparently white body is any the less apparently white because the whiteness is artificially engineered rather than natural. So we are dealing here precisely with an ontology of appearance, of surfaces.)

Is the difference that we think of the first three persons' surface whiteness as real (because genetic), whereas Mr. Oreo's is unreal (because artificial)? In the first place, of course, the Schuyler Machine may work through genetic manipulation, so the etiology would still be genetic, though not hereditary. If we insist that the whiteness comes from parental genes, is this not just a repetition of the ancestral criterion, whereas we began by agreeing to consider them separately? In the second place, even if the whiteness is artificial, why is it any the less real? "Artificial" does not necessarily contrast with "real"; it just contrasts with "natural." An artificial heart is real enough and can sometimes do the job as well as (or better than) a real heart. Moreover, technological advances and the general mediation of the natural by the social make the distinction increasingly problematic.

Or is the objection of another kind, that the "whiteness" is thought of as somehow merely surface, a kind of full-bodied "whiteface" that corresponds to the blackface of nineteenth-century minstrelsy, and underneath it is the original black-skinned person? By hypothesis, the pertinent bodily parts really are transformed; it is not that the skin acquires a white sheen that will come off if Mr. Oreo goes out in the rain, for example, or scrapes himself by accident. Rather, the change is in the skin (and hair texture, facial features, etc.). Or do we unconsciously think of physiological "whiteness" as something that permeates the whole body, inhering not merely in skin color, facial features, and hair texture but also sparking in the synapses of the brain, pumping through the bloodstream, dripping through the pancreas? If so, it is a revealing indication of how, despite ourselves, lay conceptions of race affect us. Research has shown that the morphological differences between people classed as white and those classed as black are minor, quite apart from the reality that many "blacks" in the United States have largely white ancestry.

My suggestion is, then, that whether the apparent whiteness is natural or artificial should make no difference to its reality; in both cases, the person is apparently white. So the point of this exercise is to undermine conventional intuitions about the "natural" basis of whiteness and the location of its ontological depth in the biological. Race *is* ontologically deep, but its depth lies in intersubjectivity; a body that appears to intersubjective judgment to be white is all, I am arguing, that is necessary here. (The alternative would be to introduce another level and speak of bodies that "appear white," whereas other bodies "appear to appear white.") A case can be made, then, that Mr. Oreo succeeds in changing his race, especially if he moves to a part of the country where nobody knows about his black past, though admittedly if he marries a white woman, having children will be a challenge.

Problem Case VI

Consider the case of unconscious passing from the other direction: the white child in the Twain story raised as black. This is someone with a genetically white body and all-white ancestry who, unaware of his actual parentage, grows up as black, thinks of himself as black, is culturally black, and is categorized by the community as black. If the ancestral criterion is the overriding one, then we have to say that this person is really white. But what does the "really" mean other than the repetition of the point that his ancestry is white? At the novel's end, the deception is discovered and the biologically white young man resumes his place as rightful heir (though never to feel at home except in the kitchen), whereas the unconscious impostor, who has been a miscreant in various ways, is sold down the river as partial payment for estate debts. But suppose the switch had never been discovered. Would it still be true that in some deep sense, the biologically white boy was really white? Or can we say that he became black, that his race was changed?

Problem Case VII

In a vertical racial system, members of the subordinate race who assume the privileges of the dominant race are, as I have noted, usually morally condemned. Correspondingly, members of the racially privileged group who support and identify with the racially oppressed usually gain our moral approbation, if not that of their peers. Can this identification extend to race-changing? The hostile term "nigger-lover" often carried with it the threat that to persist in subversive behavior would lead one to be treated in the same way as blacks, but does this actually amount to an ontological shift? Various terms from the American and colonial experience seem to register such a possibility: the "white Injun" of the frontier period, the European explorer who "goes native," the general notion of the "white renegade" or "race traitor" who is seen as not merely betraying his race but in some sense as *changing* his race. A U.S. journal, *Race Traitor,* calls on white Americans to self-consciously repudiate their whiteness. (In the 1950s Norman Mailer wrote a famous essay on the hipsters as "White Negroes";[27] their contemporary descendants are "whiggers," or "white niggers," suburban white kids who affect the clothing, language, and musical styles of black inner-city youth.)

Imagine such a contemporary white renegade who sets out to support and identify with black struggles, steeps himself in black culture, joins nonseparatist black political organizations, and is therefore on occasion targeted for differential treatment by hostile authorities. Sometimes, of course, whites who take this course are working out personal problems, indulging in some kind of "exoticism," or "slumming." But perhaps this individual's sincerity so impresses the black community that he is even regarded as an "honorary" black. In this case, unlike that of Mr. Oreo, one's moral judgment is likely to be favorable, but is this relevant to the metaphysical issue? It could perhaps be argued that since the metaphysics depends in part on some kind of subjective decision, the moral authenticity of giving up racial privilege translates into or becomes a kind of metaphysical authenticity. But we would tend to feel, I think, that the person is at most politically or maybe culturally but not *really* black. After all, in many situations his assumed identity will not be known, and he will just be treated like any other white guy. And in any case, he can always have a change of heart and jettison his assumed identity, which in a world without a Schuyler Machine blacks in general cannot do. (But suppose that the community is small, and the authorities have an official policy to penalize racial transgressors by publicizing their identities and formally and permanently changing their racial standing. Consider the real-life case of the white author John Howard Griffin, who, in a reversal of the Schuyler Machine process, had his skin treated to darken it and on the basis of his experience wrote the bestselling *Black Like Me* in 1959.[28] If Griffin had carried out his project in a society so small that everyone subsequently was informed about his "crime" and treated him accordingly forever after, we might want to say that he really *would* have become black.)

Problem Case VIII

But let us say that he would not have become black. Consider four variations on this theme: (1) unknown to the white renegade, he actually does have black ancestry, but neither he nor anybody else ever finds this out; (2) he discovers his black ancestry, makes it public, and is officially recategorized as black; (3) he discovers it but chooses to keep it secret, wanting to "earn" his blackness through his own efforts, so that his official categorization remains white; (4) he makes the same discovery and announces it publicly, thereby being recategorized, but in fact the "discovery" is erroneous, and the supposed black ancestor is really white, though this is never found out. In all cases, assume that he identifies with black culture and supports black struggles to the same extent, so that whether public or secret, real or mythical, his ancestral blackness makes no difference to his actions. What do we judge the metaphysics of race to be in each case?

Problem Case IX

Consider now the case of biracialism. The U.S. racial system has been polarized mainly between white and black, with blackness being demarcated through the one-drop rule. An intermediate mulatto category has sometimes or in particular locales been officially recognized, and within the black community there are traditional shade hierarchies,[29] but this has been the basic division. In the Caribbean and Latin America the spectrum of statuses is more variegated. In part because of the growth in intermarriage and resulting "mixed" children, a movement is afoot in the United States to introduce a multiracial category on census forms to accommodate the experience of people who reject the bifurcation into black and white.[30] The young golfing star Tiger Woods, for example, identifies himself as "Cablinasian"—Caucasian, black, Indian, and Asian. Some blacks protest that this is merely another way for people with visible European ancestry to differentiate themselves from the "pure" black population. Historically, browns/ mulattoes/mestizos have been seen as superior to "unmixed" blacks, if not as good as whites, and as such have been privileged in various ways in mainstream white society. (This situation is recognized in black American popular discourse in the old rhyme "If you're white, / You're all right. / If you're brown, / Stick around. / If you're black, / Stand back." Moreover, within the black American population in some cities there were somatically exclusive clubs—for example, the blue-vein or brown paper bag clubs—from which dark-skinned blacks were excluded.)

As before, however, the focus is on the metaphysical question. The question is not whether such a tri- or multipolar racial system is possible, because the Latin experience shows it is, and one could imagine a United States with an alternative history that had evolved with such a system. If racial constructivism is correct, then by definition the same human population can be demarcated and constructed into different "races" in many ways. The question is whether, in the face of majority white resistance to such a revision, subgroups within the existing bipolar system can successfully construct themselves as biracial. My endorsement of constructivism has been predicated on a uniform national system. But it might be argued that certain circumstances could promote a racial relativism in which particular subcommunities could reject official categorizations and construct their own identities.

In his book *Who Is Black?* for example, F. James Davis discusses the history of "American Mestizos": Brass Ankles, Red Legs, Yellow-hammers, Red Bones, Guineas, Jackson Whites, Moors, Creoles, and other groups with black ancestry who have historically refused the status of blackness. "These so-called American Mestizo groups have protected themselves from the one-drop rule by remaining as isolated as possible, which has become more and more difficult. Within their own communities they are presumably all equal, whatever their racial composition, and they are very cautious in their dealings with the outside.... [They] continue to try to avoid being defined as blacks by remaining isolated and wary."[31]

We are talking, then, not of individual voluntarism (racial subjectivism) but of a group decision to challenge dominant conceptions. But as Davis's account makes clear, to the extent that their deviant self-definition has been possible, it has required social exile, which is not a desirable option for contemporary bi- and multiracial individuals. So the question is whether such a self-chosen hybrid identity can be sustained on the basis of group endorsement in the face of the majority's adherence to the traditional principle by which any black blood makes one black. Would such people really become another race, or, because of their interactions with the larger society, would they really just stay black?

Problem Case X

Finally, an interesting challenge has been posed by the philosopher Naomi Zack—the argument that the admitted absurdity of racial classifications should push us to endorse neither race 1 nor race 2 nor even bi- or multiracialism but no race at all: we should simply repudiate racial categorization. "The concept of race is an oppressive cultural invention and convention, and I refuse to have anything to do with it.... Therefore, I have no racial affiliation and will accept no racial designations."[32] Whereas bi- or multiracialism has some objectivist base, though a local rather than global one, this position seems to be a nonstarter, for it ignores the fact that in a racialized society people will continue to have racialized experiences, whether they acknowledge themselves as raced or not.

We have seen, then, that there are issues pertaining to race and racial identity that are well worth the time of philosophers to address. Doubtless they will become more pressing as the nation's racial composition shifts. Most Western philosophers have been white and have taken their racial standing for granted, not seeing how it enters into their identity and affects their relationship with the universe. Race may not be real in the sense that racial realists think or would even like, but it is real enough in other senses. The metaphysics of racial identity is thus a metaphysics well worth investigating.

4 Dark Ontologies

Blacks, Jews, and White Supremacy

To what extent can the ideas of Immanuel Kant, or at least some kind of modified Kantianism, help us to understand the problems of race, and the racial and ethnic tensions that continue to plague the modern world? For minority philosophers who work on issues involving race, of course, there are general conceptual obstacles to the appropriation of *any* of the classic figures of the Western canon. Western philosophers have not historically been interested in theorizing about these issues; their writings may reflect racism, but they do not analyze it. With Kant, however, the challenge is particularly acute because the potential payoff and the apparent obstacles are so great. On the one hand, the decline of utilitarianism and the apparent failure of Marxist socialism have led to the triumph of a rights-based person-centered liberalism, making Kant arguably the most important moral and political philosopher of the modern period.[1] If a Kantian framework could be employed for theorizing on race, it would obviously be of great benefit. On the other hand, how could a philosophy celebrated for proclaiming the irrelevance to full personhood of anything but rationality have anything useful to say on a subject as seemingly morally irrelevant and "phenomenal" as race?

Here I will outline a strategy for bringing race and Kantian—or perhaps "Kantian"—theory together. My focus is black-Jewish relations. The subject is of interest in its own right, but its ultimate value for this discussion is the instrumental illumination it sheds on a background political structure whose contours are barely acknowledged, let alone mapped, in mainstream Anglo-American political philosophy: white supremacy. For most white philosophers, race (if it is noticed at all) is essentially conceptually residual, a "deviation" from ideal practice to be theoretically handled through discussions of affirmative action, compensation, reparations, and so forth. Racial privilege, as a normatively backed political system, needs to be taken far more seriously by white moral and political philosophers as we approach the twenty-first century, and Kantian theory can be adapted to provide a philosophical blueprint of its architecture.

Ontologies Light and Dark

Tensions between the African-American and Jewish-American communities, a constant subterranean presence in recent decades, surfaced once again with the infamous speech delivered by Khallid Muhammad in November 1993 at Kean College, in which he accused Jews of being "bloodsuckers" of the black community. This was, of course, only one in a long series of unhappy episodes, going back in the most recent cycle to the 1960s (though ultimately older), which have worsened relations between black and Jewish Americans: the Nation of Islam's publication of *The Secret Relationship between Blacks and Jews;* the murder of Yankel Rosenbaum in Crown Heights; Jesse Jackson's "Hymietown" remark; the firing of Andrew Young by the Carter administration for unauthorized meetings with the PLO; Israel's suspected role in giving South Africa the technology to acquire nuclear weapons; the 1968 teachers' strike in New York; and, more generally, the perceived prominence of Jewish intellectuals in the neoconservative ideological backlash to the movements and causes of the 1960s and 1970s (including affirmative action), with its well-publicized conversions, apostasies, and mea culpas. Op-ed pieces, conferences, books, and anthologies on the subject continue to multiply, and an exhibition on black-Jewish relations sponsored by the Jewish Museum in New York toured the country in an attempt to build bridges.[2]

I will take a different approach to this familiar issue, an approach that relies on a reconceptualization of the polity as a *racial* one. To this end I will use the interrelated notions of "personhood" and "respect," the conceptual apparatus central to Kant's moral and political universe. For Kant's work is the best articulation of the moral egalitarianism associated with the Enlightenment, the American and French revolutions,[3] and the rise of modernist individualism: the once-daring idea, exploding the old social hierarchies of antiquity and feudalism—patrician and plebeian, noble and serf—that all humans are moral equals, *persons,* and so, as autonomous moral agents, equally worthy of respect. "Kant's entire moral philosophy can be understood as a protest against distinctions based on the far less important criteria of rank, wealth, and privilege.... Kant's is an ethics of the people, of moral egalitarianism.... Respect is an attitude due equally to *every* person, *simply* because each is a person, a rational being capable of moral self-determination."[4] Indeed, in the *Groundwork* and *The Metaphysics of Morals* we find (at least ideally) an inspiringly ecumenical conception of personhood so far removed from the phenomenal world of prejudice and ethnocentrism (or anti-Copernican geocentrism) that even intelligent aliens from another planet can be persons, since the crucial feature for equal moral status is rationality.[5] If we speak of a "social ontology"—a mapping of the basic units of a social universe—then we can say that in Kant we have the social ontology of an ideal Enlightenment liberalism, the polity as a *respublica noumenon,* a world of abstract individuals equally deserving of respect and characterized by freedom, equality, and independence.

So much for the familiar Kantian ideal world, the world toward which he hoped we were progressing. To get a sense of the reality, we need to turn to a radically different figure, someone from the oppositional black tradition also concerned with the moral idea of respect but from an understandably different perspective. The Jamaican political activist Marcus Garvey (1887–1940) died in obscurity but is celebrated today as the organizer and leader of the largest black political movement in history.[6] At the height of its global influence in the 1920s, the organization he founded, the Universal Negro Improvement Association, "could boast over 1200 branches in over 40 countries, with 700 branches flourishing in the United States alone," others being spread across the Caribbean, Central America, Canada, and Africa. Garveyism was thus a "subversive" ideology of significant concern to many governments of the white world.[7] Garvey's anticolonial and antiracist political program failed during his lifetime, but his ideas lived on to inspire later generations of African and African-American activists. And his basic message to the millions of Africans at home and abroad who read his *Negro World* newspaper and tried to follow his political guidance was "A race without authority and power is a race without respect."

The reality, of course, is that the world in which Garvey was politically active—the world of the early twentieth century, as indeed the world for many previous centuries and, some would argue, the world even today—was not in conformity with the raceless Kantian ideal. The norm was what one could term global white supremacy, the formal/juridical domination of the planet by white people.[8] The United States had the official system of segregation known as Jim Crow, with systematic disenfranchisement of blacks, thousands of unpunished lynchings, inferior housing and education, pervasive job discrimination, and a color line running through most everyday transactions (separate and inferior dining, traveling, and entertainment facilities) and extending even into death (separate hospitals and cemeteries).[9] Elsewhere, the world was dominated by European colonialism, which in 1914 "held a grand total of roughly 85 percent of the earth as colonies, protectorates, dependencies, dominions, and commonwealths,"[10] a political system justified by an ideology of master and subject races.[11] And everywhere in lay and academic opinion, popular consciousness and respectable scholarship, the inferiority of nonwhites, particularly blacks, was taken to have been "scientifically" established—whether by craniometry, Camper's facial angle, recapitulationism, social Darwinism, or IQ theory.[12]

In this world it would be quite wrong to assume that the ideal Enlightenment Kantian social ontology—people as abstract noumenal individuals equally deserving of respect—was the norm, with a few unfortunate deviations. Rather, the opposite was the case. The norm was the routine restriction of full personhood to whites, and the consignment of nonwhites to a subordinate moral status. Garvey's linking of race to respect thus becomes perfectly understandable as a recognition of the state of affairs that actually obtained, the realization that the Kantian ideal was not taken seriously where nonwhites were concerned. Race was far from irrelevant to personhood; skin color, hair, and facial features were used to categorize people and determine their moral standing. So this could be said to be the "dark ontology" that is the unacknowledged dark side of the Enlightenment ideal. Simply put: one set of rules for whites, another for nonwhites. All persons are equal, but only white males are persons.

The claim is, then, that whatever the merits of the Enlightenment social ontology of Kant as an ideal, the reality is this dark ontology. It could be said to be triply dark. First, it is dark in the sense of being color-coded, consigning nonwhites to a lower rung on the ontological ladder. Second, it is dark in the sense of being sinister, a social ontology of domination and subordination. And finally, it is dark in the sense of being largely unacknowledged in Western political theory. Little theoretical attention has been paid to the fact that the polity and Western moral and political philosophy were structured in this way, so that the ideal might seem to have been realized, admittedly with some unfortunate deviations. (The analogy here is to the dark matter in the universe that can be detected only by inference, by the way it bends light and twists gravitational fields. Or think of the term "black economy," used to describe the underground economies of some Third World countries, where in some cases the unofficial economy of drugs, smuggling, higgling, and the like is the *real* economy, and the official economy is a myth.)

Official Kantianism: Ideal Enlightenment ontology

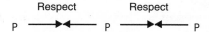

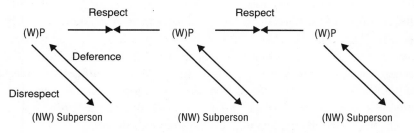

Population: Abstract individuals.
Raceless persons give each other mutual respect as individuals.
Personhood and self-respect are taken for granted, have no connection with race.

Herrenvolk Kantianism: Actual dark (unacknowledged) Enlightenment ontology

Population: Raced; white persons and nonwhite subpersons.
White persons give each other mutual respect as whites but give racial disrespect to nonwhite subpersons, who in turn are required to give racial deference to whites.
For nonwhites, personhood and self-respect have to be fought for and are intimately tied up with race.

P = person   W = white   NW = nonwhite

Figure 2. Official and *Herrenvolk* Kantianism

We can represent these ontologies diagrammatically as in Figure 2, using "personhood" and "respect" as the conceptual common denominator. This strategy provides a simple and straightforward way to translate race into the vocabulary of mainstream political philosophy. On the one hand is the official ontology of the ideal Enlightenment, where abstract raceless and colorless individuals are treated as persons equally deserving of respect. On the other hand is the actual dark, "naturalized" social ontology,[13] the ontology of the divided Enlightenment, characterized by an "exceptionalism in European thought about the non-West," an "Enlightenment dichotomization" in its normative theories.[14] This is the social ontology of the world of slavery, colonialism, and segregation, where concrete individuals are seen as raced and colored and treated accordingly. If the former is the world of abstract Kantianism, the latter can be said to be the world of "*Herrenvolk* Kantianism." I adapt this term from the sociologist Pierre van den Berghe's description of white settler states such as the United States and South Africa as "*Herrenvolk* democracies," polities that are democratic for the master race, the *Herrenvolk*, but not for the subordinate race(s).[15] Extrapolating this scheme to moral theory, as I explained in chapter 1, we can imagine a *Herrenvolk* ethics, a set of moral rules that prescribe a different schedule of norms—rights, duties, privileges, liberties—for different subsets of the human population according to racial demarcation. So if idealized Kantianism has a population of raceless persons among whom symmetrical relations of mutual respect are supposed to obtain, then we could say that naturalized *Herrenvolk* Kantianism has a population partitioned between white persons and nonwhite subpersons, with asymmetrical relations between them. Persons give each other respect but give disrespect to subpersons, who in turn, to show that they know their place in the scheme of things, are normatively required to show deference to persons. For nonwhite subpersons, disrespect is the norm, the "default mode" of this system. For blacks in the West—*contra* official, ideal Kantianism—this *Herrenvolk* ethic means that moral standing and race, whiteness/personhood/respect and blackness/subpersonhood/disrespect, have been inextricably tied up together for hundreds of years.

Finally, I want to consider the objection that however interesting such a model may be, it has very little to do with Kant and Kantianism, even in a scare-quotes sense, so that my attempt to locate it in this framework is essentially misguided. Two points may be made in reply.

The first is that in the application of Kantian moral philosophy to the real world, it is the naturalized rather than the idealized ethic that we need to grapple with and understand in our efforts to change people's moral consciousness and behavior (which is presumably the ultimate point of moral philosophy). As an academic exercise, mapping the internal normative logic of Kant's (idealized) views on personhood and respect is valuable in its own way. But it is of less use when it comes to actually engaging with and transforming human social behavior, especially if there is no corollary recognition of how systematically divergent from the ideal this behavior has been. For such a remedial moral project, one needs to map not so much the idealized normative logic (surely very familiar by now) as the nonideal naturalized logic of these notions, as *concretely instantiated* in the theories and practices of racially privileged Westerners. And even if Kant had said nothing at all about race, one could still consider this exercise to be derivatively Kantian insofar as notions of personhood, respect, and self-respect have, though in a racialized form, been central to these theories and practices.

But it turns out that Kant had a hand in both ontologies; it is not the case that his work only inspired the laudable ideal theory from which others' lamentable practice then fell short. For if Kant can be regarded as the father of modern moral theory, he is also known to some — a fact that will probably astonish many Anglo-American philosophers — as the "founder of the modern concept of race."[16] This embarrassing attribution will not be found in the average contemporary philosophy textbook or anthology, but the judgment is not new, and the evidence seems to support it. Radical and minority philosophers have perhaps more of a motivation to uncover such passages, given their conviction that even seemingly abstract and "pure" philosophy has too often been infected by racism and Western imperialism. But Kant is not some minor and obscure figure; he is the increasingly preeminent moral/political philosopher of the modern period, and it is surprising that more attention has not been paid to this aspect of his work in establishment mainstream theory.

There is, to begin with, his notorious statement in *Observations on the Feeling of the Beautiful and Sublime* (1764) that "so fundamental is the difference between [the black and white] races of man ... it appears to be as great in regard to mental capacities as in color," so that "a clear proof that what [a Negro] said was stupid" was that "this fellow was quite black from head to foot."[17] Often cited by black philosophers as a paradigm example of impure reason that stands in need of critique, this passage could, nonetheless, be dismissed as no more than a "precritical" lapse. More problematic for such a dismissive interpretation, however — as David Theo Goldberg points out[18] — is Kant's later essay "On the Different Races of Man" (1775), in which he outlines a classic hereditarian, antienvironmentalist account of innate racial difference that essentially anticipates post-Darwinian "scientific" racism.[19] In George Mosse's summary of this essay, "racial make-up becomes an unchanging substance and the foundation of all physical appearance and human development, including intelligence."[20]

But the most detailed account of the centrality of race to Kant's thought, *including* his "critical" philosophy, is to be found in an article by Emmanuel Eze.[21] Drawing on both translated and untranslated work, and greatly developing the discussions of previous authors, Eze shows that Kant's moral theory really needs to be understood in the context of his anthropology and physical geography, subjects on which he lectured for forty years, thus including his mature, "critical" period. For Kant, it turns out, there is a natural color-coded racial hierarchy of (reading from top to bottom) white Europeans, yellow Asians, black Africans, and red Americans, with corresponding differential capacities for moral educability. Europeans are basically self-starters; for Asians there is some hope, though they cannot grasp abstract concepts; Africans can at least be morally educated as slaves and servants, with the help of a split bamboo cane (Kant offers some advice on how to beat Negroes, given the obstacle to their moral education posed by the thickness of their skins); and Native Americans are just hopeless and cannot be educated at all. Thus, as Eze concludes, Kant can be regarded as putting the racial classifications of Carolus Linnaeus on a philosophical foundation: race is actually a transcendental. "The black person, for example, can accordingly be denied full humanity since full and 'true' humanity accrues only to the white European. For Kant European humanity is *the* humanity par excellence."[22] So Immanuel Kant, the theorist of abstract noumenal persons equally deserving of respect, reveals himself simultaneously as one of the founders of the very ontology of subpersons and racial disrespect that black activists such as Garvey have traditionally had to fight against.[23]

Race as a Political System

My suggestion, then, is that only by recognizing the existence of this background system of political domination and its accompanying social ontology can we really begin to understand the troubled relationships between blacks and Jews.[24] If we see these problems solely in terms of individual prejudice and bigotry, free-floating attitudes and cultural predispositions, we will miss crucial realities that need to be incorporated into an adequate explanation. In other words, we need to talk about race as itself a political system, and the differential and evolving relations of blacks and Jews to it. We need to put this relationship in a historical context and ask where Jews are located with respect to this system, where blacks are located with respect to this system, what psychology is tendentially produced in people by these different locations, how social cognition of the system is shaped by these different locations, what form ethnic affirmation and racial self-identification characteristically take under these conditions, and how moral assertions of personhood and demands for respect typically play themselves out, given this background dark ontology.

As I have mentioned, part of the problem, certainly in mainstream political philosophy and to a certain extent in political theory more generally, is that we lack a developed theoretical vocabulary and conceptual framework for this enterprise. Categories, distinctions, and theorizations do not crystallize of themselves; they have to be developed by people who think long and hard about the matter, make mistakes, try out ideas, correct themselves, have an epistemic community to go back and forth with on theoretical innovations. Cognition is, contra the Cartesian paradigm, essentially social, reliant on an already developed network of concepts and paradigms. Without a constituency with a motivational interest in developing this understanding and with the educational training to facilitate it, certain realities will remain largely uninvestigated and unmapped. Cognitive psychologists have documented the remarkable extent to which our perception of the world is theory-driven rather than data-driven.[25] We have macro- and micro-theories about how things work and tend to filter, process, and assimilate information accordingly. Perceptions that are not in keeping with or are actively contradictory to preexisting theories tend either to be ignored or to be suspended as puzzling anomalies, viruses epistemically quarantined from the body of existing theory, which eventually perish for want of a sustaining conceptual environment. Whites have generally taken their domination of the planet for granted and so have either ignored it or positively valorized it, not seeing it as a negative system of oppression whose mechanisms need investigation. Nonwhites have generally been cognitively disadvantaged by being either deprived of formal education or socialized into a white conceptual framework whose internal logic is refractory to an investigation of these realities. And where attempts *have* been made to develop oppositional understandings of the racial order, they have generally been marginalized by mainstream thought.

So the result is that the body of critical theory on the racial structuring of the polity cannot compare in depth, detail, and sophistication to the tremendous volume of work which, by taking *whites* as the norm, assumes an essentially "raceless" system. Yet, as George Mosse has written, "racism as it developed in Western society was no mere articulation of prejudice, nor was it simply a metaphor for suppression; it was, rather, a fully blown system of thought, an ideology like Conservatism, Liberalism, or Socialism, with its own peculiar structure and mode of discourse," indeed "the most widespread ideology of the time."[26] For hundreds of years, race was a political system in its own right: it was through race that whites came to understand their identity, their position in the world, their manifest destiny, their civilizing mission, their burden, their entitlements and privileges, their duties and responsibilities. The term *white supremacy* is usually associated with localized regimes, particularly with the American Old South and apartheid South Africa. But as I pointed out earlier, in a broader sense the history of the world has long been a history of white supremacy, in that Europeans basically controlled the globe and were the privileged race, the *Herrenvolk*. A historian of anti-Semitism, Léon Poliakov, argues that the horrors of the death camps produced an expedient amnesia about this truth in the postwar European intelligentsia, so that the centuries-old centrality of racist ideology to the mainstream of Western thought was erased and attributed instead to scapegoat figures, such as Arthur de Gobineau and Houston Chamberlain: "A vast chapter of western thought is thus made to disappear by sleight of hand, and this conjuring trick corresponds, on the psychological or psycho-historical level, to the collective suppression of troubling memories and embarrassing truths."[27]

Thus, to the traditional vocabulary of modern Western political theory —absolutism and constitutionalism, dictatorship and democracy, capitalism and socialism—we need to add such concepts as white supremacy, pigmentocracy, a *racial* polity. For even if we assume complete good faith and sincere commitment on the part of whites to eradicate the legacy of this system of de jure racial privilege, the world of European expropriation, slavery, and colonialism, there will be a period of continuing de facto white advantage, sustained by—if nothing else—cultural lag, institutional momentum, accumulated wealth, and attitudinal inertia. Whites on the whole will generally be privileged with respect to nonwhites, in terms of economic opportunities, political input, and dominant cultural representations. (For the sake of simplicity, I am going to ignore the class and gender differences in both populations.)

Let's look at race as a *politically constructed categorization*, then, the marker of locations of privilege and disadvantage in a set of power relationships. (One book actually talks about "the invention of the white race.")[28]

1. Race is essentially *relational* rather than monadic—there have to be at least two groups characterized as races for the categorization to be motivated. (One could say that without two races, there could not be one race.)

2. Race is *dynamic* rather than static—the relations between races change over time, as do the rules for racial membership.

3. Race is only *contingently* tied to phenotype: a given appearance is neither necessary nor sufficient for inclusion in the privileged race, R_1, or the disadvantaged race, R_2. The Japanese, for example, have been classified as honorary whites (in South Africa under apartheid), so phenotypical whiteness was not necessary to be white. Other peoples, however, who would today be thought of as uncontroversially white—the Irish, Slavs, Mediterraneans, Jews—have in the past been seen as borderline whites or sometimes even nonwhites. And in the United States, where genealogical criteria are crucial, there are people who are phenotypically white, who could pass for white, but who, by the one-drop rule, count as black.

4. Race is usually *vertically* defined, in terms of hierarchy and subordination, with R_1 over R_2 over R_3. Although it is certainly logically possible for investigation to be carried out for purely taxonomical reasons, the mo-

tivation for the project has usually been to arrange the "races" in some kind of moral/evolutionary/intellectual/aesthetic hierarchy.

5. For individuals of a given phenotype, race may vary both *temporally* in a given system (membership rules shift over time) and *geographically*, through entry into a different system (different membership rules in different racial systems). People of mixed black and white heritage who count as browns, mulattoes, or even whites by local Caribbean and Latin American rules thus become black in the United States.

6. Race is *unreal*—in the biological/anthropological sense, race does not really exist, and though the categories continue to be used, most scientists agree that it is actually a category like phlogiston.[29]

7. Race is *real*—in the sociohistorical/political sense, race does exist as a categorization with a massive effect on people's psychology, culture, socioeconomic opportunities, life chances, civil rights.

8. Race as a system has to be *maintained* through constant boundary policing against both the contestation of members of subordinate races who seek inclusion in the privileged race and, more radically, those who wish to dissolve the system altogether.

9. Finally, although there are local systems with different rules, historically the most important *global racial system* has been the system of white domination, structured on a white/nonwhite axis.

Given such a background, where the basic divide is between privileged whites and disadvantaged nonwhites, the crucial question obviously becomes: Who gets to be white? And to anticipate the following discussion, the simple answer is: Blacks never get to be white; Jews get to be white, or nearly white, most of the time.

The Position of Blacks in This System

First, the straightforward case—that of blacks. This case is straightforward because blacks have the dubious honor of being the paradigm representatives of the darkness in these dark ontologies. In the racial taxonomies drawn up by Europeans from the seventeenth century onward, blacks are almost always at the bottom, the last quasi-human link (or sometimes the missing link) in the Great Chain of Being before it descends unequivocally into the animal kingdom.[30] Kant's derogatory judgment has already been mentioned, but (confining ourselves just to philosophers) there is also Hume's, which it echoes, that "negroes, and in general all the other species of men" are "naturally inferior to the whites"; Voltaire's polygenist conclusion, in "The People of America," that blacks (and Native Americans) are a different species, unrelated to Europeans, whose understanding is "greatly inferior," "not capable of any great application or association of ideas"; and Hegel's denial, in *The Philosophy of History,* that sub-Saharan Africa *has* any history, so that since Negroes are "capable of no development or culture," European slavery at least has a civilizing influence: "we may conclude *slavery* to have been the occasion of the increase of human feeling among the Negroes."[31]

The native peoples of the Americas are also disparaged in Western theory, of course, appearing in most of the classic social contract theorists' writings as the paradigm savages of the state of nature. But they at least get to be "noble savages" some of the time; blacks are almost always *ignoble* savages. Similarly, whereas Europeans have sometimes grudgingly valorized the civilizations of other nonwhites, such as those of China and India, they have almost never expressed a corresponding respect for African civilizations, and black African claims to the most famous civilization on the continent, that of ancient Egypt, continue to be contested.[32] So conceptually linked are blacks with the ground floor of racial hierarchies that when other nonwhite races of higher status are contingently forced downward because of conjunctural circumstances, the process is sometimes described by race relations theorists as "niggerization."

What explains this unhappy distinction? One argument is that on practically all the major theories offered to explain white racism, blacks are at the antipodes; they are the polar opposites to whites, so that — to the extent that these theories are complementary, and *multiple* causation may be involved — there is a devastating confluence of mutually reinforcing causes.

Culturalist Explanations

It has been argued that the historic source of white racism lies in a combination of religious intolerance and cultural predispositions to see nonwhites as alien, Other. The medieval battles against Islam are then the precursors of the racism that was to accompany European expansionism into the world. African religions were seen as devil worship, black culture and customs viewed as "mumbo jumbo," paradigmatically bizarre.[33]

Psychosexual Explanations

Other explanations focus on the *body* and the psychological associations, linked with European, particularly English, color symbolisms, of nonwhite flesh.[34] And of all human bodies, blacks' are the farthest from the Caucasoid somatic norm, not just in color but also in hair texture and facial features. So whereas at various times other races have on occasion been seen as physically attractive, sexually "exotic," the black body has usually been portrayed in grotesque and negative terms, caricatured and denigrated in seventeenth- and eighteenth-century illustrations of European travelers' tales, the later representations of "scientific" racism, American postbellum "blackface" imitations, nineteenth- and twentieth-century cartoons and advertising.[35]

Politico-economic Explanations

Finally, Marxist explanations attribute racism to the ideological need to rationalize the political and economic projects of privileged classes.[36] African slavery thus arguably demands the most severe kind of racism, since slavery reduces people to things, to property, and requires their depersonization for the atrocities that necessarily accompany it. Moreover, blacks are the only people to have been enslaved *as a race*—African slavery, unlike the systems of ancient Greece and Rome, was tied to phenotype—so that African features became the stigmata of subordination.

Overall, then, blacks have been at the bottom of these dark ontologies or, more strongly, have usually defined where the bottom is. Other races have shown more mobility and have been able to move up the ontological ladder. But for centuries Western consciousness has been imprinted with the image of blacks as the paradigm subpersons: ugly, uncivilized, of inferior intelligence, prone to violence, and generally incapable of serious contributions to global culture.

The Position of Jews in This System

Compare this position with that of Jews. In medieval Christendom, Jews were traditional outcasts, victims of the Inquisition, pogroms, expulsions, forced conversions, massacres. But this persecution was carried out under the sign of the cross. Though there are some precursors of what we would today call racism—for example, the fifteenth-century deployment in Spain of the criterion of *limpieza de sangre,* or purity of blood, against Marranos, Jews who sought exemption through conversion[37]—religion rather than race is the central category of identification. Only with the the rise of secularism in the modern period and the diminished significance of faith as a social marker does race become for Europeans a central category of other- and self-understanding. Although, as I pointed out at the start, the bourgeois revolutions flatten the normative social hierarchies within Europe, producing in the ideal limit the noumenal Kantian individual, an ontological gap begins to open up (in what is also the Age of Discovery) between Europe and non-Europe. A social ontology gradually crystalizes around race, an ontology in which Europeans ("whites") are opposed to and raised above the rest of the world.[38]

And in this social ontology, Jews basically get to be white. This is not to say that they are *fully* white — as Winthrop Jordan has pointed out, "If Europeans were white, some were whiter than others."[39] Internal, fine-grained exclusionary distinctions continue to be made, coinciding often with subordinated minority status or with undeveloped nation or region, and giving rise to more restrictive conceptions of entitlement: Teutonism, Anglo-Saxonism, Aryanism. And some of these distinctions, of course, were later drawn on by private racist groups (in the case of the Nazis, a group that gained state power) to rewrite a more exclusionary definition of whiteness. But for the official, state-backed racial system, the fundamental conceptual cut, the main line of cleavage in this global dark ontology, is that between white European and nonwhite non-European. And Jews generally end up on the white side of the line. As George Mosse notes, "The Jews were either ignored by anthropologists during most of the eighteenth century or considered part of the Caucasian race, and still believed capable of assimilation into European life.... Ideas of cosmopolitanism, equality, and toleration operated for the Jew as they could not for the Negro; after all, the Jew was white.... No one seemed to feel such [ambivalence] toward blacks. Blacks, unlike Jews, had a fixed lowly position in the 'great chain of being,' " a position "close to the animal world."[40] Thus in the racial taxonomies that were increasingly devised in the period, Jews were generally subsumed under whites, not identified as a separate category. So though European Jews continued to be the victims of prejudice and ostracism, they benefited from being *Europeans,* from being citizens of the continent that increasingly dominated the world. They benefited materially, as all Europeans did, from European imperialism. They benefited culturally, by being considered citizens of the superior global culture. And they benefited "ontologically," being classed with the privileged global race of whites. Within this framework, then, one could argue that from the modern period onward, Jews really become nonwhite only under the Third Reich, which was precisely why the Nuremberg Laws came as such a shock to German Jewry.

Even in Europe, then, the situation of Jews differed from that of nonwhites. But in North America the contrast was even sharper. Here, of course, the legacy of medieval Christendom was much weaker, and new political systems were erected on the expropriation of Native American civilizations. So from the start, there was an explicit commitment to an egalitarianism of a *Herrenvolk,* racially exclusivist kind, which — more clearly than in the Old World, where nonwhites were part of the distant empire — was structured around an axis of crucial differentiation from the *domestic* nonwhite population. And, again, Jews counted as whites. Particularly in the United States, where mass turn-of-the-century Jewish immigration from the Eastern European Pale of Settlement coincided with the formal introduction of Jim Crow/de jure segregation after the 1896 *Plessy* v. *Ferguson* Supreme Court decision, Jews were juridically categorized as white. The signs read "White" and "Colored," not "White," "Jewish," and "Colored." This is not by any means to deny the stigmatization of Jews by the Klan, the wave of anti-Semitism in the 1920s that led to a limitative rewriting of the immigration laws, the prevalence of discrimination in the form of restrictive housing covenants, job advertisements that specified "Christian" applicants, exclusion from private clubs, and university admission quotas. It is to point out the qualitatively worse character of oppression for those *formally* subordinated by the racial polity. Of the thousands of U.S. lynchings from the 1880s to the 1930s, for example, only one victim (Leo Frank in 1915) was a Jew.[41] The ontological whiteness of Jews gave them an edge that gradually enabled them to assimilate and enter the northern industrial economy in a way that the millions of black migrants from the sharecropping South were not able to emulate.

With the discrediting of anti-Semitism after the war, the Jewish success story came to a remarkable climax in the present financial standing of American Jewry, whereas the civil rights victories over formal segregation in the 1950s and 1960s did not produce a comparable material success for blacks. Now uncontroversially white (except in the eyes of racist fringe groups), favored by the system, many Jews can no longer see that system's continuing racial character. In comparing black American to Jewish-American history, they look at their own success and ask why blacks can't achieve the same, an analysis encouraged by the dominant school in U.S. race relations theory, which assimilates race to ethnicity and represents the black experience as a variant of the traditional immigrant European experience.[42] The feeling grows that blacks are asking for special treatment. But as two sociologists, Douglas Massey and Nancy Denton, argued in *American Apartheid*, to understand the causes of the continuing existence of a black "underclass," one must realize that from the 1920s onward, no European immigrant group in the big American cities suffered a rate of ghettoization that reached even the lowest degree blacks suffered, so that in a sense the term *ghetto* can properly be associated only with black Americans.[43] It is the difference between the fate of a religiously stigmatized but white group, still part of the European family, and that of a nonwhite group that after hundreds of years in North America remain strangers at the gate, the paradigm representatives of subpersonhood. One could say that Jews in the West essentially became white from the modern period onward, became nonwhite for a restricted period under the localized racial system of Nazism, suffering racial mass murder, and then became white again in Europe after the war. This ontological trajectory is quite different from that of blacks, who, because of their original location as chattel in a slave system, were nonwhite practically from the beginning and remain so today.

Blacks and Jews: Similarities and Differences

It is a mistake, then, just to assimilate the histories of blacks and Jews, as many well-meaning liberals do, pointing to a common experience of suffering and racism, and then expressing bewilderment at the tensions between them. There are similarities in the histories, to be sure, but there are also significant differences. And many of these differences stem, I suggest, from their differential location in this racial system and its social ontology. The idea here is not to get into one of those repellent "Holocaust competitions" ("My Holocaust was worse than yours"). As the philosopher Laurence Thomas, a black Jew, has argued, the differing goals and structure of American slavery and the institutionalized genocide of European Jewry obviate totalizing comparisons anyway, apart from the inherent odiousness of such an exercise.[44] Rather, the aim is to try to explain the divergence in the subsequent fates of the two groups. Some of the important similarities and differences may be summarized as follows.[45]

Similarities
1. Both peoples have been forcibly displaced from their original homelands.
2. Both have a history of slavery.
3. Both have been the victims of state apparatuses of subjugation: oppressive laws, government-sanctioned ideologies of inferiority.
4. Both have been the victims of mass murder at the hands of white, Christian, Western civilization.
5. Both have been theologically stigmatized, Jews as Christ killers, Africans as devil worshipers.
6. Both have been morally stigmatized in Western culture as paradigm outsiders, scapegoats, pariahs.
7. Both have been aesthetically stigmatized, so that women of both groups have sometimes changed or tried to soften their "racial" features to facilitate sexual competition with the shiksa/white woman.

8. Both have been discriminated against in North America in employment, housing, education.
9. Both continue today to be the victims of individual hate crimes: personal attacks, defacements of houses of worship, cross burnings.
10. Both draw on the Old Testament to make sense of their experience, Jews viewing its account as literal, blacks viewing it as an analogy (though some blacks do see themselves as the "real" Jews).
11. The language of oppression and redemption used by Jews has sometimes also been employed by blacks: "Egyptian bondage," "ghetto," "diaspora," "Exodus," "promised land," "children of Zion."
12. They have sometimes been depicted in racist literature (Klan, Nazi, Aryan Nations) as cooperating to overthrow and take over white Western civilization.
13. They have actually cooperated in the founding and staffing of civil rights organizations (the NAACP, the National Urban League) and alliances against racist laws and practices in the United States.
14. Both populations are politically generally more liberal than the white Gentile majority.
15. Early twentieth-century Pan-Africanism and Zionism have significant similarities as redemptive nationalist political movements, seeking, respectively, black liberation/African decolonization and a homeland for the Jews. (Garvey was sometimes characterized as a "black Moses.")[46]

Differences

1. Jews were displaced from their homeland but generally retained their identity, traditions, and family structure, and cultural control of their lives. "Black" is a *new* identity forged out of the forced bringing together in the West of many different African peoples with no common language, whose families were often broken up by slavery and who were, until recently, largely deprived of literacy and told that they had no real culture or history.
2. The enslavement of Jews occurred thousands of years ago; the enslavement of blacks was a reality little more than a century ago and is a much more powerful *living* memory in shaping contemporary consciousness.
3. Jews were enslaved at a time when slavery was standard practice throughout the world and was not linked to race; blacks were enslaved during the modern period, when slavery was dead or

dying out in the West, so that "slavery acquired a color" and black features became the racial stigmata of subordination.

4. Israel received reparations from Germany for the crimes of the Jewish Holocaust; African-Americans and Caribbeans have yet to receive reparations from the American government or Europe generally for the crimes of slavery and the African Holocaust. (In fact, it was the former slave owners who, after emancipation, were compensated for the loss of their property.)

5. Though the Christian church has a long, culpable history of anti-Semitism, the mainstream Western religious tradition is still a *Judeo*-Christian tradition, not an *Afro*-Christian tradition.

6. Correspondingly, Judaism is today respected as one of the main global religions (with Christianity, Islam, Hinduism); African religions are generally not respected, and most blacks in the West are converts to Christianity (though often in a syncretized version).

7. European Jews are phenotypically sufficiently similar to other Europeans that in North America they can assimilate with a change of name ("Funny, you don't look Jewish"). In the felicitous phrase of one writer, Jews have "protective coloration."[47] Thus under the Third Reich, when Jews were classified as racial subpersons, *Untermenschen,* they were forced to wear a yellow Star of David so that they could be identified as such. Blacks, by contrast, are identifiable by phenotype no matter how they try to assimilate; permanent subpersonhood is written on their faces.

8. Because of the phenotypical closeness of Jews and Gentile whites, as against blacks and whites, the perceived need (given the internalization of a racist aesthetic) for transformative cosmeticization is much more foundational and pervasive for the black body than for the Jewish body (a technologically unrealizable change of skin, to begin with, as against occasional rhinoplasty).

9. The classic racist stereotypes differ crucially in that Jews are generally credited with (sometimes supernormal) intelligence,[48] whereas blacks are traditionally represented as bestial, subnormal. Thus the most famous anti-Semitic document, the forged *Protocols of the Elders of Zion,* credits Jews with the ability to plan and carry out a takeover of the world. Insofar as racist propaganda allocates blacks a contributory role in such an enterprise (however worthy), by contrast, it is basically as foot soldiers, muscle.

10. From the time race becomes an important category in the European colonization and settling of North America, Jews have

generally been socially categorized as "white," albeit stigmatized "off-whites." Blacks, on the other hand, have always been "nonwhite," indeed the *paradigm* nonwhites on whose subordination the system has been based.

11. In North America today, Jews are economically successful, whereas blacks continue to be at or near the bottom of the ladder.[49]

12. In North America today, Jews are successful and influential in the worlds of "high" intellectual culture (the academy, scholarly books, highbrow fiction, literary magazines) and middlebrow culture (Hollywood movies, television); blacks continue to be greatly underrepresented in both spheres. Where blacks have made a significant contribution to popular culture—in black or black-derived music (jazz, blues, rock and roll), which has been the single greatest force in shaping American popular music—their lack of *economic* control over the industry has meant that they have often not reaped the rewards they deserved for their work.

13. As a result of the preeminence of the Jewish community, Jews—in the words of Laurence Thomas—have greater "group autonomy," cultural control of representations of themselves, than blacks do.[50] By a fundamental asymmetry, Jews are regarded as the foremost interpreters of their experience in a way that blacks are not, and far more Jews are seen as experts on the black experience than vice versa.

14. The tragedy of the Jewish Holocaust is commemorated in popular culture (movies, TV), and thus imprinted on mass consciousness,[51] in a way that the African Holocaust is not, though the latter's effects continue to make themselves felt in the degraded position of Africa and African-Americans. *Roots*, the 1977 television dramatization of Alex Haley's novel (which was in its time, admittedly—and is still, all these years later—the highest-rated miniseries ever),[52] is the exception rather than the norm. In general, there has been relatively little serious exploration of the ordeals of slavery and Jim Crow, despite their obviously fundamental shaping effect on both black and white Americans. The most famous big-budget Hollywood films about slavery and the postbellum period either overtly demonize blacks (*Birth of a Nation*, 1915) or romanticize plantation life from the whites' perspective (*Gone With the Wind*, 1939). In addition, demeaning portrayals of blacks as servile "Toms," comic "coons," and threatening "bucks" were routine for decades in Hollywood movies (and continue to some extent to appear in disguised form today) long after anti-Semitic portrayals

of Jews ceased to be permissible, an indication of the differential status of the two groups in the white racial polity.[53]

15. In North America, the Jewish community is on the whole far better politically organized than the black community, a reflection variously of class differences, a greater degree of assimilation, and (given black disenfranchisement) a longer history of political activism. In addition, in the United States for many decades, Jews were a prime source of funding for black civil rights organizations, on the one hand a tribute to the antiracist commitments of many Jews but on the other, the foundation of a differential power relationship. The overall result is that Jewish-black political relations have generally *not* been peer-to-peer relations but have been viewed by many blacks as paternalistic.

16. Israel is seen as part of the West; the decolonized African nations are not.

17. In the postwar period, after the revelations of the death camps, racist ideology of the anti-Semitic kind ceased to be respectable in the West. By contrast, antiblack racist ideology never died, and from the late 1960s onward it has had a dramatic resurgence in the form of IQ theory (alleged lower black intelligence)[54] and some interpretations of sociobiology (alleged greater black propensity for violence).

18. The overall judgment of the historian George Mosse: "[I]f, under the shock of the holocaust, the postwar world proclaimed a temporary moratorium on anti-Semitism, the black on the whole remained locked into a racial posture which never varied much from the eighteenth century to our time.... Moreover, nations which had fought against National Socialism continued to accept black racial inferiority for many years after the end of the war."[55]

19. The overall judgment of the philosopher Lawrence Blum: Blacks are both vulnerable and subordinated; Jews are vulnerable, but they are not subordinated.

Narratives of Identity and Oppression, Negotiations of Personhood

Against this background, let us examine the dynamic of the degeneration of black-Jewish relations and its source in the different ways in which personhood is characteristically negotiated in a racial polity.

The logic of the racial polity is that personhood cannot be taken for granted by everybody. In the ideal Kantian ontology, the presumption is that all humans are persons (this is our starting point), and one expects respect as a matter of course. But in a system of white domination, supported by a dark ontology of master and subordinate races, members of the subordinate races will routinely *not* get respect. It will be an immanent part of the culture and social structure that they get a disrespect that is not at all contingent but, especially in the de jure phase of racial subordination, is mandated by the system as part of its reproductive dynamic. In other words, treating nonwhites as equals would jeopardize the racial order by violating the *Herrenvolk* ethic that is its moral economy. So this dark ontology has to be continually maintained through transactions at the boundaries. Correspondingly, the most salient feature of the experience of those classified as subpersons in this system will be the need, for their own self-respect, to assert their personhood, to contest the racial disrespect that they routinely receive. For if they accept it without protest, they are accepting the official definition of themselves as less than human, not really persons.

In a section of *The Metaphysics of Morals* titled "On Servility," Kant points out that a person's feeling of "his inner worth" and "inalienable dignity" "instills in him respect for himself" and likewise demands "*respect* for himself from all other rational beings in the world": "He can measure himself with every other being of this kind and value himself on a footing of equality with them. Humanity in his person is the object of the respect which he can demand from every other man, but which he must also not forfeit.... And this *self-esteem* is a duty of man to himself."[56] But in the racial polity, where historically servility is precisely what has been expected and required of subpersons, their demands for equal respect from the population of official persons will be actively resisted, and their duty to themselves of self-esteem will be much harder to fulfill. Personhood, respect, and self-respect thus have to be fought for by nonwhites in a way that they do not for whites or for abstract individuals in the race-free polity of an ideal Kantianism.[57] And to the extent that whites remain committed to a racist self-positioning of superiority over nonwhites, their self-respect and personhood will be jeopardized by this contestation from below. This reciprocal interlinkage of definitions of personhood in terms of race may give rise to a zero-sum game of conflicting ontologies. Relations between blacks and Jews, paradigm nonwhites and borderline whites, need to be examined against this background.

For blacks in North America, the basic conceptual divide, the one around which their lives have historically been structured, will naturally be that between whites and blacks. They will be less attentive to differences among whites—language, customs, religion—because their experience has been that these differences are eventually rendered irrelevant by the objective logic of the racial system. The rules of the American racial order, predicated on the subordination of the expropriated reds and the enslaved blacks, offer even borderline whites—Irish, Slavs, Mediterraneans, Jews—the chance of whitening themselves.[58] The experience of ethnic oppression in Europe could have contradictory psychological outcomes. Although it did make some immigrants more sensitive to racial oppression in their new home, for others it had the converse effect. Precisely because their status was shaky, precisely because their group had originally been beyond the pale, they rushed to demonstrate their whiteness, their worthiness to be admitted into the club. Most of the millions of newcomers eagerly embraced the system with the militant assertion of their bona fides as legitimate white people, fully deserving of respect.

The strategy of negotiating personhood therefore characteristically plays itself out differently in these two locations—unambiguously nonwhite, ambiguously white. One could say that it is the difference between outside outsiders and inside outsiders. For blacks, with no hope of attaining whiteness, the tendency is to challenge the system of racial privilege and racialized personhood. Because of their antipodean location—the standpoint of chattel seeing Western civilization from the bottom—black critics are forced in radical directions to make sense of their experience and to attain respect. For Jews, the situation is significantly different, since they have a choice. As victims of Christian persecution in the Old World, they may agitate for the dismantling of the system of racial persecution in the New, demanding that respect and personhood be unlinked from race. And, to their credit, Jews have been the European ethnic group most active in the founding and staffing of civil rights organizations in the United States. But as Europeans, whites, they also had the option of entering the racial system, even if the barriers were higher for them than for some other groups. And as Cornel West points out, "Like other European immigrants, Jews for the most part became complicitous with the American racial caste system."[59]

Moreover, as Europeans, even borderline ones, their standpoint is from within the system, so they have difficulty seeing the project of the West from outside, as epistemically privileged blacks, along with Native Americans, the West's primary victims, have always been able to do. For them, the dominant narrative is the history of persecution of Jews by Gentiles and the basic conceptual division that between Jews and Gentiles (of all colors). They recognize, of course, that blacks have been subordinated within Christian civilization, but their personal experience naturally sensitizes them more to anti-Semitism than to antiblack racism. It is unsurprising, then, that though some Jews were antiracist activists, most were content to assimilate to majority white Gentile society and, in some cases, to collaborate in the creation of the *Herrenvolk* cultural products necessary to maintain the racial order.[60] For these Jews, the dominant strategy for negotiating personhood is to insist, against anti-Semitic slanders imputing to them an alien nature, on their *Europeanness,* their rightful membership in the West, with either no awareness of or indifference to the way in which Europeanness has come to be tied up with claims to white supremacy.

Blacks' hostility to Jews needs to be seen within this context. My suggestion is that the historic black struggle against white oppression generates, as an ideational accompaniment, conspiracy theories centered on race, and that over time, Jews increasingly become the prime suspects.

Fredric Jameson suggests that the conspiracy theory is a kind of half-baked Hegelianism, a degraded attempt to think the whole.[61] There is a lot to this, but I would add that it is an attempt to think the whole with the political and psychological virtue of *highlighting human agency.* This is particularly important for subordinated groups, since there is a general tendency in complex modern societies for their human-made character to disappear, so that their causality becomes impersonal, fetishized, like a force of nature. Things happen, but no one is to blame. Or, even worse, blame for group subordination is attributed to the group (their culture, their innate biological deficiencies). Conspiracy theories of the oppressed refuse this causal evisceration, or causal misdirection, by expressly categorizing the group's plight as a state of *oppression* (which presupposes the hostile agency of other humans). *Racial* conspiracy theories are then a subset of conspiracy theories in general, involving the racial identification of the oppressed and oppressor group and the imputation of some kind of racial motivation to the latter.

It is important to realize that racial conspiracy theories are nothing new and that historically the most influential of such theories have come from the dominating groups. If we think back to the various "colored perils" that have historically haunted the white imagination — the Red (Indian) Peril, the Yellow Peril, the Black Peril — clearly they are racial conspiracy theories of rulers worried about the insurrection of their subjects. Europeans in the late nineteenth and early twentieth centuries, worried about race wars of revenge, produced popular literature about nonwhite alliances to challenge colonial white supremacy. As Gary Okihiro points out, "Fundamentally ... the idea of the yellow peril does not derive solely from the alleged threat posed by Asians to Europeans ... but from nonwhite people, as a collective group, and their contestation of white supremacy"; thus it was "expounded most vehemently at the height of imperialism and at the start of Third

World nationalism and decolonization."[62] In the United States, similarly, the intellectual legacy of the Indian wars and the watchfulness for slave uprisings generated what Gary Nash and Richard Weiss call "the great fear — race in the mind of America."[63] Books such as Lothrop Stoddard's *Rising Tide of Color against White World-Supremacy* were favorably reviewed and influential in the 1920s.[64]

So racial conspiracy theories come in many versions. The racial conspiracy theories of the oppressed, blacks in particular, draw on the undeniable fact — no paranoid fantasy, this — that colonialism, the slave trade, and segregation were developed and institutionalized through the concerted and planned actions of whites. These things did not just happen; they were made to happen. In these historical cases, of course, no reasonable person could deny the role of racism. But in contemporary mainstream sociological analyses of the plight of blacks in the United States, racism tends to drop out as an explanation, and recourse is increasingly had to the "culture of poverty," genetic propensity, and transformations of the local and global economy with racially differentiated, though not racially motivated, effects. Black popular discourse, in contrast, spreads detailed theories explaining, for example, political assassinations, the prevalence of drugs in the ghetto, the origins of AIDS, the targeted marketing to a black clientele of particular products (cigarettes, soft drinks, fast-food stores, footwear, sportswear), and the perceived persecution of elected black officials and black celebrities in the United States (Marion Barry, Mike Tyson, Michael Jackson, O. J. Simpson) as the result of white conspiracies.[65] Such theories have the psychological and political function of insisting on the continuing existence of racism as a determining factor in black lives and representing the plight of blacks as something avoidable, something that is the result of oppressive human causality, of individual choices and public policy decisions made one way rather than another. The causality may be short-circuited, structural trends voluntarized, the locus of ultimate responsibility misidentified, details or the central thesis completely wrong, but in a sense this is irrelevant: what collectively they do is to reaffirm the *human-*created character of the black situation.

My suggestion, then, is that a lot of black hostility to Jews may be cognitively explained as a reaction to the system of racial disadvantage for which Jews are at least partly a symbol. Traditional anti-Semitism is, among other things, a set of conspiracy theories about Jewish attempts to capture Christian virgins, pollute Gentile blood, take over the world, and so forth. So there is, so to speak, a preexisting *legitimized* trope in mainstream culture with a slot for Jews as the prime agents of a sinister, behind-the-scenes, globally efficacious social causality. Black antiwhite feeling and theory, seeking a template to categorize, understand, and protest black oppression, and traditionally inclined toward conspiracy theories rooted in historical fact, intersects with the formal structure of conventional anti-Semitism. But the content and motivation are obviously significantly different from those of the classic European variety.

Moreover, this unfortunate cognitive synthesis is encouraged by the ambivalences and shifts in black-Jewish relations arising out of the two groups' divergent positions in the white polity, especially the increasing assimilation and material success of Jews since World War II, which, together with the rise of black nationalism and (sometimes) separatism, pull the two politically apart. Because established WASP capital and exclusivist ethnic networks blocked Jewish immigrants' access to certain investment opportunities and professions, available jobs brought them differentially into contact with blacks, so that white oppression then often wore a Jewish face. The cognitive impact is deepened by the fact that Jews are already somewhat differentiated from other whites, and as cognitive psychologists have shown, "vividness" is a factor in determining what sticks in our heads, what we remember.[66] The distinctiveness of Jews then gives rise to a specifically black anti-Semitism: blacks seize on Jews as the key agents responsible for their ongoing subordination. In James Baldwin's famous judgment, "Negroes are anti-Semitic because they're anti-white."[67] Jews here serve as a confused cognitive proxy for the real targets—the system of racial political power and a set of exclusionary mechanisms that, with the demise of de jure racism, are much harder to identify. Affirming black personhood and racial self-respect requires a narrative of racial exploitation to preempt dominant narratives of racial inferiority; narratives of racial exploitation become racial conspiracy theories; and Jews, especially Jews whose situation in North America has dramatically improved over the century and who have turned politically right, become the paradigm conspirators.

From the Jewish side, of course, things seem quite different. To begin with, some Jews are simply racist, an unsurprising development given their assimilation into a culture that for hundreds of years took black inferiority for granted. But even liberal, antiracist Jews are understandably hurt, puzzled, and outraged when they seem to hear from blacks, people with whom they have allied in the past, the same language and rhetoric that they have heard for centuries from traditional anti-Semites. A detached analysis of such a psychological phenomenon is obviously easier to develop when one is not likely to be a victim of the phenomenon. When Jews hear that black American youths in Crown Heights chanted "Kill the Jew!" before Yankel Rosenbaum was stabbed to death, of course they are alarmed; the chant recalls the Russian pogroms, the Nazi *Kristallnacht*. Khallid Muhammad's accusation that Jews control the Federal Reserve Bank brings back memories of the *Protocols of the Elders of Zion* and the accusations of a Jewish conspiracy to take over the world. When they hear that they are responsible for the African slave trade, they remember the medieval Christians' portrayal of Jews as the main source of all human evil. Within a narrative of Jews versus Gentiles, within a framework where a Jew's personhood and right to respect and equitable treatment characteristically have to be asserted against Gentile attack, the color of the accusers is less significant (except to sharpen the pain) than the familiar message.

Jewish self-respect therefore demands the denunciation of those who, yet again, are singling out the underdog Jews for special blame. But within the conflicting narrative of whites versus blacks, this denunciation is read by *blacks* as white racists' familiar denial of responsibility for their racist policies of oppression and the persecution by the powerful of those courageous enough to speak the truth and expose their role. So *black* self-respect demands that one stand up to the agents of white racism, the architects of the dark ontology, and prove one's personhood by not buckling and giving in to white criticism. The result, obviously, is a disastrous clash of narratives and negotiations of personhood, in which the ranks close, the categories lock into place, the reflexive tropes harden, and the affirmation of self-respect increasingly manifests itself in racial accusation. Rival conceptions of the social order and racially conflictual views of personhood collide and feed on each other, establishing a self-sustaining degenerative cycle of mutual recrimination, in which each side's self-conceived moral duty of affirming their humanity constitutes proof for the other precisely of their *immorality* and *inhumanity*.

I have focused on the narrow question of blacks and Jews, but of course the problem of racial and ethnic conflict in the world today is much broader. What is the solution? The threat of the balkanization of the polity into competing tribal groups, with all for each and none for all, may suggest that these local particularistic identities are too dangerous and should perhaps be dispensed with altogether in the name of an encompassing universalism. But the problem, at least in the West, is that historically this kind of universalism has usually turned out to be a white particularism in disguise, in that it is really the "other" ethnic/racial groups (the groups who are designated *as* "ethnic," *as* "raced") who have to give up their ethnicity/race and assimilate to the majority population. What we really need to strive for is a rainbowed rather than an abstract—in effect a white—universalism.

Moreover, ethnic and racial identities are not going to be given up as long as they condense narratives of history and origin, meaning and personhood. The challenge, as Cornel West points out, then becomes the moral *rethinking* of these identities so that they can be disarmed, stripped of the exclusionary commitments that lead to antagonism and conflict: the revision of what it means to be white, black, Jewish. And the main obstacles to such a revision are not conceptual—there is no intrinsic consistency problem with the simultaneous valorization of different ethnic/racial identities—but *political/psychological;* that is, whether as a matter of contingent fact, given present patterns of subjugation, such a moral transformation is really likely.

The crucial issue is therefore the connection between racial/ethnic identity and the structure I have delineated. These group identities will continue to come into conflict not out of logical necessity but through their shaping and reshaping by a context of relative access to and blocking from economic opportunities, cultural image-making, and political input. As long as a structure of racial privilege exists in the United States (and elsewhere), claims to racial identity will essentially be coded ways of affirming and challenging differences in privilege. To affirm whiteness in this context is to affirm white entitlement to privilege; to affirm blackness is to challenge black exclusion. Appeals to moral toleration of difference will do no good if the system remains intact, because no matter how subjectively sincere people's intentions, the objective structure keeps recoalescing the identities in their old, antagonistic forms. Race becomes an innocent identity and is most safely affirmed precisely when there is no longer any need to affirm it, when there is no connection between race and structural advantage or disadvantage. In an ideal Kantian world, unlike the world of *Herrenvolk* Kantianism, respect will be detached from race, and its present explosive moral charge will be defused.

But achieving such a world—bringing into existence Kant's *respublica noumenon*—requires an honest look at the world that actually exists. Kant's "two viewpoints" dichotomization assumes that our freedom as noumenal moral agents to do our duty can always overcome empirical disinclination, that we can always see and do the right thing.[68] Contemporary Kantians are justifiably more dubious about such a metaphysics of moral agency, recognizing the many ways in which our upbringing and this-worldly empirical obstacles can deform our moral development, impeding recognition and performance of our duty. The point of identifying and mapping a *Herrenvolk* Kantianism, as I have done, is not, of course, to endorse the actual, naturalized, nonideal practice of the past and present but to make ourselves self-consciously aware of the history and structure of these practices and how they have affected and continue to affect our moral psychology. Solving the problem of how to get there from here, of how to realize the ideal, requires an accurate delineation of the obstacles on the route. Epigrammatically, one could say, following Justice Blackmun, that the ideal world *beyond* race can be reached only by going *through* race, not by trying to go *around* race.[69] Less figuratively: white moral and political philosophers need to recognize the centrality of race to the past few hundred years of global history, and how white domination has shaped not only the moral topography of our world but their own moral theorizing and moral practice. To reflect these realities, we need, as Onora O'Neill has argued, theories that abstract without idealizing, that register the radical historical differences between agents rather than subsuming them under abstract, colorless individuals.[70] And in constructing such a theory, we can greatly benefit, I suggest, from drawing on black and Third World oppositional traditions, the theorizing about race of those persons whose personhood has historically been denied because of race.

In conclusion, then. To the black community, to my own community, I would say this. The narrative of oppression we have inherited from hundreds of years of slavery and subjugation in the West is in danger of degeneration and needs to be redirected against the appropriate target. We betray those who gave their lives in the struggle against racism if we embrace racist and anti-Semitic ideas. The Jewish community are not the enemy; the enemy is white racism and the present legacy of a historically exclusionary racial structure. To the extent that *some* Jews are now actively complicit with this structure, they should of course be criticized. But there is no genealogical connection between this structure and the Jews; they did not create it, and they have been victimized by it. Nor should criticisms be global accusations that ignore the history of the many Jews who have fought against racism directed at blacks as well as at Jews. To accuse Jews as a group of such conspiracies puts us morally on the same level as traditional white racists—Nazis and Klansmen—and deprives us of the moral authority the black community, as victims rather than victimizers, have traditionally had. The assertion of black personhood and the demand for black respect, far from leading us to condone black wrongdoing and black anti-Semitism in the name of black solidarity, require us to condemn them for the sake of our own self-respect.

To the Jewish community, I would say this. While always keeping alive the memory of the Jewish Holocaust and recognizing the continuing danger of anti-Semitism, including black anti-Semitism, you need to update the traditional narrative of Jewish victimization. North America at the turn of the twenty-first century is not the Third Reich, nor is it likely to be transformed into it. Although individual blacks may commit anti-Semitic acts, blacks as a group do not have power, so that this kind of ideational and behavioral racism cannot be put on the same plane of social significance as the *institutional* racism, directed primarily against people of color, of the centers of political and economic power. Nor should the justifiable criticism of the former be used as a pretext to blind oneself to the existence of the latter. History moves on, and one's group narratives, negotiations of personhood, and moral responsibilities must keep pace. If because of the horrors of Nazism we think of Jewishness as being classically in part a disadvantaged location in a system of racial power, then we could say that in North America the real Jews have never been the Jews. The real Jews are Native Americans. Or the real Jews are blacks. In an anthology published many years ago, Rabbi Alan Miller, a member of the Jewish Reconstructionist Movement, made this very point: "[The black man] is the one who, on the American scene, has been the persecuted. He is, in truth, the American 'Jew'."[71] In North America today, it cannot realistically be claimed that Jews are Untermenschen.

So there is an ironic turnaround that is surprising only to those who see race as fixed rather than fluid. On this continent, whether one speaks angrily of white supremacy or more gently and nonconfrontationally of white privilege, the system of racial advantage is divided on an axis of white/nonwhite, and Jews are on the privileged side of that line. Difficult and astonishing as it may be to accept, then, unthinkable and incongruent as it is with the defining Jewish narrative, the fact has to be faced that Jews in the West are now unequivocally part of the privileged race. As Nat Hentoff says in his introduction to the same anthology, "We are, all of us who are white, the *goyim* in America."[72] Updating your narrative means realizing this fact and recognizing that—in addition to your own heroic efforts—part of the reason for your success on this continent is that doors have been opened for you that were closed to nonwhites. Whatever your personal feelings and political views, you are objectively socially advantaged by your racial characterization. Your moral responsibility now, as privileged members of society —indeed, the moral responsibility of all whites of goodwill—is to throw your political and organizational weight behind the opening of these doors to everyone, so that whiteness, blackness, and Jewishness will be equally connected to—and thereby equally disconnected from—personhood; all races and ethnicities will have an equal chance in a nonracial polity; and the shameful dark ontology inherited from the shadowed and divided Enlightenment will disappear in a blaze of egalitarian light.

5 Revisionist Ontologies

Theorizing White Supremacy

For mainstream First World political philosophy, race barely exists. What accounts for this silence? Why shouldn't such issues be incorporable into a history of modern political philosophy course along with Hobbes, Locke, Rousseau, Kant, Mill, and Marx, or a contemporary thematic course that looks at contractarianism and communitarianism, welfare liberalism and laissez-faire libertarianism, at Rawls, Nozick, Walzer, Sandel? Why this ghettoization of race and the Third World, as if nonwhites were on a separate planet rather than very much a part of one world interconnected with and foundationally shaped by the very region studied by First World theory? What exactly is it about the way political philosophy has developed that encourages this kind of intellectual segregation?

The problem in part seems to involve a kind of exclusionary theoretical dynamic, in that the presuppositions of the world of mainstream theory offer no ready point of ingress, no conceptual entrée, for the issues of race, culture, and identity that typically preoccupy much of black and Third World theory. (The issues of Third World poverty and economic underdevelopment *can* be handled, if the will exists, within the framework of discussions of international justice, through an expansion of moral concern beyond the boundaries of First World nation-states.) The assumptions are so different that one may seem to be caught between two heterogeneous intellectual universes, with no ready way of transporting the concerns of the one across the boundary of the other. And when racism in European thought *is* mentioned, the discussion is usually limited to the writings of marginal theorists such as Arthur de Gobineau; the biases in the views of the central figures in the pantheon are not examined.[1]

Typically, what one gets (insofar as any effort is made at all) is an attempt to piggyback the problem of race onto the body of respectable theory. One looks at racism as a *violation* of the ideals of liberal individualist ideology, for example, or one *explains* race and racism within a Marxist paradigm. But race is still really an afterthought in such deployments. That is, one starts from a preexisting conceptual framework—an overall characterization of the system ("constitutionalist liberal democracy," "capitalism"), a set of large-scale and small-scale theories about how this system works or should work, and an array of corresponding concepts—and then tries to articulate race to this framework.

Unsurprisingly, then, these efforts are usually unsatisfactory. I want to propose an alternative approach as an innovation in political philosophy. Suppose we place race at center stage rather than in the wings of theory. The idea is to follow the example of those feminists of the 1970s once characterized as radical (as against liberal or Marxist), who, inspired by the U.S. black liberation movement, decided to put gender at the center of their theorizing and appropriated the term *patriarchy* to describe a system of male domination.[2] So rather than starting with some other theory and then smuggling in gender, one begins with the fact of gender subordination.

Of course, some crucial disanalogies need to be noted. For one thing, gender as a system of power has been seen as practically universal, and it dates back, if not to the origin of the species, at least to an age thousands of years before ours, whereas white domination is clearly a product of the modern period. Moreover, many radical feminists appeal to varieties of biological determinism to explain patriarchy and regard it as the source of all other oppressions—claims I would certainly not make for race. But with these and other caveats registered, it still seems that one may fruitfully consider race as a political system. We would treat this system as a particular mode of domination, with its special norms for allocating benefits and burdens, rights and duties; its own ideology; and an internal, at least semi-autonomous logic that influences law, culture, and consciousness.

As I suggested in Chapter 4, I use the term *white supremacy* to conceptualize this system.[3] But I intend a latitudinarian conception, one that encompasses de facto as well as de jure white privilege and refers more broadly to the European domination of the planet that has left us with the racialized distributions of economic, political, and cultural power that we have today. We could call it global white supremacy.[4] And the idea would then be to locate both oppositional black/Third World theory and establishment white/First World theory in the conceptual space of this expanded political universe. From this perspective, we would be able to appreciate that black and

Third World theory have characteristically been concerned to map the *whole* of this system, whereas mainstream theory has preeminently focused on a very limited section of it, either ignoring the rest of the world or squeezing it awkwardly into the categories developed for this restricted mapping.

Global White Supremacy as a Political System: Replies to Objections

This idea of global white supremacy as a political system may seem problematic, so I want to address some objections that might be raised to it.

First, there might be the friendly amendment that we already *have* a politico-economic term with the same approximate referent, in the form, say, of *imperialism* or *colonial capitalism*.

But in the first place, of course, this isn't true, because these terms aren't usually taken to apply (apart from upholders of variants of the "internal colonialism" thesis) to the *internal* politics of white settler states such as the United States and Australia, or the Iberian colonies in the Americas, which became independent at a relatively early stage. Moreover, colonial capitalism is by definition restricted to the period of formal colonial rule, whereas I contend that in a weaker sense, white supremacy continues to exist today.

In the second place, and perhaps more important, these terms are, for my purposes, not sufficiently focused on the *racial* dimension of European domination. Both in the standard liberal and the standard Marxist analyses of imperialism there has been an economism that fails to do theoretical justice to race, with race being seen as irrelevant to the ontology of the liberal individual or the class membership of workers and capitalists. But the racial nature of the system is precisely what I want to highlight. As Walter Rodney points out, imperialism has to be seen as bringing into existence a "White Power" that is international in character and that became global by the time of World War I: "At that point, everywhere in the world, white people held power in all its aspects — political, economic, military, and even cultural. . . . The essence of White Power is that it is exercised over [nonwhite] peoples — whether or not they are minority or majority, whether it was a country belonging originally to whites or to [nonwhites]."[5]

Still in the spirit of a friendly amendment, it might then be argued that, in that case, *racism* or *white racism* is the term appropriate to the conceptual task.

My response here is, first of all, that after decades of divergent use and sometimes abuse, the term has become so fuzzy and has acquired such a semantic penumbra of unwelcome associations that unless a formal definition is given, no clear reference can be readily attached to it.

Second, one of the crucial ambiguities in its usage is precisely that between racism as a complex of ideas, values, and attitudes and racism as an institutionalized politico-economic structure for which the ideas are an ideological accompaniment. If the term *white racism* were consistently employed in the latter sense, we might not need another locution, but this is not at all the case. On the contrary, the *ideational* sense is usually intended. And this has the theoretical disadvantage of making it possible for everybody to be "racist," in a Hobbesian scenario of equipowerful atomic individuals with bad attitudes, thereby deflecting attention from the massive power differentials actually obtaining in the real world between nonwhite individuals with bigoted ideas and institutionalized white power. *White supremacy* and *global white supremacy*, in contrast, have the semantic virtues of clearly signaling reference to a system, a particular kind of polity, so structured as to advantage whites.

A more hostile objection might be that to speak of white supremacy as a political system necessarily implies its complete autonomy and explanatory independence from other variables. But I don't see why this follows. The origins of white racism as an elaborated complex of ideas (as against a spontaneous set of naive prejudices) continue to be debated by scholars, with various rival theories — ethnocentrism on a grand scale, religioculturalist predispositions, the ideology of expansionist colonial capitalism, the rationalizations of psychosexual aversions, calculated rational-choice power politics — contending for eminence. We don't need to make a commitment to the truth of any of these theories; we can just be agnostic on the question, bracketing the issue and leaving open the question which explanation or complementary set of explanations turns out to be most adequate. All that is required is that, whatever the origins of racism and the politico-economic system of white supremacy, they are conceded to have attained at least a partial, relative autonomy, so that they are not immediately reducible to something else.

Correspondingly, I am not claiming that white supremacy as a political system exhausts the political universe. The idea is not that white supremacy must now *replace* previous political categorizations but that it should *supplement* them. In other words, it is possible to have overlapping, interlocking, and intersecting systems of domination. The concept of white supremacy focuses attention on the dimension of racial oppression in these systems; it is not being claimed that this is the *only* dimension. In some contexts, the focus on race will be illuminating; in other contexts it will not.

The idea is to correct the characteristic methodological omissions of past and present, not to prescribe an exclusivist theoretical attention to this one aspect of the polity.

Nor does use of the term imply that white supremacy is either synchronically uniform or diachronically static. White supremacy will take different forms in different parts of the world—expropriation and enclosure on reservations here, slavery and colonial rule there, formal segregation and antimiscegenation laws in one place, mixing and intermarriage in another. The privileging of whites is compatible with a wide variety of political and institutional structures: this privileging is the key element. Similarly, the status of nonwhites within the system can vary tremendously—from exterminable savage to colonial ward to second-class citizen—without threatening the crucial premise of nonwhite inferiority.

Moreover, white supremacy evolves over time, in part precisely because of the other systems to which it is articulated, in part because of nonwhites' political struggles against it. In a detailed treatment, one would need to develop a periodization of different forms, with one obvious line of temporal demarcation being drawn between the epoch of *formal* white supremacy (paradigmatically represented by the legality of European colonialism and African slavery) and the present epoch of de facto white supremacy (the aftermath of slavery and decolonization, with formal juridical equality guaranteed for whites and nonwhites). The basic point, then, is that it would be a mistake to identify one particular form of white supremacy (e.g., slavery, juridical segregation) with white supremacy as a family of forms and then argue from the nonexistence of *this* form that white supremacy no longer exists. The changing nature of the system implies that different racial organizations of labor, dominant cultural representations, and evolving legal standings are to be expected.

This argument would also preempt the objection that if global white supremacy ever existed, it is clearly long past now, since—especially with the demise of apartheid in South Africa—we live in a world where yellows, browns, and blacks rule their own countries, and nonwhites in First World "white" nations are no longer formally subjugated. The answers would be as follows.

First, even if global white supremacy were completely a thing of the past, it would still be a political system of historical interest.

Second, even if whites agreed on the desirability of abolishing this system in complete good faith, the recency of its *formal* demise (slavery in the Americas ended little more than a century ago, and global decolonization and U.S. desegregation are essentially postwar phenomena) would ensure that it would continue to affect the new world for a long time to come simply through institutional momentum and unconscious attitudinal lag.

Third, it is politically naive to argue from the mere fact of the abolition of de jure racial subordination to the reality of genuine de facto equalization, and to conclusions about the genuine commitment of all or most whites to relinquish their racial privileges. An objective look at the world reveals that independent Third World nations are part of a global economy dominated by white capital and white international lending institutions, that the planet as a whole is dominated by the cultural products of the white West, that many First World nations have experienced a resurgence of racism, including biologically determinist ideas once thought to have been definitively discredited with the collapse of Nazi Germany, and that in general the dark-skinned races of the world, particularly blacks and indigenous peoples, continue to be at or near the bottom of the socioeconomic ladder in both metropolitan and Third World polities.

So a case can easily be made that white supremacy continues to exist in a different form, no longer backed by law but maintained through inherited patterns of discrimination, exclusionary racial bonding, cultural stereotyping, and differential white power deriving from consolidated economic privilege.[6] Kimberlé Crenshaw emphasizes (with specific reference to the United States, though the point is more generally valid) the importance of distinguishing between "the mere rejection of white supremacy as a normative vision" and "a societal commitment to the eradication of the substantive conditions of Black subordination." She notes that "a society once expressly organized around white supremacist principles does not cease to be a white supremacist society simply by formally rejecting those principles. The society remains white supremacist in its maintenance of the actual distribution of goods and resources, status, and prestige."[7]

A different kind of objection might be not to the principle of the notion of race as a political system but to the details; that is, to the *white* in *global white supremacy*. The racial rules in the United States basically dichotomize the polity according to the one-drop principle, but in the Caribbean and in Central and South America the ladder has many rungs rather than just two. Moreover, in the postcolonial period, there is at least a partial transition in which "browns" come to rule rather than just whites. The response here would have to be as follows.

The color and shade hierarchies in many Latin American countries have been established by global white supremacy, in that ascent up the ladder is strongly correlated with a greater degree of white ancestry and a greater degree of assimilation to European culture, so that these systems are essentially derivative and still need to be related to it. And—it needs to be underlined, against the widespread myth of Latin "racial democracy"—they *are* hierarchies. Though differently structured than the bipolar northern model, they privilege the lighter-skinned, with the official ideology of a race-transcendent *mestizaje,* race mixture, being undercut in practice by the ideal of *blanqueamiento,* whitening.[8]

Moreover, even if in many of these countries "browns" govern, economic power often continues to be controlled by a white corporate elite, whose presence and interests constrain the dimensions of the political space in which browns can operate, thus delimiting the real possibilities for independent action and the democratizing of racial access to socioeconomic opportunities.

In addition, the larger world—the global economy, the international financial institutions—is dominated by First World powers, which (except for Japan) are themselves white and are linked by various political, economic, and cultural ties to local whites, thus differentially privileging them.

Another objection might be to the imagined theoretical presuppositions of such a notion. The invocation of "race" as explanatory in politics has historically been most strongly associated with discourses (nineteenth- and twentieth-century imperialism; Nazism) explicitly predicated on biologically determinist assumptions (social Darwinism; *Rassenwissenschaft,* or race science). These doctrines were, of course, officially (though never completely or thoroughly) discredited with the collapse of the Third Reich and postwar decolonization. The widespread employment of a racialized discourse in oppositional popular black and Third World theory may then be assimilated by hostile critics to racist theorizing of this kind, even if the charge is sometimes softened by prefatory references to "reverse racism" or "antiracist racism."

But this preemptive rejection of race as a respectable theoretical category is illegitimate, because the dichotomy between a mainstream methodology (liberal or radical) that is largely insensitive to race and a racial determinism with ludicrous pseudoscientific assumptions (whites as evil "ice people" driven to dominate the planet) does not exhaust the actual alternatives. A growing body of literature in critical race theory is beginning to recognize both the reality (causal significance, theoretical centrality) and the politicality (socially constructed nature) of race.[9] It is not the case, in other words, that a focus on race, white supremacy, and corresponding "white" psychology necessarily commits one to racist assumptions about whites, though admittedly lay thought does not always make these distinctions. So although I said earlier that I wanted to bracket and suspend the question of theoretical explanations for racism, I am at least theoretically committed (as detailed in Chapter 3) to the extent of seeing race in constructivist rather than biologistic terms.

For "whiteness" is not natural; rather, infants of a certain genealogy or phenotype growing up in a racist society have to learn to be white. Correspondingly, there have always been principled and morally praiseworthy whites who have thrown off their socialization and challenged white supremacy, whether in the form of imperialism, slavery, segregation, or apartheid, in the name of a color-blind humanity.[10] They could be described as whites who have rejected "whiteness." The important point—as "race men" have always appreciated—is that a racial perspective on society can provide insights to be found in neither a white liberalism nor a white Marxism, and when suitably modified and reconstructed, such a perspective need not imply biological generalizations about whites or commit the obvious moral error of holding people responsible for something (genealogy, phenotype) they cannot help.

A specifically left objection, correspondingly, might be that to see race as theoretically central implies a return to a pre-Marxist conception of the social order and ignores class.

To begin with, of course, in today's largely postcommunist world, Marxism's explanatory credentials are hardly unchallengeable. But in any case, the constructivist conception of race presupposed does leave open the possibility that a convincing historical materialist account of the creation of global white supremacy can be developed. To make race central is not to make it foundational; it is simply to take seriously the idea of an at least partially autonomous racial political system. (For those with left sympathies, the traditional explanatory route will be through the European Conquest, the imposition of regimes of superexploitation on indigenous and imported populations, and the differential motivation and cultural/ideational power of local and metropolitan ruling classes to ensure that race crystallizes as an overriding social identity stabilizing the resultant system.)[11]

Nor does the idea of white supremacy imply that there are no class differences within the white and nonwhite populations or that all whites are materially better off than all nonwhites. The implication is rather that whites are differentially privileged *as a group,* that whites have significantly better life chances. This implication is compatible with the existence of poor whites and rich nonwhites. It also leaves the way open for the Marxist case to be made that in the long term, white supremacy is of greater political and economic benefit to the white elite than to the white working class, and that though by the baseline of existing white-supremacist capitalism, white workers are better off than nonwhites, they are poorer than they would be in a nonracial order. Since white supremacy is not being put forward as denoting a comprehensive political system, it does not, as earlier emphasized, preclude the existence of other systems of domination (based on class or gender, for example).

Finally, it might be objected that the concept of global white supremacy is pitched at a level of abstraction too high to be useful. But one has to differentiate appropriate realms of investigation. "Capitalism" as a concept has obviously been found useful by many generations of thinkers, both lay and academic, as a general way of categorizing a certain kind of economic system with a core of characteristic traits, despite the vast differences between the capitalism of a century ago and the capitalism of today, and among the capitalist systems of Japan, the United States, and Jamaica. For detailed case studies, one must descend empirically to the investigative level of the political scientist, the economist, the sociologist. But for the purposes of supplementing the conceptual apparatus of the political philosopher, this distance from empirical detail does not seem to me to be problematic. At this level, one is concerned with the general logic of the abstract system, the overarching commonalities of racial subordination between, say, colonial Kenya and independent Australia, slave Brazil and the postbellum United States, which warrant the subsumption of these radically different polities under a general category. "White supremacy" captures these usually ignored racial realities, and on this basis it should take its rightful place in the official vocabulary of political theory, along with such other political abstractions as absolutism, democracy, socialism, fascism, and patriarchy.

Having considered all these objections, I should point out that the great virtue of this account is that race is no longer residual, a concern to be awkwardly shoehorned into the structure of a theory preoccupied with other realities, but central, so that any comprehensive mapping of the polity must register this feature. And by virtue of its social-systemic rather than ideational focus, this analysis directs attention to the important thing, which is how racial membership privileges or disadvantages individuals *independently* of the particular ideas they happen to have. (In that qualified sense, race is objective. Even so-called white renegades need to acknowledge that, no matter what their racial politics, they are privileged by their social classification.) The attitudinal and atomistic, individualist focus of at least some varieties of liberalism reduces the issue to bigotry, which needs to be purged through moral exhortation; the class-reductivist focus of some varieties of Marxism reduces the issue to a variant of ruling-class ideology, which needs to be purged through recognition of class identity. In neither case is the system's racial character adequately registered: that it has its own dynamism and autonomy, its own peculiar social ontology.

Moreover, whereas Marxism's claims about the intrinsically exploitive character of capitalism and the viability and attractiveness of socialism as a solution have always been—and are now more than ever—highly controversial, all good liberals should oppose racism and should want to eradicate its legacy. If, as many now argue, the events since 1989 have conclusively demonstrated that capitalism is the only feasible option for humanity, then what one wants is a capitalism that lives up to its advertising. Liberals as well as radicals should therefore enthusiastically *endorse* rather than object to the exposure of global white supremacy as a political system, since it clearly contravenes the ideal of a color-neutral, racially accessible market society. The Marxist anticapitalist goal is currently of severely limited appeal, but in theory at least one would like to think that all people of goodwill would support the critique and ultimate elimination of white supremacy, including the whites privileged by it. Doubtless, then, the project will be broadly supported, insofar as it is consonant with the proclaimed values of the liberal ideology that is now triumphant across most of the globe.

The Politics of Personhood

Suppose, then, that this concept is accepted as a useful one that needs to be taken account of in orthodox political philosophy. How then, would mainstream theory have to be transformed to include race—that is, global white supremacy—in conventional discourses? What would it mean for the standard terminology, scenarios, frames of reference, characteristic terms, and favorite preoccupations of Western political philosophy? What new phenomena would come into theoretical view, and what old phenomena would have to be transformed?

Obviously, there are many ways to approach these questions. Here my focus is on an issue that, as I argued in Chapter 4, is central to these concerns—the issue of *personhood*. As Kant states most eloquently, persons are rational self-directing entities whose rights must be respected and who must be treated as ends in themselves rather than merely instrumentally.[12] Kant is the philosophical spokesman for the Enlightenment moral and political egalitarianism that ushered in the modern epoch. Thus in the eighteenth-century revolutions, American and French, which resonated around the world, it was classically stated, "We hold these truths to be self-evident, that all men are created equal." By contrast with ancient and medieval hierarchies, the starting point is the freedom and equality of "all men." (Feminist theorists have long since demonstrated that the "men" in these theories are indeed male rather than gender-neutral "persons.")[13]

The social contract tradition that dominates political theory over the period (1650–1800: Hobbes, Locke, Rousseau, Kant) begins from a social ontology of the equality of (those counted as) persons. Though contractarianism then disappeared for a century and a half (to be surprisingly revived by Rawls's *A Theory of Justice* [1971]),[14] this equality is henceforth installed as the normative ground floor of the edifice of Western political philosophy. All humans within the scope of the theory are persons, and the preoccupations of First World theory then center on different theories of justice, competing constitutional models, and rival economic arrangements for this population.

What difference does taking race seriously intrude into this picture? Basically, it directs our attention to what is happening *beneath* the normative ground floor, in (so to speak) the moral/political basement. My claim is essentially that for most of Enlightenment First World political theory, what seems like a neutral starting point, which begs no questions, is actually *already* normatively loaded, in that the population of persons has been overtly or covertly defined so as to be coextensive with the white male population. They are the respectable occupants of the building. So in the period of de jure global white supremacy (European colonial rule, African slavery), the scope of European normative theories usually extended just to Europeans at home and abroad. That is, theories about the rights, liberties, and privileges of "all men" were really intended to apply only to all white men, nonwhites being in a moral basement covered by a different set of rules.

The present period of de facto global white supremacy is characterized by a more complicated normative arrangement, an abstract/formal extension of previously color-coded principles to the nonwhite population. But genuine equality is preempted by lack of mechanisms and resources to enforce antidiscrimination law; by the evasion of juridical proscriptions by legal maneuverings;[15] and by the continuing educational, cultural, and financial handicaps suffered by nonwhites disadvantaged by the race and class concentrations of economic power established under the previous system, which in a capitalist economy violate no laws. Thus, even though such an extension is a real normative advance, by no means to be despised, it does not constitute a genuine challenge to white supremacy unless and until the means to correct for the effects of past racial subordination are included in the rewriting. And this requires, inter alia, a formal recognition of the white-supremacist nature of the polity.

To take Rawls as an example: even if Rawls declares (as he would) that race is morally irrelevant to personhood, and that knowledge of it is accordingly stripped from us by the veil of ignorance, policies prescribed on this basis will not be sufficient in the real-life, nonideal polity of the United States to redress past inequities.[16] Failure to pay theoretical attention to this history will then just reproduce past domination, since the repercussions of white supremacy for the functioning of the state, the dominant interpretations of the Constitution, the racial distribution of wealth and opportunities, as well as white moral psychology, conceptions of self-respect, willingness to sacrifice, and notions of entitlement, are not examined. One is then beginning from a starting point whose structural influences are untheorized, thereby guaranteeing that the corrective measures objectively necessary to overcome these obstacles and achieve genuine equality will not become theoretically visible. (Compare Susan Moller Okin on the illusory, merely "terminological" gender neutrality of most contemporary political theory, such as Rawls's, and the need to develop concepts sensitized to the specific situation of women in the nonideal family, for example, to reflect the ways in which women are made "vulnerable by marriage.")[17] In other words, one does not confront a history of racial domination by ignoring it, since to ignore it is just to incorporate it, through silence, into the conceptual apparatus, whose genealogy will typically ensure that it is structured so as to take the white experience as normative.

A more realistic starting point, one that registers the history of white supremacy, would be the "dark ontology" of *Herrenvolk* Kantianism discussed in Chapter 4. Here the political population is explicitly characterized as it was originally conceived, as a two-tiered, morally partitioned population divided between white persons and nonwhite subpersons.[18] (See Fig. 2, p. 71.)

From this cognitively advantaged perspective—the view from the basement—First World political theory can be seen for what it is: primarily the limited theorizing of the privileged "person" subset of the population about itself. For those in this tier, personhood is not in contention in any way; personhood is taken for granted, so that in the internal dialogue between members of this population, the real-life second tier can generally drop out of the picture. Abstract, raceless, colorless persons—*who are concrete, raced, white persons*—will then, in their egalitarian moral/political theories, such as Kant's, relate to one another with reciprocal respect as moral equals. Because of their representation of this system—because the basement second tier is usually presupposed as invisible—they will think of this respect and this personhood as disconnected from everything but rationality; race, color, history, culture will generally play no role in the overt theory, not because they play no role overall—they are in fact crucial to the architecture of the two tiers—but because their commonality to the white population means they can be eliminated as a factor.

One can appreciate, then, why this conceptual terrain is so apparently inhospitable to the concerns of Third World theory. For if race is not even acknowledged to make a difference, how can these two discourses be located in the same universe? The way to bring them together, accordingly, is to point out the illusory character of abstract Kantianism and to recognize the actual *Herrenvolk* moral theory appropriate for a white-supremacist polity, in which the difference race makes is to demarcate persons from subpersons. Individuals are raced or colored bearers of a certain history and culture, and this is what indicates their location in the racial polity. And if paradigmatically in the Kantian normative framework, persons are not to be treated merely instrumentally, as means to others' ends, then subpersons (Native Americans, blacks) can be regarded as precisely those for whom such treatment *is* morally appropriate.

It should be noted that this equation has always been recognized by black and Third World theory—antislavery, antisegregationist, anticolonial. Thus in the introduction to his classic *Black Skin, White Masks,* Frantz Fanon says bluntly, "At the risk of arousing the resentment of my colored brothers, I will say that the black is not a man."[19] As he points out elsewhere, the colonial world is "a Manichean world," "a world cut in two," "divided into compartments ... inhabited by two different species," and "it is evident that what parcels out the world is to begin with the fact of belonging to or not belonging to a given race, a given species"—on the one hand the "governing race"; on the other, inferior creatures to be described in "zoological terms."[20]

Correspondingly, from the other side, so to speak, a white Alabaman addressing a northern audience in 1860 describes with admirable clarity the founding principles of the United States: "Your fathers and my fathers built this government on two ideas; the first is that the white race is the citizen and the master race, and the white man is the equal of every other white man. The second idea is that the Negro is the inferior race."[21] And this, of course, far from being an idiosyncratic perception, is accurately reflected in the *Dred Scott* decision, that blacks "had for more than a century before been regarded as beings of an inferior order, and altogether unfit to associate with the white race, either in social or political relations; and so far inferior, that they had no rights which the white man was bound to respect."[22]

So I am not making any claims to theoretical discovery here; I am arguing for the formal recognition of these realities within the framework of an orthodox theory that generally ignores them. Race has been a problematic "deviation" for both liberal individualist and Marxist class-centered mappings of this system, because both have failed to take seriously the objective partitioning in the social ontology produced by global white supremacy. Bill Lawson points out that a "lexical gap" in mainstream liberal moral/ political discourse obfuscates the distinctive history of black Americans. By simply assimilating them to the general category of citizens, it conceptually blurs the legacy of slavery, so that there is an inadequate "semantic basis" for "the framing of policies for implementing programs to bring about true citizenship for blacks."[23] More generally, the danger of the universalist and colorless language of personhood is that it too easily slips over from the normative to the descriptive, thus covertly representing as an already achieved reality what is at present only an ideal, and failing to register the embedded structures of differentiated treatment and dichotomized moral psychology that "subpersonhood" captures. An ideal is realized through recognizing and dealing with the obstacles that block its attainment, not through pretending they are not there.

For once this expanded moral topography has been acknowledged, and not evaded or defined out of existence, it immediately becomes obvious that the transactions in moral and political space are far more complicated, involving many other dimensions, than those sketched in the standard First World cartography. Focusing exclusively on the lateral person-to-person relations of the ideal Kantian population, mainstream theory misses the dense vertical network of person-to-subperson relations and also elides the ways in which even horizontal relations are structured by their positioning with respect to the vertical relations. So political struggles will arise which are, if not invisible, at least not readily detectable by the lenses of orthodox theory's conceptual apparatus. Or if they are seen, the tendency will be to assimilate them to something else, and their true significance will be missed; it will not be appreciated that they constitute struggles around (affirmations/repudiations of) the *Herrenvolk* ethic, because the existence of this ethic is not formally acknowledged in mainstream philosophy.

Here, then, are some theses on the politics of personhood within the framework of white supremacy.

1. Personhood and subpersonhood are reciprocally defined and are manifested on several planes. In ideal Kantianism (predicated on a population of white individuals), persons can be abstract, raceless, colorless. In *Herrenvolk* Kantianism, the criteria for being a person necessarily have to be developed in contrast to the criteria for being a subperson. There is a dy-

namic interrelation between the two. As Richard Drinnon observes about the early colonial settlements in the United States, "Indian-hating identified the dark others that white settlers were not and must not under any circumstances become."[24] Moreover, whereas abstract Kantianism is focused solely on rationality, *Herrenvolk* Kantianism has a richer set of metrics of assessment—cognitive, moral, cultural, somatic—numerous axes along which one can measure up to or fall short of full personhood. The result, in part, is that (white) persons look to (nonwhite) subpersons as an inverted mirror, a reflection of what they should not be, and (nonwhite) subpersons who accept the *Herrenvolk* framework in turn have (white) persons as their (unreachable) ideal, a norm that by definition can never be achieved but can at least be aspired to.

2. Subpersonhood has to be enforced and racial deference from subpersons maintained. Because of its self-sustaining symmetry, ideal Kantianism is inherently stable, since it rests on reciprocal relations between persons of acknowledged equal worth, involving a respect voluntarily given. *Herrenvolk* Kantianism, in contrast, requires that a subset of the human population learn to regard themselves as subpersons and, as such, not fully human, not of equal worth. Thus the system will be potentially unstable, requiring subjugation and ideological conditioning to ensure its ongoing reproduction. Subpersons are not born but are made, and the making is not a once-and-for-all event, like slave-breaking or even the extended process of indoctrination known as education in colonial societies, but an ongoing political operation involving routine daily transactions of various kinds.

Moreover, people's sense of self-worth will obviously be influenced by the peculiarities of this system. In the ideal Kantian community, self-respect is fortified by reciprocal symmetrical relations of respect from others who are our moral equals. But in this nonideal, racially hierarchical "community," the self-respect of those designated as full persons will be linked with moral relations on two levels, white peers and nonwhite inferiors. Not merely must one's fellow persons respect one, but one must also be paid what could be termed *racial deference* from the subperson population. Failure to receive this deference then becomes a threat to one's sense of self-worth, since self-worth is defined hierarchically in relation to the class of inferior beings. So it is crucial to the maintenance of the system that the moral economy of deference is maintained, with a watchful eye for signs of insubordination in the subperson population. By posture, body language, manner, speech, and gaze, subpersons need constantly to demonstrate that they recognize and accept their subordinate position. In Richard Wright's famous characterization of his boyhood in Mississippi, one has to learn "the ethics of living Jim Crow," or one may not go on living at all.[25]

3. Resistance to subpersonhood becomes an ongoing subterranean tension within the racial polity. The persons of mainstream philosophy, being ghostly disincorporate individuals, can take their personhood for granted, because they are really *white* persons conceptualized without reference to the nonwhite subperson population. Subpersons, however, have to fight for their personhood (against the opposition of the white population, who, insofar as they maintain their racist beliefs, have a vested material, psychic, and ontological interest in continuing nonwhite subpersonhood). Sometimes this struggle will be overt; at other times, circumstances will make it necessary for resistance to be clandestine, coded. But in all these white supremacist states, it will be a constant presence, a standing threat to the dark ontology of racial hierarchy.

Because the stigmatization of nonwhites is multidimensional, resistance to it has to be correspondingly broad: moral, epistemic, somatic. Morally, one has to learn the basic self-respect that white Kantian persons can casually assume but that subpersons can attain only by repudiating the official metaphysic. Thus, in his analysis of Frederick Douglass's famous fight with the "slave-breaker" Edward Covey, Bernard Boxill argues that Douglass's point is that the slave, the enslaved person, "would not be free of mental constraints," "would not know himself to [be] the moral equal of others, unless he resisted his enslaver."[26] Epistemologically, a cognitive resistance to *Herrenvolk* theory will be necessary, the rejection of white mystification and the sometimes painful and halting development of faith in one's ability to know the world, and the articulation of different categories, the recovery of vanished or denied histories, the embarking upon projects of racial "vindication." Somatically, since the physical body has become the vehicle of metaphysical status, since physiology has been taken to recapitulate ontology, resistance may also involve a transformation of the flesh or of one's attitude toward it. Because of the deviant standing of the flesh of the nonwhite body, the body is experienced as a burden, as the lived weight of subordination. So one gets what could be called a "somatic alienation," more central to one's being than any Marxist notion, since what is involved is not the estrangement of the worker from his product but the estrangement of the person from his physical self. The subperson will then not be at home in his or her body, since that body is the physical sign of subpersonhood; one will be haunted by corporeal spirits, the ghost of the white body. Resistance to subpersonhood thus requires an exorcism of this ghost and a corresponding acceptance and celebration of one's own material being.

Revisionist Ontologies

This model provides a generally useful trope for expanding and transforming traditional political philosophy, extending our conception of what is to count as political. If global white supremacy is conceptualized as a political system, then a wide variety of phenomena can be seen as attempts variously to enforce and to resist this system. In particular, once we recognize that personhood has been overtly or tacitly racially normed, we can appreciate that a central focus of the struggles of the colonial peoples, particularly Native Americans and Africans, has always been the defiant assertion of their personhood, the repudiation and reinvention of the selves imposed by white supremacy (the white man's Negro, the white man's Indian).[27] One will be able to see as political the fact that, as Gordon Lewis put it, "the mere act of rebellion required, on the part of the slave-person, the capacity to purge himself of the white bias, and its accompanying slavish deference to everything that the white system stood for; to perceive himself, in his self-image, as equal, or even superior, to the white master-person."[28]

Revisionist ontologies can then be taken in one or both of two ways: the necessary formal recognition in political theory of the actual dark ontologies constructed by the *Herrenvolk,* the metaphysical infrastructure of global white supremacy; and the revisionist challenges to these ontologies by the subordinated population contemptuously categorized as subpersons. As Rex Nettleford has pointed out about the Rastafari, "At the heart of his religious system is the notion of his own divinity and the first-person image of self. As if for emphasis the terms 'I-n-I' and 'I-man' are used as a constant reminder of the final transformation of a non-person (as the old slave society and the new Babylon would have it) into a *person,* as is defined by 'Jah Rastafari' and asserted by the Rastaman himself."[29]

Conceptualizing personhood as a battlefield, a terrain of political contestation, enables us to locate and understand as political an array of phenomena not readily apprehensible as such through either the liberal or Marxist prism. Whatever their other differences, these theories are both predicated on taking personhood for granted. But Native Americans' personhood was in doubt from the time of the first European incursion into the Americas; the controversy over whether they were human culminated in the great 1550–51 debate at Valladolid.[30] And throughout the period of African slavery, abolitionists and antiabolitionists continued to ask whether blacks were really equal to whites. So the historical record is clear enough; I am not revealing anything that people don't know. The burden of my claim is that the *philosophical* and *political* significance of these well-known facts has not been appreciated sufficiently. I am arguing for an explicit reconceptualization of political philosophy that would enable us to situate these struggles appropriately—as defenses and subversions of a political system of global white supremacy that is insufficiently, if at all, discussed within the body of theory within which most of us have been trained and within which we continue to operate intellectually.

I want to conclude by indicating some possible directions of research for political theorists.

Herrenvolk History

The black oppositional tradition in the Americas has always pointed out the significance of what has been called the "bleaching" or "whitewashing" of history. It would be worthwhile to take this as a theoretical object for political philosophy. Thousands of articles have been written in the Marxist tradition on so-called bourgeois ideology and its influence on diverse fields of study. But Third World political theorists need to theorize self-consciously about what could be called "white settler ideology," "*Herrenvolk* ideology," and its Eurocentric influence on representations of the European Conquest and accounts of world history ("discovery," "colonization," "founding of a new world," "the civilizing mission," etc.).[31]

It would be an interesting exercise, for example, to investigate and chart a history of holocaust denial, not the familiar neo-Nazi denial of mass murder of Jews during World War II but white scholars' depiction of the fate of indigenous peoples, from the response to the original claims of Bartolomé de Las Casas onward through characterizations of the Indian Wars of the eighteenth and nineteenth centuries. David Stannard's *American Holocaust*, an important revisionist work timed for the Columbian quincentenary, draws on demographic research that has dramatically increased estimates of the pre-Conquest population of the Americas, so that—with figures ranging possibly as high as 100 million victims—this would be, Stannard says, "far and away, the most massive act of genocide in the history of the world."[32] The historic downplaying and even moral justification of this foundational feat of mass murder would repay study for what it reveals about *Herrenvolk* theory.

Similarly, the distortions about Africa's past—the "invention of Africa"—need to be contextualized not as contingently racist descriptions by individual bigots but as an organic part of the project of denying African personhood.[33] Correspondingly, we need to research and valorize the long "vindicationist" tradition in the Pan-Africanist movement, locating it as a crucial part of the intellectual political struggle against the system of global white supremacy.[34]

Language and Culture

Colonization has standardly involved the denigration as barbaric of native cultures and languages, and the demand to assimilate to the practices of the superior race, so that one can achieve whatever fractional personhood is permitted. "The Negro of the Antilles," explains Fanon, "will be proportionately whiter—that is, he will come closer to being a real human being—in direct ratio to his mastery of the French language."[35] The educational systems imposed have usually overtly sought to suppress indigenous tongues. Moreover, the colonized have often argued that the languages of the mother countries are not neutral but to a significant extent are the carriers of imperial culture. For this reason, the Kenyan writer Ngugi wa Thiong'o no longer writes in English, choosing instead to write in his native Gikuyu.[36] In the Caribbean, where creoles of various kinds have developed, part of the resistance to white racism has simply been the affirmation of the worth of these languages, from the work of J. J. Thomas onward.[37] But it might also be illuminating to examine them for evidence of conceptual opposition to dominant semantics, alternate categorizations of reality that to a certain extent challenge existing frameworks—an "antilanguage" appropriate for an "antisociety."[38] And if not here, in the creole languages that developed more or less spontaneously, then certainly in the self-consciously created "dread talk" of the Rastafari.[39]

In the case of the United States, with a white settler population representing themselves as creating a world out of wilderness, the construction of an exclusionary cultural whiteness has required the denial of the actual multiracial heritage of the country, what the black American writer Albert Murray calls its "incontestably mulatto" character.[40] Whites have appropriated Native American and African technical advances, language use, cultural customs, and artistic innovations without acknowledgment, thereby both reinforcing the image of nonwhites as subpersons incapable of making any worthwhile contribution to global civilization and burnishing the myth of their own monopoly on creativity.[41] Culture has not been central to European political theory because cultural commonality has usually been presupposed. But once cultures are in contestation, hegemonic and oppositional, and linked with personhood, they necessarily acquire a political dimension.

"Raced"/Third World Epistemology

Mainstream liberal political theory has seldom been epistemologically self-conscious, taking for granted the universal perceptiveness of the abstract Enlightenment cognizer. The challenge of Marxism was seen in part as an attempt to develop a radical theory from the putatively epistemically privileged position (with respect to possibilities for differential experience, alternative conceptualization) of the proletariat.

A plausible case can surely be made, correspondingly, that a racially informed/"black"/"Third World" epistemology can be developed as part of this political project, an epistemology that would self-consciously take the standpoint of those racially subordinated by the system of white supremacy as a source of conceptual inspiration and experiential guidance. Such a project would recognize that there is a "black" experience and perspective on reality while simultaneously, through a social-structural rather than biologistic conceptualization, repudiating the mystifications of contemporary "melanin theory." In this spirit, Lucius Outlaw, although sympathetic to the task of a cognitive rethinking of dominant "discursive formations" in the light of the history of Euro-American racism, urges a careful critical analysis of the normative claims of Afrocentrism and "Africology," and he is wary of "a restrictive cultural nationalism" that is cavalier about "refined norms for truth, objectivity, and justification."[42]

The Body

In the racial polity, by contrast with the colorless polity of abstract Western theory, the body necessarily becomes politicized, giving rise to a "body politics." White supremacy subordinates the body as the indicator of diminished personhood, a subordination manifested both in the derogation of the nonwhite body, particularly the black body,[43] and, especially during the regime of slavery, the impositions of certain postures, body languages.

Resistance to these negative valorizations and somatic inflictions has perhaps most strikingly been manifested in the case of the Jamaican Rastafari: the deliberate transformation of the black body and its revisionist reinscription into an alternative narrative of captive warriors in Babylon. The very fact that the flashing locks of the strutting dread are now a media cliché is a remarkable testimony to the abrogation of the original rules of the somatic space of the white polity.[44] In addition, popular dance could be scrutinized for signs of reinventions of the postures of the body, micropolitics of assertion, and stiffenings of the spine against the imposed deference required of subpersons.[45]

More generally, of course, Ralph Ellison's famous trope of invisibility, already cited several times, relies on the notion of a peculiar class of bodies that appear only to disappear. Thus within this expanded vision of the subject matter appropriately to be investigated by political philosophy, an evolving phenomenology of the black body would no longer seem out of place, being clearly tied in with the contested flesh of politicized (sub)personhood. Lewis Gordon employs Sartrean ideas of embodied consciousness to explore how, in an "antiblack world," the white Other determines that black presence becomes absence, so that one is seen as the unseen: "He is not seen in his individuality. To see him as black is to see enough. Hence to see him as black is not to see *him* at all."[46] One's nonwhite body excludes one from full membership in the white body politic.

Folk Religions

This new framework also implies the explicit political recognition of folk religion—vodun, Santería, obeah, Rastafari, candomblé—as a primary locus of resistance to the ideology and practice of the regime of white supremacy. (Indeed, this recognition is, ironically, more clearly manifested in the suppressive policies of colonial governments toward these religions than in academic intellectual theorizing.) The crucial role black religion historically played in slave uprisings is well known, but even well into the postemancipation period these religions have continued to be important as oppositional sites. The church or the informal meeting place has functioned as an epistemological fortress, a place where the community could freely meet away from the white gaze and collectively synthesize insights to forge a countervailing ideology. It has served as a source of spiritual strength, reinforcing conceptions of self-worth within an alternative narrative, a different cosmology, in defiance of the official status of subpersonhood.[47] And in some cases, as we have seen, it has arguably contributed through the rituals of song, dance, and spirit possession to the generation of oppositional physicalities, the rebuilding of an alternative self differently related to its material body.

Intersection with Gender

Finally, all of these issues need to be examined in connection with the intersecting system of gender domination, which necessarily shapes both the structures of oppression and the patterns of resistance.[48] The valorization of precolonial tradition against European erasures, for example, may foster an uncritical embrace of a past remembered less fondly by women assigned to traditional roles, so that a double rethinking may be necessary. The male assertion of personhood in a sexist society becomes the assertion of manhood, a manhood that is likely to be at least partly conceptually conflated with a certain positioning over subordinated women. Sexuality and sexual relations are necessarily racialized in a white-supremacist order and involve the privileging of certain somatotypes in a hierarchy of desirability and prestige.[49] Thus nonwhite women will in general be engaged in a politics of both transgender unity and intergender division, fighting on shifting fronts that are both racial and sexual.[50]

The idea, then, is for black philosophers in political theory—or rather all philosophers interested in the elimination of racism and in bringing mainstream philosophy down from its otherworldly empyrean musings—to take global white supremacy as a political system and begin to map its contours. An interdisciplinary approach is obviously called for, in which one moves back and forth across the boundaries of formal philosophy, drawing on work in cultural studies, critical race theory, and socioeconomic research to keep the abstractions in touch with empirical reality. (The problem is not abstraction itself but an idealizing abstraction that abstracts *away* from crucial determinants. No serious theorizing is possible without abstraction.)

There is nothing at all new in the observation that for the past few hundred years, race and racism have been central to the histories of the Americas in particular and the West in general. But the profound implications of this fact for the categories and explanatory schemas of mainstream Western political philosophy have not properly been worked out. In effect, Anglo-American theory needs to catch up with what the racially subordinated in the West have always perceived: that the local intra-European ontology was never the general one, and that the revision in both theory and practice of the actual *Herrenvolk* ontology has always been as worthily "philosophical" an enterprise as any of the preoccupations of orthodox textbook white theory.

6 The Racial Polity

A new paradigm is beginning to emerge across a variety of subjects, a paradigm that takes race, normative whiteness, and white supremacy to be central to U.S. and indeed recent global history.[1] The rate of emergence is by no means uniform, far advanced in cultural studies, retarded in, say, political philosophy. Nor are the theoretical presuppositions always the same. (If this is a prerequisite for paradigmhood, one might want to speak more cautiously of an "orientation" or a "perspective" instead.)[2] Some authors draw on deconstruction and discourse theory, on Derrida and Foucault. Others seek to modify and update old-fashioned Marxist frameworks to give race an autonomy—and perhaps even a "material" status—not usually conceded to it in more class-reductivist accounts. Still others would consider themselves traditional liberals, though with a nontraditional appreciation of how racialized actual liberalism has been. And a few view themselves as working toward new theorizations that do not readily fit into any of the standard metatheoretical taxonomies. But what they all have in common is that they see race as central (though not foundational) and as sociopolitically "constructed," thus distinguishing themselves from earlier theorists of race, who usually took it to be a transhistorical biological essence and whose assumptions were in fact often simply racist. The term originally associated specifically with minority viewpoints in legal studies is being used more generally by some writers to refer to this new paradigm: *critical race theory.*[3]

For racial minorities and Third World scholars long interested in the theorization of race and Western domination, this is, of course, a welcome development, providing them with a recognized academic space for work previously regarded as marginal. It holds out the prospect of ultimately mounting a challenge to the conceptualizations of orthodox theory that would parallel the impressive achievements of several decades of feminist scholarship. My particular interest here is in that unfortunate area of backwardness: political philosophy. How would ostensibly raceless but actually white First World political philosophy need to be rethought and transformed so as to formally incorporate race into its anatomies of the body politic, instead of, as at present, tacitly taking the white body as normative?

Gender and Race Theory

Many years ago, in his pioneering work on race and racism, Robert Blauner pointed out that "the colonial order in the modern world has been based on the dominance of white Westerners over non-Western people of color; racial oppression and the racial conflict to which it gives rise are endemic to it.... [I]n the United States, as elsewhere, it was a colonial experience that generated the lineup of ethnic and racial division.... [T]he colonial system brought into being races, from an array of distinct tribes and ethnic peoples."[4] Yet First World political philosophy has not shown much interest in critically analyzing this historic system of domination or its contemporary legacy. There was a flurry of articles and books in the 1970s and 1980s specifically about affirmative action; there were and continue to be general declarations about the evils of discrimination in work essentially focused on other themes. But the historic contradictions between European liberalism at home and conquest, slavery, and imperialism abroad, the inconsistencies of a color-coded white American egalitarianism that rests on nonwhite subordination, have received little systematic exploration in the discipline.

Where gender is concerned, the picture is much brighter. There has been such a burgeoning of feminist scholarship in philosophy — articles, books, special journal issues, anthologies, series — that it now merits its own category, whereas race (as against routine condemnations of racism) has yet to arrive. Thus, to cite one reference work, Robert Goodin and Philip Pettit's nearly 700-page Blackwell *Companion to Contemporary Political Philosophy* (1993) has feminism as one of the six entries in the "major ideologies" section (along with anarchism, conservatism, liberalism, Marxism, socialism), but no entry on, say, black nationalism or Pan-Africanism.[5] Nor does either appear, or the related subjects of race, racism, and white supremacy, in the subsequent list of twenty-eight "special topics," though this list extends all the way to such nontraditional political topics as environmentalism and sociobiology. Frantz Fanon and W. E. B. Du Bois do not even make the index.

So even though feminism is by no means completely respectable yet, in contrast to this kind of silence it clearly represents a comparative success story. The revisionary feminist cartography—the redrawing of the map of the political so that what had formerly been taken to be natural, personal, unchanging becomes the object of political discourse—has shifted the terms of the debate. It has become possible to see male domination as political and to categorize Plato and Aristotle, Hobbes and Rousseau, Locke and Marx, Rawls and Nozick as *male* theorists in a sense deeper than their mere possession of one kind of genitalia.

What I want to suggest, elaborating on the theme of Chapter 5, is that the feminist challenge to mainstream political philosophy may provide a useful model to be followed by those who wish similarly to theorize race. So let us examine the evolution of this challenge as it developed out of the "second wave" of feminism.[6] It is possible to distinguish three separate aspects of feminist theory, though in practice, of course, they are often found together.

First, there is the discovery, analysis, and critique of the sexism of the major figures of the canon. This can be seen as a kind of cognitive awakening, the initially hesitant and then increasingly self-confident perception that this supposedly universalist tradition is not really speaking for you, that the "men" really are male. The aim is not muckraking for its own sake (though muckraking is not without its peculiar pleasures) but a demonstration of how deeply embedded in the tradition are assumptions of the naturalness and rightness of male domination. It is not that these theorists just happen to be male but that their maleness enters into and seminally penetrates their theories, a conceptual DNA that reproduces a template of particular concerns, foci, values, and perspectives.

Second, there is the parallel enterprise of the excavation and rediscovery of oppositional political texts or fragments by women: Olympe de Gouges's "Declaration of the Rights of Woman and Citizen," Mary Wollstonecraft's *Vindication of the Rights of Woman*, Simone de Beauvoir's *Second Sex*.[7] The aim is to demonstrate the existence of a tradition of resistance, a "usable past." This goal is important not merely on the symbolic level but also because of the actual value of the substantive insights of past theorists. One finds in nascent or developed form contestations of male theory that later generations may be able to draw upon intellectually.

Finally, there is the attempt to develop new conceptions of the polity that make explicit, through their mapping of the full dimensions of female subordination, what would be required to incorporate women into the body politic on a basis of real moral equality. For some, these conceptions involve the reworking of distinctions within a traditional framework, on the assumption that existing theory, when purified of its gender biases, can be adopted by women. For others, it is not merely that the application of the theories has been contingently sexist but that the very way of looking at the world is necessarily corrupted by its male origins, so that one almost needs to start anew, rejecting "malestream" thought. Thus the innovation—coming originally from radical feminism, later more broadly adopted—of reconceptualizing the polity as a patriarchy, a politico-economic system of male domination, so that the political is extended to include the personal and the dynamics of gender relations (heterosexual intercourse, marriage, pornography, rape) emerge as political practices in need of theorization. Within this framework, the sexism of traditional male political thinkers is seen no longer as contingent, embarrassing but conceptually insignificant prejudices to be quickly passed over, the rest of the theory remaining intact, but as the organic ideational outcome of a structure founded on female subordination and as such affecting the character of the theories.

Can this feminist strategy for rethinking Western political philosophy be emulated by those of us who seek to theorize race and First World/Third World relations? I believe it can, and that the differences on some points should actually make the task of rethinking easier. The origins of patriarchy remain a subject of bitter dispute, but even if it is not, as radical feminists claim, traceable to the origin of the species, it is obviously far older than white racial domination and arguably more foundationally embedded in human interrelations. Thus in some respects, at least, racism has been less taken for granted than sexism and so requires less work to be made conceptually visible. Moreover, the long struggle against racism and European domination has been documented amply. So a reconceptualization of orthodox political philosophy that takes this history into account is the task to be addressed.

As far as reexamination of the canon is concerned, a body of literature that constructs genealogies of racism[8] and analyzes the racist views of various famous philosophers already exists, though it does not approach in volume and depth the body of feminist revisionism. Such research needs to be expanded. On the empirical level, what is needed is an equivalent to what was done for women many years ago—the putting together of an anthology collecting Western philosophers' statements on race and the non-European world.[9] On the theoretical level, what is required is a framework for situating such views and showing that—at least in the modern period—they are not incidental but are linked to a crystallizing sociopolitical system.

With respect to locating oppositional texts as both symbol and resource, theorists of race have the tremendous advantage of being able to draw on a huge body of work: Native American resistance; the abolitionist and antisegregationist movements; slave narratives; nationalist and anticolonial struggles in Latin America, Asia, Africa, Australasia; and already articulated ideologies such as Pan-Africanism and *indigenismo*. Western political philosophers do not usually consider these writings when they map the political, arguably because of the deficiencies of the mapmakers rather than those of the writers.

Finally, perhaps the most interesting point of differentiation is that, with respect to revisionary theorizing, the necessary global reconceptualization of the polity that would correspond to the feminists' "patriarchy" is already at hand, in the form of "white supremacy." Feminist theorists had to learn to see male domination as a political system and redefine an old term that once had quite a different meaning in order to name this system. But white supremacy, the domination of whites over nonwhites, was originally proclaimed quite openly and under that very name. In a sense, then, the initial work has already been done, though when the perspective shifts, the system will be negatively rather than positively valorized, the survival of white supremacy beyond its officially proclaimed demise will have to be demonstrated, and the mechanisms by which it sustains and reproduces itself will have to be mapped.

So one strategy for developing critical race theory within political philosophy will entail self-conscious theorizing of a *racial polity*—in this case, a *white-supremacist polity*—and a rethinking of the political around the axis of race.

Why are these questions of reconceptualization important for political philosophy? After all, in the orthodox Anglo-American analytic framework, political philosophy is usually represented as properly concerned only with normative claims, as against the factual claims of political science. But in the classical Western tradition, political philosophy has always sought to explain as well as to prescribe. Thus Jean Hampton, invoking this tradition, rejects an exclusivist focus on normative questions and argues that political philosophy also seeks to "understand at the deepest level the foundations of states," how political societies arise and how people in those societies are bound together. Matters of fact do legitimately enter the ambit of political philosophy, though usually at a higher level of abstraction than in political science. One needs, in Hampton's words, to go beyond mere "surface description" to excavate the "deep structures" that generate "not only forms of interaction that make certain kinds of [resource] distributions inevitable but also moral theories that justify those distributions."[10]

And these factual questions (low-level empirical assertions or, more usually, abstract theoretical claims) will almost always play some role in the normative disputes also. Only rarely is there a factual consensus among political philosophers about the social picture, with the debate being purely about rival sets of values. Instead, there will typically be disagreement about what the facts are. And once there is any kind of radical normative challenge to mainstream political thought—as, famously, with Marxist or feminist theory—it is usually precisely in the systematic *contestation* of the ostensibly neutral, "apolitical" empirical and theoretical assumptions that have hitherto framed and underwritten the debate that the clash of political philosophies reveals itself. Different political philosophies will have different stories about the past and present of the polity, its origins and its workings, and these divergences will have implications for its moral assessment also.

Consider, for example, the minimal statement that "women are oppressed," which Alison Jaggar takes to be the common premise defining of all feminisms, no matter what their other theoretical differences.[11] The claim is descriptive as well as normative. It makes a moral and political judgment about the situation of women that is predicated on a narrative alternative to conservative accounts that would represent women's position as the result, say, of free and informed choice, innate cognitive deficiency, or natural sex roles. Different feminisms offer different accounts of the origins of this oppression, see class or gender or both in tandem as foundational, have rival perspectives on domestic labor, heterosexuality, rape, the market, the state, male political theory. But in all cases, the findings of social theory and different views on those findings are indeed relevant to the normative enterprise. In the words of Jane Mansbridge and Susan Okin, "Feminist theory ... has one overarching goal—to understand, explain and challenge [men's systematic domination of women]."[12] And for feminist political philosophy, as noted, one theoretical key to conceptualizing this domination and developing this normative challenge is provided by the idea of patriarchy.

Diana Coole suggests, "It is the concept of patriarchy which marks the most distinctive and innovative contribution by feminism to political thought.... By using patriarchy as a descriptive term, all the interlocking structures which had been previously identified as constituents of sexual domination could be integrated."[13] By bringing the household and all that comes with it—the family, sexual relations, the division of reproductive labor—into the realm of the political, feminists not only radically transform our mapping but also give us an external metatheoretical vantage point from which to understand the previous (male) mapping. The sexism of the tradition is seen to be not at all contingent but structurally related to the unnamed system of patriarchy that the tradition—whatever else it is doing at the moment—generally serves to rationalize, since male freedom and equality in the public sphere are overtly or tacitly predicated on female servitude and inequality in the private sphere, a "functionalist attitude" toward women that pervades the assumptions of political theory.[14] In this deep and interesting sense the theorizing is "male," as against the superficial sense in which the authors all possess a characteristic set of chromosomes: "maleness" as a location in a system of power that generates a certain corresponding outlook.

The point is, then, that a political philosophy necessarily involves factual (descriptive and theoretical) assumptions as well as normative claims about the polity, and if the former are not explicitly stated and highlighted as integral to the political philosophy, it is often simply because they are part of a conservative, background "common sense" that its proponents take for granted. And radical theory, whether of class, gender, or race, typically contests these "commonsensical" assumptions. The Blackwell editors' inclusion of entries on economics, history, law, political science, and sociology shows that they recognize this descriptive dimension of their subject. But as one would expect, these entries are no more neutral and politically disengaged than the listing of major ideologies. The economics and history of imperialism, colonialism, slavery — the law, politics, and sociology of imperial rule, white settler states, Jim Crow, apartheid, racial polities — make no appearance here, either. The "whiteness" of the text, of this vision of what political philosophy is and is not, inheres not in the biological whiteness of (the vast majority of) the authors but in the political whiteness and Eurocentrism of the *outlook,* one that takes for granted the truth of a certain account of world history and the centrality and representativeness to that history of the European experience. The pattern of exclusion is thereby epistemically complete, the theoretical circle closed. Given such a framework, it is hardly surprising that issues of race and Western domination are mentioned neither in the political philosophy nor special subjects sections, and that a political reference work produced in the last decade of the twentieth century can make next to no reference to the political issues that have for several hundred years engaged the majority of the planet's population.

Determining the cartography of the political is therefore a political act, insofar as it demarcates what is judged political, worthy of theoretical attention, central, interesting, perhaps subject to a transformational human causality, from what is dismissed as apolitical, residual, marginal, uninteresting, naturally ordained. Correspondingly, reconceptualizing the polity can be a radical, even revolutionary undertaking, because it names differently, it identifies different ontologies and alternative categorizations, it brings to light connections unknown or ignored, it offers different spatial and temporal maps, it privileges a subordinated set of experiences, it raises different questions, it points factual and normative inquiry in different directions. From the perspective of race, one can then see the events of the past few hundred years as bringing into existence a polity of a kind not described by Plato or Aristotle, Hobbes or Rousseau, Locke or Marx, Rawls or Nozick. It is thus unsurprising that the political philosophies of these writers, at least in their unmodified form, are of limited use in theorizing this polity, and that contemporary philosophers who see themselves as part of this tradition ignore its existence. And the name of this polity is "white supremacy," a political structure both global and national.

Race as a Global System and
Modern Western Political Philosophy

In this analysis of race it is appropriate to begin at the global level. The idea of race as a global system, far from being new, can be found practically at the inception of the oppositional black tradition. The pioneering Pan-Africanist Martin Delany complained in the mid–nineteenth century that though "there are two colored persons for each White man in the world ... the White race dominates the colored."[15] Half a century later, Du Bois's appeal "To the Nations of the World" at the Pan-African Conference in 1900 described the global problem of "the color line, the question as to how far differences of race ... are going to be made, hereafter, the basis of denying to over half the world the right of sharing to their utmost ability the opportunities and privileges of modern civilisation."[16] In our time, Frantz Fanon observed that "it is evident that what parcels out the world is to begin with the fact of belonging to or not belonging to a given race."[17]

Radical black and colonial intellectuals have always seen race in international terms, as a set of relations to be understood not merely locally, in the particular setting of the Caribbean or the United States or Africa, but as the global outcome of a historic process of European imperialism, settlement, and colonialism. Where the white left has tended to treat race as epiphenomenal, one finds in the work of black Marxists such as C. L. R. James a repudiation of both class-reductionistic Marxism and foundationalist racial essentialism: "The race question is subsidiary to the class question in politics, and to think of imperialism in terms of race is disastrous. But to neglect the racial factor as merely incidental [is] an error only less grave than to make it fundamental."[18] I take this statement as an assertion that race is both real and nonfoundational, that it is, in the contemporary vocabulary, "constructed," and that this construction, resulting as it does from European imperialism, is global.

Thus Gary Okihiro talks about the emergence of "transnational identities of white and nonwhite" linked to "a global racial formation that complemented and buttressed the economic and political world-system," thereby "transcend[ing] national boundaries." Similarly, Paul Gilroy argues for the notion of a "black Atlantic," an "intercultural and transnational formation" that reflects the reality that pan-Africanism and Black Power signified resistance to "a hemispheric order of racial domination."[19] There is no world government as such, so one cannot speak of a global polity in that formal sense. But there is a set of *transnational* relations of domination, transcending the First World nation-state, for which race is the bearer. These relations are not merely internal, between colonizers and aborigines, slavemasters and slaves, but global, between one continent and the others, between European civilization and non-European barbarism, so that one *can* speak of a "virtual" planetary polity. From the modern period onward, with the simultaneous domestic emergence of liberalism and the external expansion of Europe, pronouncements on race and the non-European world thus became theoretically significant, since they had to be seen in the context of this crystallizing racial world system. Race will in general be the marker of entitlement or dispossession, civilization or barbarism, normative inclusion or normative exclusion, full or diminished personhood.

Economically, wealth is extracted through the seizure of bullion and the expropriation of land, through slavery and colonial labor. "[W]hiteness is ownership of the earth," commented Du Bois.[20] As Eric Williams argued half a century ago and as numerous Third World and some renegade First World scholars have argued since, the profits from conquest, the slave trade, and colonial exploitation were to a greater or lesser extent crucial in enabling the European take-off now misleadingly known as "the European miracle."[21] But instead, in Jim Blaut's words, the rise of Europe is represented as resulting, "essentially, from historical forces generated within Europe itself."[22] Correspondingly, cultural myths of origin represent Europe as self-sufficient, autochthonous, with the contribution of Afro-Asia having been written out of the history books. "There never was a civilized nation of any other complexion than white," boasts Hume.[23] Ancient Greece becomes a self-contained fountainhead of wisdom, removed from its actual origins and influences, and its Enlightened heirs go out into the world as historied and cultured Europeans encountering peoples without history and culture.[24] Morally, progress, liberalism, and Enlightenment for those on the home continent rest on color-coded principles that turn out to be somewhat less applicable to those on other continents. "The slave-trade and slavery were the economic basis of the French Revolution," points out C. L. R. James.[25] Finally, the planet as a whole is tectonically divided by a racial metaphysic that partitions persons from subpersons, who are linked by a reciprocating ontological engine. "[T]here was virtual unanimity that subject races should be ruled, that they *are* subject races.... [This assumption was] buttressed by a cultural discourse relegating and confining the non-European to a secondary racial, cultural, ontological status. Yet this secondariness is, paradoxically, essential to the primariness of the European," observes Edward Said.[26] Thus white Lockean, Kantian, Millian persons who own themselves and their efficient nature-appropriating labor, who are rational noumenal duty-respecting beings, whose individuality must be respected by the modernist liberal state, emerge not merely in contrast to but to a certain extent on the backs of nonwhite subpersons thousands of miles away, whose self-ownership is qualified and whose labor is inefficient, whose phenomenal traits limit their rationality and consequent moral autonomy, and for whom, accordingly, slavery and despotic colonial rule are appropriate. As Paul Gilroy concludes, conquest, colonialism, and African slavery must then be seen not as the "special property" of nonwhites but rather as "*internal*" to the West, integral to European modernity, "part of the ethical and intellectual heritage of the West as a whole." One needs to contextualize the European Enlightenment as exemplifying "racialized reason" and to "reevaluate," correspondingly, the usefulness of the category of the European nation-state.[27] In certain respects the real political system is global.

Like gender, then, this reconceptualization provides a framework for illuminating and explaining the silences, evasions, misrepresentations, and double standards of (most of) the important figures of modern Western political theory. These phenomena can appropriately be seen not as marginal deviations uninteresting to a later and (supposedly) more sophisticated audience but as part of the general project of justifying the global white racial polity and the exploitation of the rest of the planet for the benefit of Europeans at home and abroad. Locating First World thought within the context of the consolidation and reproduction of this system then puts us in the metatheoretical position of being able to track how the dominant theories, central concepts, and crucial moves of Western political philosophy are systematically shaped by the overall European project. Essentially, a racialization is manifest in the explicit derogation of nonwhites and in the appearance of a dichotomous logic that restricts the principles of liberalism to domestic European space or its implantation as civilized outpost in non-European space.

Consider social contract theory, classically seen (Hobbes aside) as the main vehicle by which European liberalism challenged absolutism. Contractarianism grounds the polity on the consent of free and equal human beings. The basic apparatus is simple: a pre-sociopolitical condition (the "state of nature"); abstract "men" residing in this condition; a normative background of natural law; a voluntary decision to bring into existence society and the state; the institution of the constitutionalist sovereign and the corollary creation of *political* men. The writings of the four most important contract theorists—Hobbes, Locke, Rousseau, Kant—cover the period usually judged to be the golden age of contract theory, 1650–1800 (*Leviathan* [1651] to *The Metaphysics of Morals* [1797]). But this century and a half of the emergence of Western liberalism, from the seventeenth-century English "Glorious Revolution" to the eighteenth-century American and French revolutions, coincides with the period of modern (as against feudal Spanish and Portuguese) European expansionism. So even though the men who make the social contract are equal (bourgeois) persons rather than members of ascriptive feudal estates, they cannot be raceless; *they are in effect white men.*[28] "Wildness" and "savagery" are innate and necessary for non-Europeans, but external and contingent for Europeans (if they ever were in that state in the first place).

The racialization of the contractarian apparatus thus manifests itself in a pre-sociopolitical state of nature that is real and permanent for nonwhites but either hypothetical or just temporary (and in any case long past and not usually that bad) for whites; "men" who are by no means abstract but coextensive with "white men," as against "savages"; a normative moral background that only whites are fully capable of recognizing; a decision to bring the polis into existence that whites are the only ones qualified (strong version), or at least the ones best qualified (weaker version), to take; and the institution of a governmental and legal system that either is necessarily white, for they are the only ones who can be political men (strong version), or is at least the superior one that others need to emulate (weaker version). Since the realm of the political is reserved for those who are capable of leaving the state of nature to create political/civil society, nonwhites who are savages (as in the white settler state) are then permanently nonpolitical ("wild," even if superficially tamed and civilized). If they are to enter the polity, they can do so only through the intervention of the political beings, the whites, who then have the responsibility of speaking for them and, via the white sovereign, of ruling over them. As James Tully summarizes things:

> In the stages view of human history, all cultures and peoples are mapped hierarchically in accordance with their location on a historical process of progressive development. European constitutional nation states, with their distinctive institutions and cultures of manners and civility, are at the highest and most developed or improved stage.... [T]he modern

constitution and its associated concepts are defined in contrast to what Michel-Rolph Trouillot calls "the savage slot," which is filled by the non-European "other" who is defined as lower in development and earlier in time: in a state of nature, primitive, rude, savage, traditional or underdeveloped, depending on the theorist.... The founding of a modern European constitution and the existence of modern European political institutions are used to define sovereignty and so to dispossess the Aboriginal nations of their equal status.... The legitimacy of European settlement and dispossession was assured.[29]

Contract theory seemed to have expired by the end of the eighteenth century, partly in response to utilitarian and historicist critiques. But as with gender, the broader framework of metatheoretical political assumptions about race is independent of any particular contractarian/anti-contractarian commitment. There are some exceptions, but the record of the tradition as a whole is one of complicity with the establishment of the global racial system. To make a point that should be obvious but is often unappreciated: opposition to the ill treatment of indigenes is not the same thing as opposition to European expansionism. One can sincerely condemn cruelty to those viewed as less than equal while continuing to think of them as less than equal. Insofar as European racial superiority is taken for granted by Western theorists, insofar as the colonization, expropriation, and settlement of the world are seen as legitimate, these theorists are apologists for the establishment of global white supremacy, however they may differ on the particular forms it should take and on how humanely nonwhites should be treated. And to the extent that their political philosophies—and the adaptation of these philosophies to the exigencies of the states created by European expansionism—take nonwhite inferiority as natural and nonpolitical, or as political and justifiable, they are broadly committed to the creation and perpetuation of the racial polity, a polity that generally subordinates nonwhites to the interests of whites.

The United States as a Racial Polity

One might expect that in a nation founded as a "white man's country," where white domination has been ramified in the legal system and in the moral and sociopolitical universe, race would be dealt with systematically and given the theoretical centrality it deserves. But these expectations would, at least until recently, have been disappointed. The best-known treatment of white supremacy under that explicit name by an establishment scholar is by a historian, George Fredrickson, and, though very valuable, is an empirical rather than a theoretical work.[30] One has to turn to maverick writings by marginal black and minority thinkers or a few leftist white scholars to get a theorization of the architecture of white domination. Globally, a pattern of neglect and evasion in American sociopolitical theory has afflicted even the more empirically oriented disciplines of sociology and political science.

In sociology, whether in the influential 1920s Chicago School of Robert Park or in the postwar "melting pot" model of Nathan Glazer and Daniel Moynihan, the tendency has been optimistically assimilationist.[31] Often race has been blurred into ethnicity, with the qualitative distinctions between the nineteenth-century immigration and integration of (white) European-Americans and the exclusionary subordination of (red/black/brown/yellow) non-European-Americans being ignored or played down. Racism has been conceptualized as individual prejudice, a hangover from premodern ("caste") assumptions; attributed to ignorance, lack of education, or a certain ("authoritarian") personality type; and expected to disappear with modernization. Correspondingly, the analysis as a whole is usually confined to the level of the attitudinal and ideational. Summing up this literature, David Wellman concludes, "With few exceptions, social scientists studying racism as prejudice do not consider racial division as a form of stratification built into the structure of [American] society. In this view the roots of racial division are not located in the structure of the division of labor or in the organization of political power.... The primacy of race as an aspect of social structure in America is not recognized."[32] White Marxists who are ideologically more sympathetic to structural analyses have generally reduced race to class; black scholars who favor such accounts — pioneering Du Bois, for example, or St. Clair Drake and Horace Cayton — are marginalized.[33]

In political science, there has been a similar and, indeed, not theoretically unrelated pattern. As two black political scientists, Michael Dawson and Ernest Wilson, commented some years ago, "while the place of race in the *practice* of American politics is, arguably, quite central ... the place of race in the *study* of American politics is surprisingly peripheral."[34] Rogers Smith argues that the explanation for this silence is that from the time of Tocqueville, analysts of the American social order have been most struck by the absence in the New World of the ascriptive hierarchies of the old. Employing the transplanted categories of European sociopolitical theory, which counterpose liberal egalitarianism to feudal status, these commentators have seen the United States as a paradigmatic incarnation of the democratic dream of freedom and equality. Themselves white, inhabiting a white discursive universe, they have characteristically treated the massive exclusions of race — Native American expropriation, African slavery, Mexican annexation, Chinese exclusion, post–World War I non-Nordic immigration restrictions, World War II Japanese internment, indeed general nonwhite subordination — as marginal, minor inconsistencies in a tradition somehow essentially still inclusive and color-blind.

Hence the work of a long series of distinguished writers (Alexis de Tocqueville, Louis Hartz, Gunnar Myrdal) has a "whiggish narrative" in which the "anomalies" of systemic, juridically backed, and morally and theoretically rationalized discrimination would eventually disappear as part of the teleological working out of the universalist promise of the founding documents. "For over 80% of U.S. history, its laws declared most of the world's population to be ineligible for full American citizenship solely because of their race, original nationality, or gender," Smith notes. Yet mainstream "anomaly" theorists see no need to explain "why the exclusionary policies that have prevailed during most of U.S. history should be identified as 'exceptions' (however 'huge') to its ideals," and not as rival norms.[35]

It should be unsurprising, then, that if such cognitive myopia has been possible even in practitioners of what are supposed to be empirical disciplines, their noses pressed to the world's facticity, the room for evasion has been even greater in philosophy, traditionally regarded as inhabiting the realm of the nonempirical, the abstract, and the otherworldly. In neither of the two important American political philosophical works that originally staked out the spectrum of respectable political debate — John Rawls's *Theory of Justice* and Robert Nozick's *Anarchy, State, and Utopia* — do American slavery and American white supremacy, and what is correspondingly necessary to correct for them, figure in more than a marginal way.[36] Rawls's decision to locate himself on the terrain of "ideal theory" generates a hypothetical contractarianism in which the implications of the racial exclusions of the actual "contract" resulting from the 1776 "slaveholders' rebellion" are not confronted, and Nozick's idealized Lockeanism ignores (except for an endnote)[37] the real-life history of illicit aboriginal expropriation and property in stolen African persons. Nor has this evasion of race changed dramatically in the intervening years. Race is abstracted even more thoroughly out of the philosophical models of the polity than from their political science counterparts; those models reproduce the silences of European theory and are supported by a professional demography that makes philosophy one of the whitest of the humanities.

Bringing race into American political philosophy, then — or, more accurately, recognizing the ways in which the typical conceptualizations of white American political philosophy *already* embed and encode race in a particular evasive way, and so need to be rethought—would mean beginning from a different, more realistic starting point. The notion of a New World "fragment" of an idealized European nation-state[38] would be, if not displaced altogether, at least contextualized in the global and local relations of racial power typically minimized and abstracted away from. It would mean drawing on recent (and older) revisionist work in history, political science, sociology, legal theory, and cultural studies that, starting from the invasion of America, would recognize how the invention of the white race created a *Herrenvolk* democracy, a white republic in which the wages of whiteness motivate the division by color of the polity into two nations, so that in the moral sphere of right and wrong, whiteness itself, in this racialized universe of white *Recht*, becomes property, to be duly protected by the racial state.[39] Above all, it would mean rejecting orthodox frameworks and explicitly trying to work out the internal logic of a racial polity.

Both mainstream/liberal and oppositional/Marxist political theory have been conceptually inadequate for the theorization of race and racism. For orthodox liberalism, as I have briefly sketched, the United States is basically an egalitarian liberal democracy (though with a few admitted flaws), and racism is "prejudice" and is scheduled to disappear with enlightenment. For orthodox Marxism, the United States is basically a class society and race is unreal and ideal, attributable to the instrumentalist manipulations of the bourgeoisie to divide the innocent workers and is scheduled to disappear with class struggle. Thus in both cases, race is essentially external and ideational, a matter of attitudes and prejudicial misconceptions, having no essential link with the construction of the self, civic identity, significant sociopolitical actors, systemic structural privilege and subordination, racial economic exploitation, or state protection. In neither theory is there an adequate conceptual recognition of the significance of race as sociopolitical group identity.

By contrast, for the alternative view on race (sometimes characterized as the symbiosis view),[40] which is long established in the black political tradition,[41] the orthodox liberal picture of deviations, aberrations, and anomalies is upended. The nation's founding is placed in the demystified context of the European invasion and the conquest of America, in the course of which the earlier religious/medieval categorization of the enemy ("heathens") is gradually secularized into race.[42] In effect, the subtext already present in the classic contractarians is elevated by the Founders into the text, so that a distinction is made—in what is a white settler state—between political white men and apolitical nonwhite savages. George Fredrickson emphasizes that "liberal conceptions of polity and citizenship were originally based on the tacit assumption that 'the people' being provided with 'equal rights' were citizens of a culturally and racially homogeneous national community.... In the minds of most white Americans of the pre–Civil War era an invisible color qualification appeared between 'all' and 'men' in the [Declaration]."[43] The contract is thus a racial one, a contract between civilized whites, producing a white republic from which the "merciless Indian Savages" of the Declaration and the 60-percent-person black slaves of the Constitution are legitimately excluded. As Richard Delgado points out, critical race theory begins with the simple but politically revolutionary insight "that racism is normal, not aberrant, in American society."[44]

Race thus emerges as *central* to the American polity. Instead of counterposing an abstract liberalism to a deviant racism, one conceptualizes them as interpenetrating and transforming each other, generating a racial liberalism. The result is a universe of white right, white *Recht,* a white moral and legal equality that is reciprocally linked to a nonwhite inequality. Thus, as Herbert Blumer argues, racism should be understood not as "a set of feelings" but as "a sense of group position," in which the dominant race is convinced of its superiority, sees the subordinate race as "intrinsically different and alien," has proprietary feelings about its "privilege and advantage," and fears encroachment on these prerogatives. In effect, whites are the ruling race.[45] Race and white supremacy are therefore seen primarily as a system of advantage and disadvantage and only secondarily as a set of ideas and values. The atomic-individualist ontology is necessarily displaced by a social ontology in which races are significant sociopolitical actors. The ontology here is not "deep" in the traditional metaphysical sense of being necessary and transhistorical. As I argued in Chapter 3, it is a created, contingent ontology—the "white race" is *invented*[46]—and in another, parallel universe it would not have existed at all. But it *is* deep in the sense of shaping one's being, one's cognition, one's experience in the world: it generates a *racial* self. Biologically fictitious, race becomes socially real, so that people learn to see themselves as black and white, are treated as black and white, and are motivated by considerations arising out of this group identity.[47] Perceived group interests (not self-interest), "racial" interests, become the prime determinants of sociopolitical attitudes and behavior.[48]

Race, then, becomes the most important thing about the citizens of such a polity, for it is because of race that one does or does not count as a full person, as someone entitled to settle, to expropriate, to be free, or as someone destined to be removed, to be expropriated, to be enslaved. As white, one is a citizen; as nonwhite, an anticitizen. The two are interdefined. "Whites exist as a category of people subject to a double negative: they are those who are not non-White," summarizes Ian Haney López.[49] And since race is intersubjectively constructed, so that its boundaries are more volatile than those of class or gender, battles will be fought over race and how people should be officially (legally, socially) raced.[50] Whites whose family trees have unacknowledged roots will be terrified of losing their civic whiteness; borderline European immigrants such as the Irish will fight to have themselves categorized as white; some blacks favored by the genetic lottery will seek to pass into the white citizenry, temporarily or permanently.[51] The content and boundaries of whiteness will be shifting, politicized, the subject of negotiation and conflict.

But the bottom line, the ultimate payoff from structuring the polity around a racial axis, is what W. E. B. Du Bois once called "the wages of whiteness."[52] Particularly in the United States, usually viewed as a Lockean polity, a polity of proprietors, whiteness is, as Derrick Bell, Cheryl Harris, George Lipsitz, and others have pointed out, *property*, differential entitlement.[53] The racial polity is by definition exploitative. Whiteness is not merely full personhood, first-class citizenship, ownership of the aesthetically normative body, membership in the recognized culture; it is also material benefit, entitlement to differential moral/legal/social treatment, and differential rational expectations of economic success. For a *Herrenvolk* Lockeanism, whites' full self-ownership translates not merely into proprietorship of their own bodies and labor but also includes a share in the benefits resulting from the *qualified* self-ownership of the nonwhite population. The racial contract between whites is in effect an agreement to divide among themselves (as common white property) the proceeds of nonwhite subordination.

Thus the society is characterized by an ongoing "exploitation" whose conceptualization needs no controversial Marxist notions of surplus value, being wrong by quite conventional (nonracial) liberal bourgeois standards. From slavery, federal land grants, and the homesteading of the West through differential access to education, job opportunities, white markets, union membership, and equal wages and promotion chances to ghettoization, restrictive covenants, redlining, white flight, and differential allocation of resources to schools and neighborhoods, whites have historically been materially advantaged over nonwhites, particularly blacks.[54] In their examination of the huge discrepancy between black and white wealth, Melvin Oliver and Thomas Shapiro point out, "Practically, every circumstance of bias and discrimination against blacks has produced a circumstance and opportunity of positive gain for whites."[55] Or in the vivid phrase of Henry Louis Taylor Jr., "the black job ceiling has been the floor of white opportunity."[56] The failure to see white supremacy as a politico-economic system has blocked apprehension of this global picture. Liberals and Marxists, imprisoned in their individualist and class categories, are in general unwilling to focus on how the white population as a whole has benefited (though unequally) from nonwhite subordination.[57]

Moreover, even when the overtly discriminatory patterns of the past have disappeared, the legacy of these practices can continue so that the system is reproduced even with no racist intent. If job discrimination were to end tomorrow, for example, the fate of black Americans would be negatively affected for decades to come by the simple fact that they were, through discriminatory federal housing policy from the 1930s onward, "locked out of the greatest mass-based opportunity for wealth accumulation in American history"[58]—the chance to buy their own home. As a result of such past policies, the wealth of the median black household is less than one-tenth the wealth of the median white household, so that Oliver and Shapiro can speak of a "sedimentation" of racial inequality, a structural perpetuation of group disadvantage. Insofar as whites go along with a racially structured system that privileges them, they can be said to be complicit with it, giving a racialized tacit consent to the racial polity and indeed usually actively supporting it by their choices and by their resistance to change. Nor has the state been a detached bystander to the process. The liberal-democratic *Rechtsstaat* of an ideal Lockean or Kantian liberalism, acting to protect the property and rights of its abstract citizens, emerges here as the racial state, generally acting to protect white entitlement, whether through the original imposition of segregation or through the later failure to take the measures necessary to correct fully for the institutionalized discrimination of the past.[59]

Thus, a hundred years after the *Plessy* v. *Ferguson* decision was rendered, the United States is more segregated than it was then. One in three young black men is in prison, on parole, or on probation; "underclass" problems are seen as intractable; biologically determinist theories of race are making a comeback; and a white backlash is virtually ubiquitous. Racial polarization is as bad as it has been in decades; race has emerged as "a single profound line of cleavage" in American society, creating "divisions more notable than any other in American life," by reference to which "differences by class or gender or religion or any other social characteristic are diminutive by comparison."[60] Liberal and Marxist prognoses on the disappearance of race have been spectacularly disconfirmed. But within white political philosophy, the adequacy of the basic global categories has still not been questioned.

In conclusion: amnesiac about the history and significance of European imperialism and colonialism in shaping the modern world, disadvantaged by a conceptual apparatus inherited from officially "raceless" European theory, and blinded by its aprioristic commitment to seeing the United States as simply a flawed liberal democracy, white political philosophy has generally been hampered in its theorizations of the system, global and local. Racial exclusion, its long history ignored, has been accommodated by the categories of deviation and anomaly rather than being seen, as it should be, as *normative,* central to the system, and traceable to the European expansionist project. While the fact, if not the complete extent, of racism in the history of the West is now grudgingly admitted, the theoretical realization of its full significance is blocked by the categories of orthodox conceptual frameworks. A start toward the necessary reconceptualization of political philosophy, a start toward bringing race into the world of mainstream theory and bringing mainstream theory, accordingly, into the real raced world, will be the act of naming: the formal recognition of white supremacy—the racial polity—as a political system in itself.

7 White Right

The Idea of a *Herrenvolk* Ethics

Discussions of race in ethical theory have usually focused on such issues as the clarification of the distinctive wrongness of racism and the adjudication of the moral pros and cons of affirmative action. Racial discrimination has been taken as a deviation from liberal individualist ideals, and its character and the appropriate measures for remedying it are then analyzed accordingly. Here I want to invert this familiar approach and begin instead from the racialized, nonegalitarian *Herrenvolk* ethics. The aim is not, of course, to argue in its favor but to examine its structure in greater detail. This cognitive excursion through the looking-glass may generate insights into morality and race not so readily available from conventional reflections.

Locating and Motivating the Project

What can we gain by reconstructing an idealized version or examining an actual example of a *Herrenvolk* ethics? First, there is the simple spirit of sociological and anthropological inquiry. Studying the moral beliefs of particular societies and subcultures can be of interest in itself, and mapping a *Herrenvolk* ethics can be part of such an enterprise. Second, but still relatedly, there is the more ambitious task of developing a theory that goes beyond the merely descriptive to explain why these particular values were adopted, how they are related to social structure, and in what ways they evolve over time. Finally, and obviously more controversially, such an examination and theorization can help us to develop a normative ethics that we *would* want to endorse. So elucidating a *Herrenvolk* ethics may have implications for our own moral theory and practice, or for second-level metatheoretical reflections on that theory and practice—in the epistemology of ethics, for example, or in analyses of moral psychology.

The first two claims are straightforward enough and provide a degree of motivation in themselves. But the third claim is more interesting and provocative. Once it is conceded that the dominant moral codes in the West have in practice (if not always explicitly and self-advertisedly in theory) been influenced by a *Herrenvolk* ethics, questions arise about the adequacy of current strategies to overcome this legacy, especially when it is not usually acknowledged. Thus, the mapping of a *Herrenvolk* ethics can be seen as a potentially valuable contribution to the program of "naturalizing ethics."[1]

The naturalization of ethics follows in the footsteps of the naturalization of epistemology, a program several decades older, and many of the distinctions, arguments, and theoretical positions that have emerged there can (with appropriate modifications) be profitably applied here also.[2] In an article that gives a useful historical and conceptual overview of the epistemological debate, Philip Kitcher contrasts antinaturalism and naturalism and, within the latter, distinguishes conservative and radical camps.[3] The antinaturalist revolution exemplified by such figures as Gottlob Frege is characterized by an aprioristic conceptualization of philosophy and methodology and an apsychologistic, logical approach to epistemology. The "naturalistic return" rejects these presuppositions, seeing humans as highly fallible cognitive systems and asking: "How could our psychological and biological capacities and limitations *fail* to be relevant to the study of human knowledge?" What Kitcher calls "conservative" naturalists are committed to the retention of normativity, seeking to preserve "the normative enterprise within a naturalistic framework"; "radical" naturalists, by contrast, conclude that this framework requires the abandonment of pretenses to (objectivist) normativity for some variety of contextualized relativism, so that the prescriptive collapses into the descriptive.

Since my sympathies are epistemically and metaethically realist/objectivist, I locate myself in the conservative camp methodologically. Methodologically conservative naturalists, whether in epistemology or in ethics, endorse the traditional philosophical aspiration to the attainment of the normatively true and right. Where they differ from their antinaturalist colleagues is in claiming that this ideal is more likely to be achieved through advertence to the nonideal realities of the circumstances in which epistemic or moral agents find themselves. Many of Kitcher's strictures about mainstream epistemology can, I believe, be applied with little change to the methodology of mainstream ethics: "Analytic epistemology [and analytic ethics also, I suggest] either idealizes so far from the human cognitive predicament that its deliverances are unhelpful, or it tries to disguise substantive principles about how to proceed in a particular kind of world (that which we take ourselves to inhabit) as if they offered universal recommendations."[4] Naturalists, by contrast, are more dubious about the value of apriorism, more sensitive to the contingencies of context.

But though on the methodological question I count as conservative, in the political arena I am a radical, and this division has implications for my conceptualization of the obstacles agents face in their efforts to realize the ideal. For naturalists who are methodologically conservative and politically radical, the task of getting at the truth of the social world is more difficult than mainstream thinkers, whether naturalists or not, realize. According to political radicals, the world is systematically oppressive in ways that have far-reaching "hot" and "cold" cognitive repercussions. ("Hot" cognitive problems involve motivation and self-interest; "cold" problems involve intrinsic processing difficulties, independent of motivation.)[5] For them, the cognitive or moral agent is located within structures of class, gender, and racial power: capitalism, patriarchy, white supremacy. These structures tend to generate differential experiences of reality, vested interests in particular theorizations of reality, and dominant conceptual frameworks that rationalize the justice of the existing order. The agent's membership in a privileged or subordinated group (or both at the same time) then tendentially affects his or her cognition, illuminating some realities and obfuscating others. This is, of course, the essential burden of standpoint theory, originally developed by Marxism and successfully adopted by feminism.[6] The world "which we take ourselves to inhabit," Kitcher says, will be noncontingently related to who the "we" are, to the characteristics of the agents. Thus naturalization, whether in epistemology or in ethics, necessarily involves a greater appreciation of the *social* dimension of cognition, of the communities and subcommunities of which the agent is a member. And the "capacities and limitations" that radicals will deem most important and determining will be those that stem from socialization rather than from our natural biological cognizing equipment: "Epistemology must examine the attainment of knowledge by communities as well as by individuals.... The appropriate strategies for individuals to follow cannot be identified without considering the communities to which they belong."[7] The degree of understanding or misunderstanding of the true character of the social order will be influenced by one's social location.

Consider the case of moral knowledge. (Here and henceforth I will simply assume, without argument, moral objectivism, for which there is objective moral knowledge.) Communities systematically privileged by an unjust social order will as a rule be less sensitive to its inequities, and this insensitivity will interfere with their "attainment of knowledge." Such communities will not usually experience these injustices directly; they will have a vested interest in the system's perpetuation and thus be prone to evasion, bad faith, and self-deception about its true character. They will be more receptive to dominant social ideologies whose conceptual structure ignores, blurs over, or justifies the plight of the subordinated. Their empirical and moral beliefs about the world they "take themselves to inhabit" will therefore tend on some subjects to be misleading in various ways and thus to affect their conceptualization of that world, their prescriptions about what it is right to do, and more generally their second-level reflections on justification and epistemic norms. The moral codes of the privileged will tend to adjust to that privilege and be shaped accordingly.

From this perspective, then, a bourgeois ethic or a patriarchal ethic will be an organic product of the social order, most illuminatingly to be understood not by reference to the individual moral failings of particular wealthy individuals or particular male chauvinists but rather to occupation of a certain social location of class or gender in a system of power. And for radical theorists, one purpose of naturalizing ethics will be to bring this structural determination to light, to reveal how it has shaped our ideas, values, and concepts, dominant metaphors and intellectual framings, spontaneous patterns of affect and indifference, focal points and blind spots, in ways that are morally pernicious, thereby making clear what has to be *corrected* for in the development of "appropriate strategies for individuals to follow." For the members of these socially privileged epistemic communities, part of the process of improving their "cognitive strategies" should be a self-conscious recognition of and reflection on the ways in which their very social advantage may have fostered epistemic disadvantage in the goal of attaining moral truth. As Owen Flanagan points out, because the heterogeneity and diversity of moral problems make an algorithmic approach to them inappropriate and unworkable, it is the moral community that "trains us to possess a vast array of moral competencies.... The community itself is a network providing constant feedback to the human agent.... The community, in effect, encourages a certain complex picture of what it means to be a person, and it typically ties satisfaction of moral norms to this picture. Identity involves norms, and the self is oriented toward satisfying these norms."[8] But when this "community" has been committed to group domination, the feedback and moral training it provides its members will necessarily be shaped, in ways both conscious and unconscious, by a model of the person and an identity normatively at home with the way things are. In respect to class and gender, Marxism and the second wave of feminism have contributed insights to an impressive body of oppositional thought in Western moral and political philosophy that explores these issues. But as I have emphasized, despite the centrality of racism to U.S. history, much less has been done on racial domination and the ways in which membership in the white community may deform one's moral cognition.

Consider the following four alternative theses on the legacy of American white supremacy:

W1: The United States was *never* a white-supremacist polity.

W2: The United States was *once* a white-supremacist polity, but this regime came to an end with————(fill in the candidate of your choice: e.g., the 1863 Emancipation Proclamation that freed the slaves, the 1954 *Brown* v. *Board of Education* Supreme Court decision that ended de jure segregation), and this original racial hierarchy has left no significant moral and political legacy.

W3: The United States was *once* a white-supremacist polity, and though this regime came to an end with————, its originally racially hierarchical character continues to be a significant moral/political influence.

W4: The United States *was and continues to be* a white-supremacist polity, since despite some racial progress, the essential commitment to white domination has not altered, the change being basically a move from de jure to de facto white supremacy.

Many blacks and some white radicals believe the strong and controversial thesis W4. But note that it is *not* the case that the notion of white supremacy is useful only if this contested claim is true. If the weaker W3 is true, then the notion is of obvious assistance in enabling us to understand the contemporary legacy of the system. And even if it is only W2 that is true, the concept would still be useful in illuminating the features of an important historical sociopolitical formation that lasted hundreds of years and so, like feudalism, would merit study on its own. So it is really only if W1 is the case that a theorization of white supremacy is of no value. But W1 is in flagrant contradiction to the facts.[9] It follows, then, that for any comprehensive appreciation of the historical character of the United States and the characteristic moral blindnesses of its citizenry, the notion of white supremacy is a necessary addition to the standard vocabulary of moral/political theory.

Yet the appositeness of white supremacy as a global political concept to characterize the United States would be resisted by most whites, who, as bell hooks points out, find the notion not merely mistaken but overtly offensive.[10] But the grounds for this resistance and spontaneous rejection need to be brought to light so we can see whether they withstand scrutiny. There are, in my opinion, three main reasons for rejection, turning respectively on misunderstandings of the claim, a naive sociology, and simple factual and conceptual errors about the American polity.

First, whites might think that the claim being made is that the past two hundred years have brought no change, that conditions are as bad for blacks now as under slavery or Jim Crow. But this interpretation would be a mistake. The claim is rather the weaker one—that racial inequality between whites and nonwhites is the structuring principle of the polity, which can be manifested in a wide variety of forms. White supremacy evolves over time; in the language of analytic philosophy, slavery and Jim Crow are merely tokens of a general type that is mutable and polymorphous. The appropriate conception of white supremacy is then broader and nonjuridical, encompassing de facto as well as de jure white domination, rather than being restricted to the period of slavery and Jim Crow. The definition given by Frances Lee Ansley is often cited: "a political, economic, and cultural system in which whites overwhelmingly control power and material resources, conscious and unconscious ideas of white superiority and entitlement are widespread, and relations of white dominance and non-white subordination are daily reenacted across a broad array of institutions and social settings."[11] Note the general way in which domination is characterized, without being tied to specific manifestations.

Alternatively, it might be argued that the general claim is itself false, that although slavery and Jim Crow are admittedly systems of racial domination, we now live in a democracy where, with the civil rights victories of the 1950s and 1960s, such domination is no longer possible. But an established body of Western political theory demonstrates, or at least makes a strong case, that group domination is compatible with formal democracy, universal suffrage, and civil rights guarantees: the "ruling class" model of classical Marxism and also the "elite theory" pioneered by Vilfredo Pareto and Gaetano Mosca. Whether through ownership of the means of production, corporate wealth, military power, technobureaucratic expertise, or cultural hegemony, minority groups can exercise a decisive influence over the political system. But if this is true even when the group in question is a (powerful) minority, it should be obvious how much more easily the argument goes through when, as in the United States (as against apartheid South Africa), the group in question— whites—are a majority. Majority rule and differential economic/military/ technobureaucratic/cultural power thus coincide here rather than pull against each other, so that one gets an extraparliamentary reinforcement of the majoritarian domination already provided by formal electoral democracy.

Finally, as a last-ditch objection, it might be contended that racism is largely a thing of the past, that few whites are prejudiced against and motivated to discriminate against blacks, and that though admittedly whites have differential group power, they do not actually exercise this group power or vote by group interests. If not for the reasons advanced earlier, then for this set of reasons, it may be argued, the characterization of white supremacy is fundamentally misleading.

My answer is in two parts. First, the demise of white racism has been greatly exaggerated.[12] There are myriad competing statistics, and competing interpretations of what those statistics mean, but one simple figure seems to me to speak volumes. Interracial marriages have always been a reliable touchstone of genuine social equality and acceptance, since they symbolize a final intimacy that is not proved by willingness to accept blacks as, say, coworkers. There is a difference between being invited into the classroom, the living room, the boardroom, and the bedroom: zones of respective social distance. But as recently as 1991, one in five white Americans (20 percent) told interviewers that they thought that interracial marriages should still be illegal (as of course they were in many states before the 1967 Supreme Court decision struck down such prohibitions).[13] So one in five white Americans felt so strongly about this subject that, despite the stigma attached to being called a racist, they were willing to voice their continuing opposition to "miscegenation." It does not seem unreasonable to speculate that we could add another 5 or 10 percent who felt the same way but, because of this stigma, were reluctant to actually say so. Nor does it seem unreasonable, given the normal pattern of a standard distribution curve, to add another 5 or 10 percent in the adjacent part of the curve who, though not going so far as to advocate legal prohibition, were at least strongly opposed. Adding these numbers, one gets, say, at least 30 to 40 percent of white Americans who still do not really consider blacks as their equals and will run their and their families' lives (dating, networking, social clubs) on this principle of exclusion. Such a minority is sizable enough to block many measures of social reform even if (which is not the case) there were wholehearted support for such reform among the rest of the white population.

But the second point, which may be the more significant one, is that to a large extent white supremacy may become independent of feelings of racism. George Fredrickson pointed out long ago that a virtue of the term is that it makes no necessary reference to racism as such.[14] (In fact, it is at least logically possible, if psychologically and socially improbable, that white supremacy could be established and maintained while the subordinated nonwhites were seen as equals.) Historically, white racism certainly has been central to the genesis and development of American white supremacy, but the crucial aspects of white supremacy may be perpetuated in the absence of racist sentiments. Part of the point of employing the term and locating it as a political category is, as I explained in Chapters 5 and 6, precisely to shift the focus from the individual and attitudinal to the global and structural. Once certain socioeconomic structures are established, questions of intent and the conscious aim to discriminate become less important than their internal dynamic. The system of accumulated, entrenched privilege can reproduce itself through motivation that is simply self-and group-interested, that does not want to lose access to differential opportunities, that does not want to probe too deeply into the past (or the present, for that matter). Whites do not have to be racist to want to keep their privileges (though racism, as a rationalization, may make it morally easier); they just have to be human.

Thus in their comprehensive survey of white and black political opinion, Donald Kinder and Lynn Sanders point out that whereas most whites ostensibly and perhaps even genuinely subscribe to inclusivist liberal ideals where blacks are concerned, this support has little practical implications for what they are actually willing to do: "[W]hat Americans think about racial equality as a matter of principle must be distinguished from what they think about efforts to *apply* racial equality.... As it happens, white Americans express considerably more enthusiasm for the principle of racial equality than they do for policies that are designed to bring the principle to life.... The 'massive and wide-ranging liberalization of racial attitudes' [proclaimed by two other authors, Tom Smith and Paul Sheatsley], while real enough, applies only to principles, not to policies.... Most opinion trends on policies are flat; some policies to promote racial equality are actually less popular now than they were a decade or two ago."[15] And it turns out that whites' perceptions of their group interest *are* in fact the best predictor of white voting patterns on issues with racial implications.[16] Whites' outrage at the use of the term *white supremacy* misses the point that, whether racists or not, they are heirs to a system of consolidated structural advantage that will continue to exist unless active moves are made to dismantle it. The heart of white supremacy is this acceptance of and reluctance to give up differential racial privilege, manifested morally in a *Herrenvolk* ethics that changes form according to the evolution of the system, originally overtly racist, later not.

But most white liberal political philosophers and ethicists do not recognize these realities and their shaping effect on white moral consciousness. They explicitly or tacitly endorse instead the mainstream view — as classically represented by Gunnar Myrdal's *An American Dilemma* (1944)[17] — that racism is an anomaly within the American polity. Their descriptive and normative theorizations, correspondingly, frame black and aboriginal subordination as theoretically insignificant — a minor glitch that will eventually work its way out of the system. Operating within a white experiential and discursive universe, most white moral theorists have not deemed these racial exclusions to require significant innovation in the conventional categories of European theory. In effect, whites have been a disadvantaged epistemic community.[18] They have suffered the cognitive handicaps that usually come with social privilege. Racial privilege has been theoretically taken for granted, morally justified, or, when (in the modern period) deplored, seen as conceptually marginal.

My suggestion is, then, that taking race seriously in ethics, recognizing its centrality to people's identities and cognitive patterns, requires that we admit the foundational hybridity of a system based simultaneously on Enlightenment liberalism and aboriginal expropriation and chattel slavery. As Jennifer Hochschild points out, "Racism and liberalism are as intertwined in American history as they are antithetical," since "our politics have simultaneously affirmed the natural rights of all persons and legitimated the oppression of non-Caucasians."[19] The idea of a *Herrenvolk* ethics captures this paradoxical dichotomization.

Two minority perspectives are then possible, for both of which race is much more central than is conceded in mainstream theory. The first is the "symbiosis" view of racism mentioned in Chapter 6 (as against the mainstream "anomaly" view). Racism and racial discrimination are seen as historically symbiotic with American liberalism, so that there is little reason to expect the contradiction to be resolved any time soon.[20] This darker, more pessimistic prognosis is shared not only by many African-Americans— consider Derrick Bell's *Faces at the Bottom of the Well*, subtitled *The Permanence of Racism*—but by a significant and growing minority of disillusioned white liberals as well, as shown by Andrew Hacker's *Two Nations*.[21] The second position, delineated by Rogers Smith, recognizes "multiple political traditions" in American political culture.[22] The polity is therefore neither essentially egalitarian and raceless nor essentially hierarchical and racist. Rather, its essence is precisely its dividedness, with different aspects coming to prominence under different conditions. So the future is more open-ended, neither unproblematic Whig progressivism nor intransigent, if self-transforming, white supremacy, but a contingent working out of different possibilities inherent in the nation's conflictual past. For both positions, however, race is central rather than marginal.

The mapping of a *Herrenvolk* ethics can be useful for proponents of both of these positions, so for our purposes, it is not necessary to adjudicate between them. "Symbiosis" theorists will see the *Herrenvolk* ethic as that moral code unequivocally embraced by most white Americans through most of the republic's history. "Multiple traditions" theorists will see it as an undeniable part of the national psyche that is influential but not ubiquitous, sometimes endorsed but sometimes repudiated in favor of a genuinely color-blind universalism. But in each case the investigation of how racial privilege may systematically affect moral consciousness will obviously be valuable.

Let me now try to make persuasive the claim that naturalization can assist the normative enterprise. As indicated at the start, the line of argument will be that where nonideal practice has been the norm, a reconstruction of its guiding logic can serve as a map of danger zones, a chart of where there be moral dragons.

The spontaneous objection to the attempt to draw normative conclusions from actual practice is that an "ought" can't be derived from an "is." For those who, like Virginia Held, are dubious about what cognitive science has to offer ethics, this point is simple: "Our primary concern is not explanation but recommendation.... [E]thics is normative rather than descriptive." That a particular society's or community's epistemic and moral practice deviated from the norm does not undermine the worth of the norm. But this, at least for (methodologically) conservative naturalists, would be a mistaken reading of the purpose of naturalization. The aim is not to degrade the norm by collapsing it into squalid practice but to draw normative conclusions from degraded practice of *what to avoid* in attempts to realize the norm. As Held points out, "We need to be aware of the natural human tendencies and empirical realities that make moral recommendations feasible or not."[23] And the argument of naturalists would be that mapping these human tendencies and empirical realities (importantly, sociopolitical rather than "natural") can assist the realization of the normative ideal. The mere abstract injunction to strive for X does not tell us how best to go about it, what obstacles we are likely to encounter en route, and what kinds of failures are most frequent. One can, of course, issue general auxiliary advice, but the danger is that it may be no more than the original injunction in disguise.

Consider the following mundane example. We want to teach our children to learn to cross the street safely. Simply telling them "Cross the street safely!" is of little use, nor is the auxiliary generality to watch out for the dangers that would prevent them from crossing the street safely. This injunction is too open to be useful; it encompasses every possible hazard. What we tell our children is "Look both ways for oncoming traffic before you cross the street!" We don't tell them to watch out for passing lions; keep an eye open for falling rocks; be careful that the road doesn't suddenly collapse beneath you; make sure you're not snatched up by balloonists; look out for the telltale signs of a stray transporter beam from a starship. The hazards to be encountered when a street is to be crossed are fairly standard, and though the possibilities are infinite, we rank the most likely dangers and emphasize those when we instruct our children.

Similarly, we want to inculcate in people general moral injunctions about respecting others and treating persons equally. Since we are not angels but highly imperfect moral agents, we routinely fall short of this duty. Some of these failures are due to personal idiosyncrasy—lack of moral sensitivity, weakness of will, selfishness—and need to be remedied by the individual attention (loving or hostile) of friends, relatives, co-workers, those with whom we interact regularly. But there are also those general failures that arise from membership in a group that historically or currently has practiced an ethic of a systemically discriminatory kind, or at least has had that ethic as an influential current within its tradition. Even if one lives in a period when this ethic has officially been repudiated, it will not always be the case that one has purged oneself of its influence. If, as Larry May and his colleagues point out, moral failure can be thought of as "perceptual failure," linked with "basic abilities [and basic disabilities] of pattern completion and pattern generalization" and involving a "know-how" (and a non-know-how) that is often "supraverbal," not to be condensed into "a tractable set of summary principles or moral rules," then one will often fail without recognizing that one has failed—indeed, thinking that one has succeeded.[24] Tracking these failures and transforming one's practice so as to avoid them in the future will then be facilitated if one understands their systemic architecture, knows in advance the cognitive and affective grooves within which one's mind is likely to run. It becomes easier to do the right thing if one knows the wrong things that, to one's group, will typically *seem* like the right thing.

Writ large, then, this is merely the familiar point that men and whites often fail to recognize when they are being sexist and racist. On some occasions, bad faith may be involved: the perpetrators deny what in fact they know themselves to be guilty of.[25] But there are many other occasions when the protestations of innocence are completely genuine, when people are completely sincere in their disavowal of sexist or racist intent. In these cases, problems of *cognition* are involved, the failure to make the appropriate categorization, to identify what one is doing. Many discriminatory cognitive patterns are not transparently so, but require conceptual work to be seen as such, the education of one's perceptions. Mapping a systemically deficient naturalized ethic is therefore a contribution to the realization of the normative ideal not through its own features but through its (nonexhaustive) illustration of some important patterns to avoid and to which we are particularly prone.

Alvin Goldman lists "cognitive materials" as one of the three areas in which cognitive science would be useful for ethics. (The other two, which I will examine later, are "hedonic states" and "psychological mechanisms.")[26] A moral agent needs tools to select the morally important out of the vast field of available information: to categorize appropriately, search for the pertinent facts, make overall judgments of rightness and wrongness. Similarly, Mark Johnson argues that to do good moral theory we need to know something "about the details of mental activity, such as how concepts are formed, what their structure is, what constrains our inferences, what limits there are on how we understand a given situation, how we frame moral problems, and so forth."[27] It may seem that human cognitive processing at least roughly approximates most of the time to the ideal of recognizing appropriate conceptual subsumption through advertence to the necessary and sufficient conditions of concept definition. But quite apart from Quinean objections in principle to this notion, it turns out that people routinely operate by reference to "typicality effects," the use of "prototypes" of the concept in question. Examples, in other words, are far more important than abstract principles in teaching the logic of concept application and, correspondingly, norm application. There can be complete agreement on rules and principles but disagreement on categorical boundaries, especially if the example in question is distant from the "statistical central tendency" of the standard prototypes.[28] Moral education develops through a recognition of the instantiation of the abstract principle *in* the concrete example.

But once this demystified picture of human cognition has been accepted, it immediately becomes obvious why people who claim to accept general moral principles of egalitarianism, liberalism, and fairness continue to follow racist practices. Sometimes, of course, bad faith and other kinds of motivational factors may be involved, but often the riddle can be explained in purely "cold" cognitive terms. The moral education of whites tends to be deficient because the examples that are called upon to illustrate, make vivid, and fix in their minds the appropriate abstract moral concepts are prototypically drawn from the white experience. Thus there may be recognition problems in identifying certain racial practices as violations of those same principles or as instantiations of prohibited behaviors. Hence the familiar dispute, marked by mutual frustration and anger toward the other, in which whites and blacks disagree on how X should be categorized.

What needs to be understood, then, is that in a racial polity rationality will itself generally be "raced" — not, of course, in the biologistic sense of traditional white supremacist and Nazi theory, but in the sense that concept application and cognitive judgment are learned through examples drawn from racially asymmetrical data fields and with radically divergent background theoretical assumptions. If we were ideal cognitive processors and the pertinent concepts were sharply defined, then aprioristic epistemologies would be appropriate. But since we are fallible knowers operating with fuzzy concepts, norms for improving cognition need to be sensitized to the most likely cognitive failures, and this project requires a naturalized look at the circumstances in which cognition actually takes place.

In sum: mapping and making explicit the contours of a *Herrenvolk* ethics should be of considerable heuristic value as a cognitive aid to improving recognition of likely failings in our theory and practice. (I adopt here the honorific abstract "we"; i.e., I pretend to be white.) Mainstream academic ethics is characterized by the ever more detailed working out of the minutiae of various ideal theories. It is not that such an exercise is without intrinsic interest or value, but that one sometimes feels (or — more honestly — *I* sometimes feel) that to a certain extent these energies are misguided. One wants to know why, after hundreds of years of ever more arcane and esoteric refinement of these theories, there is still such flagrant nonconformity with their admirable norms. So much theory, one is tempted to say, and so little practice. Minority philosophers in general tend to be less interested in "ideal" theory than in the theory of the "nonideal"; they evince less interest in the fine points when even the coarse points are routinely violated. Nonwhites typically already know what whites should do; they want to know why they don't do it. A *Herrenvolk* ethics can contribute to this explanatory project and thus help in the realization of the ideal.

So I am not objecting to "abstract" theory as such. My objection is rather to the practice of abstracting from the experience of those privileged in certain ways and representing the result as abstract theory *simpliciter*. One can abstract away from race and gender when race and gender play no part in disadvantaging one; it is not because race and gender play no role in one's life that it seems natural to do so, but because race and gender play a particular kind of role. The dominant moral code in our society has evolved either directly from a *Herrenvolk* ethics (symbiosis thesis) or from a dialogue between it and abstract liberalism (multiple traditions thesis), and it continues to bear the signs of this birth and tortured evolution. Formally delineating a *Herrenvolk* ethics should then, in the Brechtian sense, be a useful estrangement technique, helping the racially privileged to distance themselves from the apparent "naturalness" of certain spontaneous categorizations and judgments and thus enabling their recognition *as* a specific pattern of racialized cognition. The white eye can thereby learn to see itself seeing whitely.

Mapping a *Herrenvolk* Ethics

Let us now reconstruct a *Herrenvolk* ethics, the moral code appropriate to the racially privileged population within a social order simultaneously committed to liberal egalitarianism and racial hierarchy. The original foundational principle is very simple, though the working out of the normative details is complex: all persons should be treated equally (by contrast with the morality of feudalism), but the racially inferior are not full persons. (As noted, this principle may change over time, so that later versions of a *Herrenvolk* ethics do not proclaim — indeed, will overtly deny — nonwhite inferiority.) In James Oakes's summary of the birth of the American republic, "The equality of all human beings could be widely proclaimed as long as it was understood that blacks were, somehow, less than human."[29] Race thus constitutes a moral dividing line by which equality and subordination are reconciled. Or as Sartre wrote in regard to the relation between Europe and its colonies, "there is nothing more consistent than a racist humanism."[30]

Racialized personhood and its lack are therefore central to this ethic. How does the racialization of personhood play itself out in the contrasting views of Locke and Kant, the two leading theorists of liberal personhood? For both philosophers, the notion of the "person" is theoretically crucial: for the first, as self-owning appropriator; for the second, as self-directing being. The idea of a *Herrenvolk* variant of the theory, predicated on drawing out the implications of the distinction between persons and subpersons, thus has a revisionist shock value (the frisson of an apparent oxymoron) *not* present in the idea of a *Herrenvolk* utilitarianism, since the standard criticism of the latter is precisely the claim that it does not take persons seriously. Note that it is not essential to my argument that Locke and Kant should have been *Herrenvolk* Lockeans and Kantians, although, as we have seen, there is some evidence that they were. Nor is it necessary that the average white moral agent should have read a single word of either author to be influenced by his ideas. The concepts of property, rights, self-ownership, appropriation, entitlement, self-respect, and reciprocated respect for others are part of the common liberal moral/political culture of the West, guiding the practice of those within its intellectual universe. Insofar as those racially privileged in the racial polities created by the West have seen themselves as acting consistently on liberal moral principles and have in fact acted in racist ways, an idealized reconstruction of a racialized version of these principles can illuminate naturalized practice, past and present. I will speak henceforth of a *Herrenvolk* Lockeanism and Kantianism to denote the racialized version of these views, without thereby implying that I am necessarily referring to Locke's and Kant's own expressed opinions.

Raced Rather Than Abstract Individuals

To begin with, an individual's racial membership is crucial for a *Herren-volk* morality, so that (originally) one does *not* start from abstract and morally equal individuals but from a population that is, before anything else, racially categorized and of *differential* moral status. For purposes of simplification, I will assume a dichotomous bipolar racial polity in which R1s are the privileged race and R2s are everybody else (so R2s are just non-R1s). This scheme corresponds roughly to the history of the American polity, where the divide between whites and nonwhites has been the most important one. If R1s are persons, then R2s are subpersons. When one talks in general about abstract persons, then, one is really talking about R1s. R1 domination may be de jure or de facto, formally recognized in law or only informally preserved through custom. In both situations, though obviously more in the former case, the R1/R2 distinction will be of central significance, ramifying throughout the social order and shaping people's moral psychology. It will therefore be of great importance to determine whether a person is an R1 or an R2. R2 moral standing may simply be zero (R2s as an exterminable population), but the more usual case is that they do have an intermediate standing, above zero, but with a ceiling depressed below the R1 level, so that they have some moral claims on the R1 population.

For both *Herrenvolk* Lockeanism and *Herrenvolk* Kantianism, the grounding of the moral distinction between R1s and R2s is a qualitative difference in rationality, though the divergence between the two views means that the internal theoretical implications are somewhat different.

Idealized Kantianism has an austere moral universe, consisting simply of "persons" (animals have no moral standing). Persons are rational, self-directing entities who must be given equal respect and not treated merely as means to an end. The threshold level of rationality is discrete and sharply demarcated, thereby constituting a clear-cut division between the world of persons, with full moral standing, and the world of nonpersons, with zero moral standing. In *Herrenvolk* Kantianism, the transition of *degrees* of rationality is fuzzier, thereby making possible the intermediate category of sub-persons, those humans whose rationality is great enough to lift them into the universe to begin with but not sufficient to elevate them to the status of full personhood. Subpersons are not capable of becoming moral agents in the full sense, directing and legislating for themselves, but require the paternalistic supervision of the person population. Precisely because one is a human of a certain "phenomenal" type, one is or is not a full person: skin color accurately determines one's standing.

Personhood is central to Lockean theory also, but Locke presupposes a "thick" rather than a "thin" version of the self.[31] Property is Locke's basic concept, and he uses it both in the conventional, narrow sense of legitimate external possessions and in the broader sense of individual rights. (For my purposes, it is both verbally and conceptually felicitous that *property* is also used metaphysically to refer to the attributes of an entity.) Abstract persons own themselves, their capacities, and their labor, and they come to appropriate the world to differing extents through the more or less rational and industrious use of their talents, thus gaining private property and becoming men of substance. Others then have a natural law–based duty to respect their property, which here includes their person (which they own), their legitimate possessions (which they have worked for), and their rights (to life, liberty, and so on).

Herrenvolk Lockeanism will then be predicated on a radical racial differentiation in the abilities (the "properties") of the R1 and R2 populations to own and enjoy property. As Cheryl Harris has argued, whiteness in effect becomes the most crucial property.[32] In the vocabulary I have suggested, R1s have the intrinsic metaphysical property of R1-ness, a property that is a prerequisite for the moral/political property of full self-ownership, for the ownership of efficient nature-appropriating labor (and thus the normative ownership of possessions), and for full entitlement to (ownership of) rights. Correspondingly, R2s' lack of the property of R1-ness negatively affects their entitlement to property in these senses — and ultimately their personhood, since the Lockean person is definitionally a self-owning, nature-appropriating, rights-bearing being.

If the racial polity evolves over time, R1/R2 relations will necessarily change accordingly. In the de jure phase of R1 domination, the inferiority of R2s is formally codified, so that there is no contradiction between official ideology and their actual standing. For later generations reading the texts of this period, R2s' inferior standing may be semantically masked by the race-neutral language of "persons" or "men," which creates the illusion that the scope of the terms is general, when in fact R1-ness was a necessary condition for full personhood. In the de facto phase of R1 domination, by contrast, the equality of R2s is officially proclaimed, and they *are* formally included in the scope of "persons." Continuing subordination of R2s is now in conflict with official ideology, so if through either unconscious custom or willful continuing commitment to the previously explicitly hierarchical racial order R2s are still treated unequally, respecting this formal constraint will require a far more complicated set of mechanisms. Think of the various means devised in the turn-of-the-century South to disenfranchise blacks while not violating the Fourteenth and Fifteenth amendments to the Constitution. Or consider the ways in which one can support integrationist principles while opposing integrationist practices. David Wellman points out that when middle-class whites are put to a "test" on racial issues, "they do not become 'prejudiced' when they resolve the contradiction between their ideals and their realities.... Instead, they develop ways of explaining their opposition to change *that do not explicitly contradict egalitarian ideals*."[33] Blacks are still being treated as raced and, in effect, of differential and inferior status, but the strategy to achieve this result has evolved. Similarly, Kinder and Sanders emphasize the importance of differentiating ideal and policy: "[A]lthough whites' support for the principles of racial equality and integration has increased majestically ..., their backing for policies designed to bring equality and integration about has increased scarcely at all. Indeed, in some cases, white support has actually declined."[34]

The basic differentiation thus remains, but for those R1s simultaneously committed to ostensible R1/R2 equality and actual continuing R1 privilege, maintaining this differentiation now involves a complex dynamic by which abstract colorless principles diverge into different color-coded practices through a prism resting on questionable background assumptions and a semantics of racially coded language and conceptual proxies. And one final irony will be that the original abstract individuals whom everybody knew were really white return recolored as (this time) genuinely colorless, *now* including everybody. In the call for a color-blind treatment of all citizens, a tacit R1-ness is positioned as the "nonraced" norm, so that the structural advantages and handicaps linked to racial difference and requiring remediation are obfuscated. A comment by a university student in a race-relations survey sums up the situation: "White people are general."[35]

Volatile Ontologies

In the ideal nonracial polity, one's personhood is guaranteed, independent of race, and as such is stable, not subject to loss or gain. In the racial polity, by contrast, the exclusionary linking of personhood to R1-ness opens the door (for R1s) to the threat of ontological decline. Correspondingly, ontological ascent for those denied personhood (the R2s, or people of currently unresolved status) will require—if, of course, it is possible at all—assimilation to R1 status, whether on an individual or a group level. And the acquisition of personhood will inevitably affect one's conception of oneself, one's notions of self-worth, and what is morally appropriate for oneself and one's children. Insofar as self-respect is central to good moral practice and full personhood is tied to race, people's efforts to preserve (or gain) full or derivative personhood will shape their crucial life decisions in a racialized way.

For R1s, the danger is that one will suffer an ontological collapse to the subperson level through the discovery of previously unknown or hidden ancestry that by existing criteria mean one is "really" an R2. For many decades after the Civil War, whites were worried about "invisible blackness," the possibility of an unrevealed black great-grandfather lurking in their genealogy, an ontological contaminant. Recall Gregory Williams's autobiographical account of the dramatic transformation of his life when he discovered he was "really" black.[36] When the criteria for R1-ness are multiple, it may be possible to jeopardize one's genealogical R1-ness inadvertently by actions deemed inappropriate for an R1, so that one needs to be careful in one's day-to-day life. Gender may also make a difference in the solidity or precariousness of one's R1-ness. Research on interracial relations in the Jim Crow period has shown that white women who married black men suffered a loss of status; they became in a sense "black," since the shakier personhood of white women is underwritten in part by the appropriate relation to the white male.

In the case of R2s, there is a roughly symmetrical inversion of this moral topography. R2s "fortunate" enough, by the roll of the genetic dice, to simulate the R1 phenotype may consciously decide to cross over, "passing" as R1s, and so in a sense defrauding the legitimate R1s. In racial polities of greater openness, there may be formally and informally recognized avenues for "legitimate" ontological elevation, if not to official R1 status, at least to some lesser standing that is still raised above that of the unreconstructed R2s. In the French colonial empire, for example, one was encouraged to master French culture and become *évolué*. Acceptance and internalization of the *Herrenvolk* ethic will therefore lead the R2s to identify full personhood with repudiation of their race and culture.

Finally, apart from these individual boundary crossings, there will be entire subpopulations (new immigrant groups and the offspring of interracial relationships) whose standing in the racial polity is not immediately obvious and whose ultimate R1/R2/Rx status may be the subject of disagreement and conflict. The children of R1s and R2s, as we have seen, may end up being classified with R1s (the Dutch policy in colonial Indonesia) or with R2s (U.S. policy), or may form an R3 category of their own (Caribbean "browns," Latin American *mestizaje*), with corresponding privileged, disadvantaged, or intermediate statuses. Some European immigrants, such as the Irish, fell into the category of the "not yet white."[37] Such ethnic groups, R2s or quasi-R2s in their domestic racial systems, had to struggle to assert their whiteness, their rightful belonging on the privileged side of the R1/R2 line in the U.S. system. And such striving has the character of a *moral* struggle, the proud insistence that one is indeed a full human, and that others had better learn to respect one's humanity and not to try to categorize one with the less-than-humans.

Racialized Moral Psychology and Value Polarities

Inevitably, then, the moral psychology of R1s will be affected by race in a racial polity, as will many of their conscious and unconscious framings of dilemmas and moral choices, generating a sense of "right" that is racialized: a white right. Alvin Goldman lists "psychological mechanisms" as one of the three areas in which cognitive science would be useful for ethics. He has in mind such phenomena as the role of empathy in the development of altruism. One's general responsibility as a conscientious moral agent is to develop a character normatively appropriate to the demands of the accepted moral code, a character that facilitates one's seeing and doing the right thing. By learning to "mimic the affective states" of others, by learning to place ourselves in their skins, we break down egoistic boundaries and develop a sensibility attuned to and caring about the welfare of other people.[38] Utilitarianism, for example, famously requires us to be sensitive to the well-being of others according to a formula in which each one counts for one.

But in a racial polity, the right thing will often be the wrong thing, so that one will need to cultivate patterns of cognition and affect suitably unresponsive to this wrongness. A felicific calculus that would register accurately the sufferings of R2s would disrupt the reproduction of the system. So here one needs a modulation of one's capacities that will use race as a trigger, a signal variously to recategorize, dampen, turn down the volume control, press the off-button, in a way appropriate for a morality where some ones count for *less* than one. In a racial polity, empathic feelings will travel weakly, if at all, across the color line; white empathy will refuse to enter black skin. "We whites have a color glaze on our imaginations that makes it hard to feel with the people we have segregated ourselves from," wrote Lillian Smith at mid-century, in her pioneering and courageous autobiographical account of a white woman growing up in the South. The racial other will be seen as Other, an opaque entity not to be identified with, and the boundaries of full membership in the community will terminate with the boundaries of the white population. And one's moral education will be consciously structured so as to be appropriate to the bifurcated ethic of racial hierarchy, producing what Smith describes as the "two-leveled existence" of her southern youth:

The mother who taught me what I know of tenderness and love and compassion taught me also the bleak rituals of keeping Negroes in their "place".... [A] terrifying disaster would befall the South if ever I treated a Negro as my social equal.... [T]he deep respect I felt for [my black nurse], the tenderness, the love, was a childish thing which every normal child outgrows ... I, too, must outgrow these feelings.... From the day I was born, I began to learn my lessons.... I learned it is possible ... to pray at night and ride a Jim Crow car the next morning and to feel comfortable in doing both.... I learned it the way all of my southern people learn it: by closing door after door until one's mind and heart and conscience are blocked off from each other and from reality.[39]

The frustration, the rage, the sense that one is going crazy, or that the world itself is crazy, which afflicts those on the other side of this *Herrenvolk* cognitive barrier have been vividly captured in the following passage by W.E.B. Du Bois:

It is difficult to let others see the full psychological meaning of caste segregation. It is as though one, looking out from a dark cave in a side of an [imposing] mountain, sees the world passing and speaks to it; speaks courteously and persuasively, showing them how these entombed souls are hindered in their natural movement, expression, and development; and how their loosening from prison would be a matter not simply of courtesy, sympathy, and help to them, but aid to all the world. One talks on evenly and logically in this way, but notices that the passing throng does not even turn its head, or if it does, glances curiously and walks on. It gradually penetrates the minds of the prisoners that the people passing do not hear; that some thick sheet of invisible but horribly tangible plate glass is between them and the world. They get excited; they talk louder; they gesticulate. Some of the passing world stop in curiosity; these gesticulations seem so pointless; they laugh and pass on. They still either do not hear at all or hear but dimly, and even what they hear, they do not understand. Then the people within may become hysterical. They may scream and hurl themselves against the barriers, hardly realizing in their bewilderment that they are screaming in a vacuum unheard.[40]

Moreover, such racialization will affect not just (Humean) empathy but the more Kantian notions of self- and other-respect. In idealized, abstract Kantianism, respect is the central moral notion from which all the others are supposed to be generated. The infinite value of a person as an autonomous being whose ends must be respected by others is the basic foundation of moral relations between humans. People may be divided by wealth and property, class and status, but their common personhood in the polity constitutes a moral equality that is supposed to be unaffected by inequalities of other kinds. One respects oneself as an abstract person; one respects others as abstract persons; and they in turn respect one as an abstract person. The result is a self-sustaining symmetry of mutual moral regard, tied to one's character as a rational and moral being.

But in *Herrenvolk* Kantianism, respect is necessarily reconstituted along racial lines. Moral egalitarianism fragments, and reflexive symmetrical relations of colorless self-respect and mutual respect are refracted in an asymmetrically color-coded spectrum. One respects oneself not as an abstract person but specifically as an R1, a being whose phenomenal phenotype is not at all abstracted away from but is used as the key indicator of full personhood. (Hence the expression that could be heard up to quite recently, simultaneously descriptive and approbative: "He's a white man," or sometimes, more extravagantly, "He's the whitest man I know.") Respect is thus linked to a certain positioning in the racial polity.

This localized symmetry of reciprocal respect among R1s is linked to a necessary global asymmetry in the appropriate moral attitude toward and from the subordinate R2 population. Giving equal respect to R2s would elevate them morally above their prescribed status and impute to them a rationality and equality they do not in fact possess. Instead, R2s are "dissed," treated with a racial disrespect that is *not* the simple nonrecognition one gives to entities not in the moral universe at all but rather a specific form of recognition: one is being recognized *as* a subperson, an inferior type of human. This disrespect will manifest itself, inter alia, in forms of address: the freedom to *tutoyer;* the language of "boy," "Auntie," "Uncle"; the use of first rather than last names (indeed, sometimes generic names bestowed in indifference to actual names). C.L.R. James made this observation of French Saint-Domingue (Haiti): "For whatever a man's origin, record or character, here his white skin made him a person of quality.... This was the type for whom race prejudice was more important than even the possession of slaves.... The distinction between a white man and a man of colour was for them fundamental. It was their all. In defence of it they would bring down the whole of their world."[41] Similarly, Derrick Bell argues that in the United States, "even the poorest whites, those who must live their lives only a few levels above, gain their self-esteem by gazing down on [blacks]."[42] Egalitarianism among R1s thus rests on inegalitarianism vis-à-vis R2s. Class differences and intra-R1 material inequalities become less important than *racial* equality, the ontological guarantee that lifts all R1s above all R2s.

In addition, in a racial polity many value polarities (freedom/slavery, equality/inequality, autonomy/heteronomy) will use the R_2s as a negative reference point, so that oppositions will be colored by racial association, and terms will have to be racially structured in such a way that the conceptual inconsistencies that would arise from according the populations equal treatment are avoided. Samuel Johnson's acerbic jibe to the American revolutionaries — "How is it that we hear the loudest yelps for liberty among the drivers of negroes?" — is famous and needs to be answered. In the intellectual atmosphere of *Herrenvolk* ethics, "freedom" will be not the abstract descendant of an ancient Greek conceptual forebear but a racialized notion that makes a reply possible. David Roediger argues that "in a society in which Blackness and servility were so thoroughly intertwined — North and South — assertions of white freedom could not be raceless."[43] The reconciliation of opposition to British tyranny and endorsement of African subordination is made possible by a definition of freedom that in effect expresses justifiable outrage that white Americans (coextensive with "Americans") should be treated as "niggers." Edmund Morgan's classic *American Slavery, American Freedom* documents the ways in which the "rise of liberty and equality in America had been accompanied by the rise of slavery," and Roediger points out that "the bondage of Blacks served as a touchstone by which dependence and degradation were measured."[44] Similarly, equality as a value comes to be linked with inequality, not merely in the obvious abstract sense of a conceptual contrast and antipode but in the specific sense of an overtly racialized foil. The equality of the R_1s — their claim to equal ontological status and civil standing — is based on their common and equal superiority to the R_2 population: it is a specifically *Herrenvolk* equality.

Finally, those R_1s who do begin to question the *Herrenvolk* morality will face moral dilemmas and moral crises. Since one's moral code has explicitly been tied to one's R_1-ness and self-respect as an R_1, the halting, agonized perception that the prescriptions of the code may be wrong is likely to be phenomenologically experienced as a betrayal of a raced rightness. One will feel oneself to be a "race traitor," a "white renegade," an apostate from civilization and moral Whiteness. Thus in Huck Finn's famous crisis of conscience near the end of the novel from which, according to Ernest Hemingway, all modern American literature springs, he considers the alternatives between which he must choose: to keep silent about Jim's whereabouts, and help him to escape; or to send Jim's "legitimate" owner, Miss Watson, a note telling her where Jim is. Helping Jim escape would, of course, leave a permanent stain on his moral character:

And then think of *me!* It would get all around, that Huck Finn helped a nigger to get his freedom; and if I was to ever see anybody from that town again, I'd be ready to get down and lick his boots for shame. That's just the way: a person does a low-down thing, and then he don't want to take no consequences of it.... The more I studied about this, the more my conscience went to grinding me, and the more wicked and low-down and ornery I got to feeling.... I was a trembling, because I'd got to decide, forever, betwixt two things, and I knowed it. I studied a minute, sort of holding my breath, and then says to myself:

"All right, then, I'll *go* to hell"—and tore [the note] up.

It was awful thoughts, and awful words, but they was said. And I let them stay said; and never thought no more about reforming. I shoved the whole thing out of my head; and said I would take up wickedness again, which was in my line, being brung up to it, and the other warn't. And for a starter, I would go to work and steal Jim out of slavery again.[45]

So a major obstacle to doing the right thing where right has been defined as white is one's vertiginous sense of thereby losing one's racial standing.

Racialized Entitlements and Baselines

In the liberal-democratic market polity, one has both a set of moral rights and entitlements and a set of rational expectations about life prospects. This twin set, moral and empirical/projective, will be involved in many issues—in one's sense of social fairness, in one's willingness or unwillingness to accept certain sacrifices, in one's comparisons of one's current level of well-being with levels of the past, in one's overall feelings about how society is progressing and what one's future in it is.

But in the racial polity, both moral rights and rational expectations will be raced, insofar as historically both will have been greater for R1s than for R2s. The differential allocation of resources and opportunities to R1s in the de jure phase of the polity has been justified as only their due. In the later de facto phase, then, R1s will in general find it very difficult to see and accept that many of their rights and expectations are grounded not in their abstract humanness but in their R1-ness, or rather their R1-ness in a system in which humanness was coextensive with R1-ness. Locke is the theorist most important for such notions of entitlement. Insofar as property, self-ownership, and rights are tied up together (the person *as* a self-owning, rights-bearing appropriator), his property-based ethic could be said to have *metaphysical* implications, in that the ability to appropriate is linked with *be*-ing in the world. R1s will see R2s as those whose self-ownership is not exercised or unrealizable, whose inferior capacities preclude appropriation of the world and thus in a sense are not fully existent as persons, their deficient properties rendering them propertyless, rightless, and with no real self to own. If R1s are men of substance, it can be said that R2s are insubstantial. One has full duties to one's fellow property owners, fellow proprietors, not to the self-less.

And historically, of course, Lockeanism of this *Herrenvolk*, racialized kind has justified both Native American expropriation and African slavery, giving rise to a white moral consciousness accustomed to full or partial ownership first of nonwhite land and bodies and later of differential opportunities vis-à-vis nonwhites, with baseline expectations constructed accordingly. The Europeans who conquered and settled the continent represented aboriginal economies as virtually nonexistent, an assessment that gave rise to the notion of a New World arising *ex nihilo* through the labor of the R1s. Francis Jennings points out, "The basic conquest myth postulates that America was virgin land, or wilderness, inhabited by nonpeople called savages," whose "mode of existence and cast of mind" made them "incapable of civilization and therefore of full humanity": "When colonists pretended that the Indians were mere nomads, the reason was to invoke international law doctrines applicable to vacant lands; such lands were available for seizure."[46] Native peoples then vanish ontologically from the *Herrenvolk* Lockean philosophical universe as an appropriate preliminary to their exit from the real one. As the only legitimate appropriators, the R1s are the real persons, the creators of civil society, the property owners.

Similarly, in the case of African slavery, the seeming breach of Lockean principles can be explained by the differential properties of R2s. If R1s are enslaved as a result of a just war, they are being penalized for their failure to abide by natural law in a specific instance, but this failure does not reflect on their general *racial* rationality, self-ownership, industriousness, and personhood. By contrast, the enslavement of R2s, and the hereditary enslavement of their wives and children under circumstances that obviously involve aggression against *them,* reflect the ways in which their R2-ness crucially modifies these moral features. Either they are not self-owning in the first place, directly assimilable to the animal population (Locke points out that God has given humanity a "Right and Power over the Earth, and inferiour Creatures in common"),[47] so that R1s would infringe no property rights in taking possession of them, or their admitted self-ownership rights have been abrogated by their failure to develop the natural resources of their home continent.[48] In either case, the creation of a polity will then formally require the nonrecognition of R2 slaves as persons, since Lockean personhood requires self-ownership, property in oneself, whereas the R2s are the property of others, the R1s. The three-fifths constitutional compromise can then be thought of as a literal quantitative representation of the reality of fractional personhood in a *Herrenvolk* polity, as can the later *Dred Scott* decision that, as "beings of an inferior order," blacks "had no rights which the white man was bound to respect."

It can be argued that this deficient or qualified R2 self-ownership carries over into the postemancipation epoch. The centrality of property to the Lockean universe means that the racial structuring of rights of self-ownership and appropriation ramifies into the broader civil and political sphere and endures after slavery has ended. R1s have the intrinsic metaphysical property of R1-ness, a property that is the foundation of the moral/political property of full self-ownership. Correspondingly, R2s' lack of R1-ness precludes self-ownership in this full-blooded sense. In abstract Lockeanism, the young person at majority becomes free and twenty-one, a full citizen; in racial Lockeanism, by contrast, where self-ownership is raced, the corresponding expression is "free, white, and twenty-one."

Moreover, property rights are linked with the general power to determine other rights, since this is, after all, a polity of proprietors. It is therefore only appropriate that property owners (those who have demonstrated their rationality by appropriating nature—or here, in the racial polity, those whose intrinsic racial properties guarantee this rationality in advance) should decide on the interpretation of natural law. In effect, in the racial Lockean polity, the R1s rule *as a whole* (remember that only R1s are capable of leaving the state of nature and forming civil society) with respect to the non-R1s, though there are, of course, class, gender, and power differences internal to the R1 population. So even though the sovereign enforces natural law as interpreted by the judiciary, it is taken for granted that this natural law is not color-blind, but is aimed at preserving the domination of the R1s. Locke says, "The great and *chief end* therefore, of Mens uniting into Commonwealths, and putting themselves under Government, *is the Preservation of their Property*."[49] The state of the *Herrenvolk* Lockean polity will be entrusted with the task of protecting the property, the rights, of its full citizens, the R1s, which means maintaining the inferior access of the R2s, since among the rights of the R1s are precisely rights *over* the persons-who-are-not-really-full-persons of the R2 population. Thus Michael Dawson outlines how, in the postbellum South,

blacks were allowed only limited property rights, and individual and group economic progress was blocked.... Letters written by blacks are filled with testimonials on the use of force to deprive entrepreneurial, successful African Americans of their property, and often their lives as well.... White economic supremacy was maintained by the use of violence, law, the local government apparatus, the credit system, and psychological oppression.... [B]lacks could not benefit from their own labor in the South.... Sundown laws—which forbade the selling of cotton between sundown and sunup ... made it exceedingly difficult for black [tenant] farmers to sell their own crops.... By manipulating the credit system, [white] merchants were able to expropriate over 10 percent of black farmers' income.... Worse, there was extreme hostility to African Americans' owning land. Whites who sold land to blacks faced severe sanctions, and blacks who owned land faced the worst forms of violence. When laws ... that actually forbade black landownership were overturned, norms about, and sanctions against, black landownership were sufficient to raise the costs to both seller and buyer.[50]

As an R1, one therefore has race-based entitlements to differential economic opportunities and political rights that come at the cost of the R2s: these are a part of one's legitimate expectations, one's property, in the racial polity.[51] As long as the state is a racial state, it has a moral responsibility to its full citizens (the R1s) to maintain their racial property rights, their common interest in R1-ness as differential privilege, whether formally codified in law or informally guaranteed by custom.

And nationally, as Cheryl Harris points out, U.S. law has generally protected "settled expectations based on white privilege": "Whites have come to expect and rely on these benefits, and over time these expectations have been affirmed, legitimated, and protected by law." In the transition from de jure to de facto white advantage, "white privilege not mandated by law remained unaddressed," so that "the status quo of substantive disadvantage was ratified as an accepted and acceptable base line—a neutral state."[52] R1s will then with complete sincerity perceive R2 agitation for the dismantling of this continuing privilege as a violation of their rights.

Correspondingly, R1s' sense of subjective well-being will be shaped in large measure by the maintenance of this racially differentiated baseline. Goldman cites research that shows that people don't draw on *all* the information available to them in making such assessments, but do a truncated search based on a particular "standard of comparison," because "people's reported satisfaction depends largely on their relative position, not only on their objective situation."[53] And although there are obviously many possible metrics for comparison, historically many whites have measured their standing by their distance from blacks. Whether overtly or covertly, it has been taken for granted that blacks should be at the bottom, society's "mudsills." As one respondent to a race-relations survey put it: "Whites feel that they should stay above blacks.... When they came into the picture, they were better off than most blacks, so that should continue."[54] When some blacks progress upward into the middle class, then, their advance is actually a source of psychic discomfort for some whites. Those whites experience a malaise that is independent of objective downward mobility or stagnation measured by more conventional economic metrics; it inheres in the sense that things are going badly because (whether they are consciously aware of it or not) they are no longer so far removed from blacks.

In their detailed survey of black and white Americans' opinions on policies with racial implications, Kinder and Sanders discovered that individual self-interest is comparatively unimportant as a determinant; what count are *collective* interests: "In matters of public opinion, citizens seem to be asking themselves less 'What's in it for me?' and more 'What's in it for my group?'" And in the contemporary United States, whites' perception is that their differential group entitlement (though it may be seen as neutral and natural rather than differential) is under attack by blacks. Kinder and Sanders conclude that "feelings of deprivation" are "relative, based less in objective condition and more in social comparison," involving notions of "group relative disadvantage."[55] Challenges to the racial status quo thus excite both moral outrage and interest-based alarm, since both the normative entitlements and the baseline of rational expectations for whites have been constructed on the basis of legitimized differential advantage that is often not even recognized as such, given the history of white right.

In conclusion, then: the reconstruction of a *Herrenvolk* ethics should help us to understand continuing white recalcitrance on race. Radical theorists, particularly of the Marxist variety, are often caricatured as claiming that morality is epiphenomenal, playing no important role in social life, since people are motivated by material interests rather than moral principles. But this crude dichotomization is misleading, for it fails to take account of the fact that social privilege and material interests manifest themselves less in deviation from abstract principles than in the *reshaping and transformation of the principles themselves,* in this case through the dynamic logic of race. Correspondingly, it is a mistake to use the language of "deviation," as if there were an abstract colorless norm from which people contingently fell short. Rather, there was an abstract norm that was generally *realized,* the norm of a more or less consistent racially structured ethic. Race did not introduce a deviation into a previously uncontaminated abstract ethic; in the construction of this ethic, race was not abstracted from in the first place. And our present moral code is, of course (whether in the "symbiosis" or "multiple traditions" interpretation), the descendant of this ethic. Understanding present debates about race requires a demystified facing up to this past and the way it continues to affect white moral consciousness and the sense of white right.

8 Whose Fourth of July?

Frederick Douglass and "Original Intent"

On July 5, 1852, Frederick Douglass delivered a speech in Rochester, New York, titled "The Meaning of July Fourth for the Negro."[1] An oratorical masterpiece, "the most famous antislavery speech Douglass ever gave,"[2] it focuses on the dualisms and (apparent) contradictions that marked the founding of the republic and that, unresolved, continue to haunt us today. The central themes of Douglass's mature thought are all present: the scornful exposure of the (supposed) gap between the noble ideals and the reality of the American polity; the insistence on black personhood and the fact of slavery's violation of natural law morality; the corresponding appeal to his audience's moral sense; and above all, the optimistic faith in the Framers' intent in shaping the Constitution as a vehicle of eventual change. The speech reveals both the strengths and the weaknesses of Douglass's critique of white oppression. Read now, in a period seen by many African-Americans as characterized by the betrayal of the "Second Reconstruction," in a United States still segregated by the legacy of *Plessy* v. *Ferguson*, it seems simultaneously inspiring and naive. The debate between the two traditions in African-American political philosophy, assimilationism and separatism,[3] has still not been settled, polarizing black Americans between hope and despair, the dream of national unity and the ongoing nightmare of division into two nations.[4] In this final chapter I want to look at some of the key assumptions of Douglass's political thought, as shown in this speech and in his other writings, and see what they may reveal to be problematic about the analysis of the assimilationist tradition.[5]

The Speech

Douglass begins by expressing his "astonishment as well as ... gratitude" that he, a former slave, should be addressing such an audience. He notes that the Fourth of July is the birthday of national independence and political freedom, and recapitulates the history of American resistance to British tyranny. But there is something odd about the language of these opening pages, whose full rhetorical significance the reader may not immediately grasp. Douglass both identifies himself with and distances himself from his audience, on the one hand addressing them as "fellow citizens," on the other hand talking about "your National Independence," "your political freedom," "your fathers," and "your nation." He points out that although it is easy in retrospect to applaud the goals of the Revolution, it took courage to do so in 1776: "They who did so were accounted in their day plotters of mischief, agitators and rebels, dangerous men. To side with the right against the wrong, with the weak against the strong, and with the oppressed against the oppressor!" He describes how the colonists "sought redress" from the home government: "They petitioned and remonstrated; they did so in a decorous, respectful, and loyal manner. Their conduct was wholly unexceptionable. This, however, did not answer the purpose. They saw themselves treated with sovereign indifference, coldness and scorn." Nonetheless, convinced of the justice of their cause, they persevered, framing at the Continental Congress in 1776 the resolution that the united colonies should be free. Douglass praises the "fathers of this republic" for their "admiration of liberty": "They were peace men; but they preferred revolution to peaceful submission to bondage. They were quiet men; but they did not shrink from agitating against oppression. They showed forbearance; but that they knew its limits. They believed in order; but not in the order of tyranny.... With them, justice, liberty and humanity were 'final'; not slavery and oppression." With these familiar words of praise for the Founders and the auspicious occasion of the birth of the republic, Douglass puts his audience off guard. One imagines them relaxing in their seats, concluding that they are, after all, just going to be treated to the standard encomium to American greatness.

But then there is a critical segue. "I need not enter further into the causes which led to this anniversary," Douglass says, for they "have never lacked for a tongue. They have all been taught in your common schools, narrated at your firesides, unfolded from your pulpits, and thundered from your legislative halls, and are as familiar to you as household words.... Americans are remarkably familiar with all facts which make in their own favor.... I think the American side of any question may be safely left in American hands." In recounting the official white narrative, Douglass may, if only for the duration, pretend to an honorifically colorless civic status. But the problem is that he is both a part of and apart from his "fellow-citizens," being a *black* American, a walking oxymoron, an unacknowledged child from the slave quarters who cannot legitimately speak of *our* white fathers. So suddenly there is a switch, and another voice begins to speak, unfolding the tale of a repudiated son that *cannot* be safely left in (white) American hands, that *has* generally lacked for an official tongue, and that involves embarrassing facts with which white Americans are not and do not want to be familiar. The significance of the earlier "fellow-"/"your" split now becomes clear. "Fellow-citizens, pardon me, allow me to ask, why am I called upon to speak here to-day? What have I, or those I represent, to do with your national independence? Are the great principles of political freedom and of natural justice, embodied in that Declaration of Independence, extended to us?" And the answer is, of course, no. In a blistering passage, Douglass goes on to lambast the hypocrisy of the divided independence:

> I am not included within the pale of this glorious anniversary! Your high independence only reveals the immeasurable distance between us. The blessings in which you, this day, rejoice, are not enjoyed in common— The rich inheritance of justice, liberty, prosperity and independence, bequeathed by your fathers, is shared by you, not by me. The sunlight that brought light and healing to you, has brought stripes and death to me. This Fourth July is *yours*, not *mine*. *You* may rejoice, *I* must mourn.

The illusory inclusiveness of abstract, colorless "citizens" is thus thrown off, and Douglass unequivocally adopts what in contemporary vocabulary would be called the "epistemological standpoint" of race: "I shall see this day and its popular characteristics from the slave's point of view." And from this demystificatory perspective, the proceedings are revealed as a fraud:

> What, to the American slave, is your 4th of July? I answer; a day that reveals to him, more than all other days in the year, the gross injustice and cruelty to which he is the constant victim. To him, your celebration is a sham; your boasted liberty, an unholy license; your national greatness, swelling vanity; your sounds of rejoicing are empty and heartless; your denunciation of tyrants, brass fronted impudence; your shouts of liberty and equality, hollow mockery; your prayers and hymns, your sermons and thanksgivings, with all your religious parade and solemnity, are, to him, mere bombast, fraud, deception, impiety, and hypocrisy.

The conceptual inversion, the rhetorical turning of the tables on the audience, is therefore complete. Douglass — the former slave meant for illiteracy, the piece of "speaking property" meant to speak only when spoken to — has learned (dangerously) well from his oratorical models: Caleb Bingham's *Columbian Orator* (1797), the Bible, the Enlightenment rhetoric of Locke and the Founding Fathers, the cadences of William Lloyd Garrison and Daniel Webster, the "antithetical prose style" of eighteenth-century England.[6] Moreover, it is a matter not merely of style and oratorical flourishes but of calculated dialogical "techniques of reversal," whose conceptual purpose is to "subvert the official monologic discourse of the dominant class" through simultaneously employing and reversing its categories.[7] The painful but epistemically privileged bifocal black vision that Du Bois would later term "double-consciousness" is seeking to reveal to a myopic white vision the injustice of the split tiers, slave and free, of Lincoln's "house divided." Douglass is trying to remove the moral scales from white eyes. His initial description of the heroic struggles of the eighteenth-century colonists for freedom has been carefully designed to be equally applicable to the abolitionist cause of his own century, so that white Americans must, on pain of inconsistency, applaud the latter as heartily as the former. He wants to put his audience in a moral and conceptual trap, to force them to acknowledge that one cause is no less noble than the other. The points made about the commitment of the Founding Fathers to justice, liberty, and humanity; the description of their patient attempts to achieve a peaceful solution, and their call for revolution when those attempts failed; the praise of their courage and adherence to principle; and the reminder that what comes to be seen as morally right may once have seemed morally controversial — all can be applied equally well to the abolitionists in their struggle against slavery. So if one believes in "natural justice," if one agrees with Locke that "man is entitled to liberty" and that "he is the rightful owner of his own body," then — since blacks are equally "men" who should be self-owning — there must be an end to the "dividing" and "subdividing" of the "discourse" of liberty that the countenancing of slavery requires. It is a call for universalization in the classic humanist tradition, for an end to the color-coding of moral principles and the pattern of "national inconsistencies": "The existence of slavery in this country brands your republicanism as a sham, your humanity as a base pretense, and your Christianity as a lie."

Finally, and crucially, Douglass claims that this universalization is one to which the Framers themselves were committed. It is important to appreciate that the irony and doubleness of his account were never meant to be targeted against the "Fathers of this Republic."[8] Rather, he sees the accusation that slavery is "guaranteed and sanctioned by the Constitution of the United States" as a "base" "slander upon their memory." And he further praises the Constitution "interpreted, as it ought to be interpreted," as "a glorious liberty document.... I defy the presentation of a single pro-slavery clause in it. On the other hand, it will be found to contain principles and purposes, entirely hostile to the existence of slavery." The significance of an earlier remark—"America is false to the past, false to the present, and solemnly binds herself to be false to the future"—emerges more clearly here. For Douglass, slavery is a *betrayal* of the revolutionary past; it is an institution "false" to the Framers' intent. Thus he concludes on a positive note, rejecting despair, "drawing encouragement from 'the Declaration of Independence,' the great principles it contains, and the genius of American Institutions." Because of what he sees as this initial commitment to universal equality, he finds reason to believe that upon these foundations a new, nonracial America can and will eventually be built.

Four Theses of Douglass's Assimilationism

To examine the background assumptions of Douglass's argument and his resulting conclusions, I will draw not only on the speech but on statements he makes elsewhere. The following four theses (comprising what may illuminatingly be seen as two roughly linked enthymematic arguments, 1 and 2 implying 3, 3 implying 4) are central:

1. Natural law is the appropriate framework for considering moral and jurisprudential issues.
2. The "original intent" of the Framers is of primary importance, and this intent was antislavery and anti–white supremacy.
3. The actuality of the American polity is therefore inconsistent with its founding principles, and those who are agitating for racial equality can use that inconsistency to exert moral suasion on white Americans.
4. Thus there is reason to anticipate that blacks will eventually be accepted as full citizens in the American polity.

Douglass is thus a classic representative in the black American political tradition of the dominant assimilationist view.[9] Embodying "both militant protest and integrationism," he has been seen as the "patriarch," the "nineteenth-century father," of the twentieth-century civil rights movement.[10] Waldo Martin's biography characterizes Douglass's guiding assumptions as universal and egalitarian humanism, Protestant and Enlightenment optimism, reformist and idealist social meliorism, combined in a "fundamental

Americanism."[11] There have always been opposing separatist currents in black political theory, from Martin Delany in the nineteenth century through Marcus Garvey in the early twentieth century to the radical nationalists of the 1960s and 1970s. Skeptical that blacks will ever really be accepted as equals in America, they have agreed with the negative diagnoses of nineteenth-century white colonizationists and have historically advocated emigration to Africa or the formal partitioning of the United States to create the "two nations" that already exist informally. But the mainstream movement, represented by Douglass, the NAACP, and Martin Luther King Jr., has been integrationist.[12] Most blacks have viewed the Constitution more ambivalently than Douglass did, and few today would endorse his interpretation of "original intent." But most *have* been committed to a Christian moral objectivism (if not to an articulated concept of natural law) by which black subordination is clearly wrong, and confident that "the genius of American Institutions" has the potential to change America through a moral and constitutional appeal to white Americans to eradicate this "inconsistency." Douglass's integrationism, anti-emigrationist Americanism, and overt hostility in the last years of his life to the "positive evil" of "race pride," which made him insufficiently radical for some black nationalists of the 1960s and 1970s (a "reformist" figure or even [remarkably] a "good nigger"), establish him as a preeminent standard-bearer of the optimistic assimilationist school.[13]

The overturning of Jim Crow legislation seemed to vindicate assimilationists, since it was precisely the principles in the founding documents that were being appealed to. Thurgood Marshall argued that if blacks had been enslaved, disenfranchised, and segregated by law, it was also true that they had been emancipated and had begun to win equality by law.[14] But the setbacks of the 1980s and 1990s made the radical analysis seem credible again. Although there is no mass separatist movement today—where would one go?—the sentiment that would support it has revived, manifested not in emigration schemes but in a deep pessimism about the possibility of change. In a bitter memoir, Kenneth Clark, the black psychologist whose testimony about the harmful effects on black children of segregated education was so pivotal to the *Brown* v. *Board of Education* decision, and who in the 1960s derided Black Power as "a sour grapes phenomenon,"[15] looks back at his life: "I write these words in my seventy-sixth year. My beloved wife is dead and my career is nearing an end. Reluctantly, I am forced to face the likely possibility that the United States will never rid itself of racism and reach true integration. I look back and I shudder at how naive we all were in our belief in the steady progress racial minorities would make through programs of litigation and education.... I am forced to recognize that my life has, in fact, been a series of glorious defeats."[16]

What, then, was the cause of those defeats? If the promise of *Brown* was illusory or at least overstated, it is obviously important to understand why. To the extent that Douglass's progressivism and social optimism may be taken as emblematic of the mainstream integrationist position, investigating his views may be more broadly enlightening about possible weaknesses in this position. If he is wrong—if this tradition is wrong—then where exactly does the mistake lie?

Thesis 1: Natural Law as the Appropriate Theoretical Framework

First, the theoretical framework. Like most political and legal theorists of mid-nineteenth-century America, and like the Founding Fathers, Douglass believed in natural law.[17] Natural law theory has its origins in the classical world, the *nomos/physis* distinction of ancient Greece, the writings of Plato and Aristotle, and the Greek and Roman Stoics.[18] It evolves and changes over the next two millennia, Christianized by Aquinas, shifting in emphasis from natural duties to natural rights by the time of the Enlightenment. But throughout these changes, its distinctive feature remains the identification of law with morality. In the words of A. P. d'Entrèves, "The relation between law and morals is the crux of all natural law theory.... Law is an indication of what is good and evil.... Thus the doctrine of natural law is in fact nothing but an assertion that law is a part of ethics." And ethics is conceived of in absolutist as well as objectivist terms: natural law theorists "believed in absolute values, and they conceived of law as a means to achieve them."[19] In the Stoic philosopher Cicero's *De republica,* for example, we find the statement "True law is right reason in agreement with Nature; it is of universal application, unchanging and everlasting; it summons to duty by its commands, and averts from wrong-doing by its prohibitions.... [O]ne eternal and unchangeable law will be valid for all nations and for all times."[20] Natural law is universal and unchanging, and reflects the immanent moral structure of the universe. And for the Stoics, "human equality is the direct consequence of natural law, its first and essential tenet."[21]

The idea of natural law thus contains several distinct theses: the view sometimes called moral realism, that morality is objective, so that acts may be moral independently of what moral agents actually deem to be moral; the stronger thesis of moral absolutism, that moral principles are exceptionless and eternal; the commitment to human equality as the first and foundational element of these principles; and the idea that these principles are embodied in a natural law, to which human law must conform if it is to be valid.

The reasons for Douglass's embrace of a natural law position should be obvious, aside from the fact that it was, in any case, the dominant view at the time. The great virtue of natural law and natural rights theory, as it became in the modern period, is that it provides a preexisting and enduring Archimedean moral vantage point from which to denounce existing human laws and practices. Its commitment to moral realism and jurisprudential denial of the validity of immoral positive law make it immensely attractive to a political opponent of an immoral but institutionalized system. Might, even when legally backed, does not make right; a crime is still a crime, though it may have the support of the highest court in the land. The uncompromisingly absolutist character of natural law prohibitions precludes any appeal to contingent circumstances (for example, the claim that slavery was justified to keep the union together). Moreover, the Framers were themselves natural lawyers, sharing with Locke and Aquinas the ideological authority of a tradition that went back to classical civilization. So Douglass could locate himself in the jurisprudential discourse central to the intellectual history of the West, and appeal as well to a Christianized version that his fellow citizens and coreligionists had (theoretically) no choice but to recognize. By their own standards, his white fellow Americans, fellow Christians, were guilty of ignoring the implications of the truth that all men were created equal. Finally, there is an undeniable rhetorical grandeur to this tradition — compare Cicero with Bentham — that fits well with the pulpit, the political platform, the abolitionist speech. The eternal rights of man, the contemptible violation of God's principles, the sacredness of human freedom — these are far more inspirational and likely to set the heart pounding than the niggling plusses and minuses of the felicific calculus.

Nevertheless, even given his political and moral commitments, there was no conceptual necessity for Douglass to have adopted this framework. The legal positivism initiated in Europe by Jeremy Bentham and John Austin was not an influential presence in Douglass's America, but there would have been no inconsistency in a political abolitionist and moral realist's endorsement of its competing approach. Positivism is sometimes associated with a conventionalist view of morality, but this is in fact a misrepresentation, since there are several varieties of positivism, not all of which are committed to such a position. The essential positivist thesis is simply that law and morality ought to be separated; that, as Austin pointed out, the task of analytical jurisprudence needs to be distinguished from the task of normative jurisprudence. The question whether a law is valid should be disentangled from the question whether a law is morally good.[22] So Douglass could theoretically have taken a positivist position and conceded that proslavery legislation was *legally* valid while still condemning it from a *moral* point of view.

It is obviously far easier for us, with the benefit of more than a century of intervening legal theory, to appreciate the wide range of possible positions, with their respective implications, on the relationship between morality and law. But the point is important because Douglass ended up endorsing some strange interpretations and arguments, probably because he believed they followed from natural law. His train of reasoning seems to run something like this. Natural law links law to morality; natural law upholds human equality and opposes slavery; the Founders were natural lawyers; blacks are humans; therefore the Declaration and the Constitution that the Founders wrote must also have been intended to uphold human equality and oppose slavery. So any appearance that they do not must be illusory.

What has gone wrong here? The problem is that natural law theory, with its rationalist and idealist emphasis on the eternal character of natural law and its relatively slight interest in historical causes, is going to be singularly unhelpful on the *social* sources of law. As d'Entrèves points out, "Natural law theorists would never have admitted that law is merely the expression of the standards of a particular group or society."[23] By contrast, the great merit of positivism, which opens the conceptual door to more politically sophisticated and sociologically informed variants such as the American legal realism of the 1920s and the critical legal studies and critical race theory of the present,[24] is its demystified focus on actual laws and lawmaking, and their embeddedness in social context and power relations. Douglass, understandably, wanted to retain the moral high ground from which to launch thunderbolts of condemnation. But one can reject the amoralist position that power determines justice, that might makes right, while still accepting the unhappy truth that power and might often determine what is legal and what is *taken* to be right. And one can concede the natural law insight that there is a relation between law and morality, between the laws that people accept and the laws they see as morally right, without ignoring the fact that moral views may be sociohistorically determined. The points of value in naturalism can be retained in a more sophisticated contemporary framework without the implausibilities that Douglass took to follow from natural law theory.

Thesis 2: Original Intent as Anti–White Supremacy

These implausibilities emerge most clearly in his views on original intent, views that put him sharply at odds with most contemporary African-American legal thinkers and in the embarrassing company of, inter alia,

Reagan's attorney general, Edwin Meese, and his defeated Supreme Court nominee Judge Robert Bork.[25] Douglass saw original intent as crucial; he saw it as antislavery; and—I think it can be more generally extrapolated from what he says—he saw it as anti–white supremacy. (As will become clearer below, this is really the more significant question.) So I suggest that there are three issues here: (*a*) What and whose original intent is important? (*b*) In what ways could it be important? (*c*) What evidence is there that the original intent was antislavery and anti–white supremacy?

(*a*) What is called originalism (and intentionalism, preservatism, and historicism, among other things) was the accepted, axiomatic model of constitutional interpretation from the birth of the republic to the New Deal in the 1930s, before it suffered an apparent demise at the hands of legal realists such as Oliver Wendell Holmes. Since then, however, it has undergone a surprising resurrection through the writings of Judges Bork and Rehnquist.[26] The simple guiding principle, which comes down from the medieval juristic tradition, is that "all legal instruments should be construed in accordance with the intent of their makers."[27] When constitutional scholars talk about original intent, it is usually the original intent of the Framers that they have in mind, and this is what Douglass meant also. But there are numerous ambiguities and alternative possibilities, both in the nature of the intent and in the pertinent "intending" population, that need to be taken into account (and whose breadth contributes to the *anti*-intentionalist case). Bruce Ledewitz, for example, distinguishes between "original intent" and "textual intent," and between the "general intent" of the Constitution and the "specific intent" with respect to blacks.[28] Even more complicatedly, Gregory Bassham differentiates under the category of intent "scope beliefs, counterfactual scope beliefs, semantic intentions, and constitutionalized extratextual intentions," and under the category of intenders "the drafters, the Framers, the ratifiers, the people of the United States, or some combination of the preceding four."[29] So there are varieties of originalism, and a case has to be made for one's particular choice. It is by no means a simple matter of pointing uncontroversially to an unequivocal statement made by a unanimously designated speaker.

Because of these and other problems, anti-originalists argue that the search for original intent is pointless. Cass Sunstein suggests that the idea of a pristine, apolitical, uninterpreted text, which we can recover by sanding away the accumulated layers of subsequent readings and reviews, is a myth. "Constitutional interpretation inevitably requires us to use principles external to the Constitution. There is no such thing as interpretation without interpretive principles, and these cannot be found in the Constitution."[30] The words actually written down exercise some semantic constraint, but the text is not foundational, since its meaning partly comes from the shifting readings, the evolving consensual (or hegemonic) conceptual frameworks, and the changing and unchanging value commitments of the interpreters. Unlike conventionalists or deconstructionists, however, who would infer from this indeterminacy that meaning is *completely* open-ended, determined simply by power or whim, Sunstein insists that rational criteria in legal argument can still be reconstructed. I agree, but I claim that this rationality is a *raced* rationality that reflects the normative structure of the actual polity—a structure that Douglass denies. And once one recognizes the racial element, it becomes clear that the original intent of the official white citizenry, or the reading of that intent by the Supreme Court, may be just as important as or more important than the Framers' own views.

(*b*) My meaning will become clearer if we ask why original intent should be considered important in the first place. I suggest that there are two basic (but not mutually exclusive) alternatives: original intent is important simply as a *normative* foundation (moral/juridical) for evaluating the character of the polity; and original intent is important as part of a larger *descriptive* causal story ("idealist" or "materialist") about the evolution of the character of the polity.

The first claim is that original intent should be the normative reference point for adjudication of possible changes in the polity. In the Western Enlightenment tradition, the ideal liberal state is committed to protecting the rights and liberties of its citizens. The Constitution then sets the moral tone, acting as a normative beacon, making a statement about what the polity essentially should be. The presumption is, of course, that the founding principles can be given an independent moral justification. But this may not necessarily be the case. A moral objectivist, then, should not automatically feel bound by original intent even if it can be unambiguously determined, since if original intent was unjust to begin with, the mere fact that it becomes constitutionally enshrined does not make it any the less wrong. Douglass read original intent as antislavery and anti–white supremacy, and on this basis he sought to indict his fellow citizens and the government for straying from its prescriptions. But if original intent is actually proslavery and pro–white supremacy, then his appropriate response as a natural lawyer, and thus a moral objectivist, should have been to condemn it. In that case original intent should not have been normatively most important for him, nor should it be for us.

The second claim needs to be clearly differentiated from the first, since it is a *causal* claim about social dynamics. Original intent is seen as important in the historical evolution of the polity, not just as a basis for evaluating it. The contrast standardly invoked in sociohistorical theorizing is between idealist theories of history, which take ideas and moral values to be decisive in determining social evolution, and materialist theories, according to which the causal hierarchies run the other way, so that group interests and power politics are more important. (It is, of course, also possible to see them as equally significant, or as so intertwined that the categories become inapplicable.) Suppose the Framers really did intend to create a color-blind America. If it is true that moral motivation generally overrides countervailing group interests or (not always the same thing) perceived group interests, then campaigns of moral suasion appealing to this original intent will be able to bring about radical changes, despite a preponderance of vested material interests in the established racial order.

On the contrasting materialist view, of course, this will not be the case. A plausible materialist theory will not consign morality to the epiphenomenal (that is, zero causal efficaciousness) but will make it secondary, subordinate to (perceived) group interests, so that when they come into conflict, the latter are likely to triumph. This position by no means commits one to amoralism, though it is sometimes interpreted that way. Rather, it simply points out that the issue of the objectivity of moral judgments needs to be separated from the issue of the social efficacy of moral motivation. One can judge a society to be oppressive without believing that this oppressiveness will lead to social change. Nor, of course, does sociological materialism imply (what a glance at world history would show to be clearly false) that moral progress is impossible. Oppressed groups seeking to advance their interests may become strong enough to force change; technological progress and socioeconomic shifts may alter the cost/benefit balance sheet of an unjust social order; and moral motivation may play a real if secondary role. The claim is simply that such progress will not for the most part be the result of a self-contained moral dynamic. In this framework, the character of the Framers' original intent will be shaped by the imprinting of group interests on dominant moral conceptions. Its significance will then inhere less in its putative role as a detached and independent moral vector lifted above the political fray than in its epistemic role as an indicator of the balance of underlying social forces.

(c) With that said, let us turn to the third issue—Douglass's claims about what original intent actually was. It needs to be emphasized, to begin with, that the mature ideas he articulated on July 5, 1852, which he promulgated for the rest of his life, were by no means his original view; they reflect a reversal of his earlier position. He had once endorsed the orthodox view of the William Lloyd Garrison abolitionists, that the Constitution was a "proslavery document," a "compromise with tyranny." The masthead of Garrison's abolitionist weekly, the *Liberator*, proclaimed, "Resolved, That the Compact which exists between the North and the South is a 'covenant with Death, and an agreement with hell,' — involving both parties in atrocious criminality, — and should be immediately annulled."[31] As late as 1851, Douglass was still agreeing that the slaveholders "are doubtless right so far as the [proslavery] intentions of the framers of the Constitution are concerned," though he wondered whether "we [may] avail ourselves of legal rules which enable us to defeat even the wicked intentions of our Constitution makers.... Is it good morality to take advantage of a legal flaw and put a meaning upon a legal instrument the very opposite of what we have good reason to believe was the intention of the men who framed it?"[32]

This use of the Constitution would have moved him closer to twentieth-century African-American legal activism, where the question of original intent is subordinated to the idea of a living and evolving document whose meaning alters over time. Thus one author points out that to the extent that racial progress has been made, it has been "because of fundamental changes in the *interpretation* and implementation of that Constitution."[33] Or in the blunt words of Thurgood Marshall, " 'We the People' no longer enslave, but the credit does not belong to the framers. It belongs to those who refused to acquiesce in outdated notions of 'liberty,' 'justice,' and 'equality,' and who strived to better them."[34]

But Douglass came to disagree, bringing upon himself the fury of the Garrisonians, as well as the puzzlement of some later generations. What were his arguments? Over the next few years he named several different considerations as decisive. In his "change of opinion" statement, he cited a "careful study of the writings of Lysander Spooner, of Gerrit Smith, and of William Goodell" as having brought him to this conclusion.[35] In the July 5 speech, as we have seen, he argued that "the Constitution is a glorious liberty document" and denied "the presentation of a single pro-slavery clause in it." Indeed, "neither slavery, slaveholding, nor slave can anywhere be found in it."[36] A year later he denied that the word *citizen* is qualified by the word *white:* "The word '*white*' was unknown to the framers of the Constitution of the United States in such connections.... It is a modern word, brought into use by modern legislators, despised in revolutionary times."[37] Similarly, he later claimed that the "constitution knows no man by the color of his skin. The men who made it were too noble for any such limitation of humanity and human rights. The word white is a modern term in the legislation of this country. It was never used in the better days of the Republic, but has sprung up within the period of our national degeneracy."[38] He argued that the Constitution must recognize slaves either as persons or as beasts of burden — "It cannot regard them as men and regard them as things at the same time" —

and repeated his contention that there is not a "word, sentence or syllable" about slavery in the Constitution.[39] In response to the *Dred Scott* decision, he insisted that the "well known rules of legal interpretation" bore out the claim that slavery was not formally recognized, reiterated the natural law position that "law is in its nature opposed to wrong, and must everywhere be presumed to be in favor of the right," and rejected the interpretation of Chief Justice Roger Taney as "discrediting and casting away as worthless the most beneficent rules of legal interpretation; by disregarding the plain and common sense reading of the instrument itself; by showing that the Constitution does not mean what it says, and says what it does not mean."[40]

So Douglass's evidence involves several claims: (*a*) the Constitution makes no reference to slaves and slavery; (*b*) the Constitution does not distinguish between blacks and whites — indeed, that distinction is a modern development; (*c*) it would be contradictory both to recognize black manhood ("personhood" for us) and to relegate blacks to the status of property, since they must be either men or things, but cannot be both; (*d*) law must be morally right, so the Framers as natural lawyers could not have intended something clearly wrong.

It should be obvious that these claims are at best problematic and at worst obviously false. Consider, to begin with, points *a* and *b*. Constitutional scholars such as William Wiecek have pointed out that the Framers made a deliberate decision to use circuitous and euphemistic language so as to avoid formal reference to slavery, but everybody knew what they were talking about. The anti-Federalist critic who signed himself "Brutus" commented sarcastically on the "strange and unnecessary accumulation of words" being used "to conceal from the public eye" what could be expressed more concisely.[41] As Wiecek puts it:

> To evade introducing the words "slave" or "slavery" into the document, they chose ambiguous and inelegant phrases that clouded their meaning.... Repeatedly in the ratifying conventions they stated that "in plain English" the euphemisms referred to slaves.... Why then the muddy language if everyone knew what was meant?... [One contemporary commentator] explained that the framers avoided "expressions which might be odious in the ears of Americans, although they were willing to admit into their system those things which the expressions signified."[42]

In fact, "the Philadelphia Convention inserted no less than ten clauses in the Constitution that directly or indirectly accommodated the peculiar institution." Wiecek cites Article I, section 2: the three-fifths clause; Article I, sections 2 and 9: taxation on this basis; Article I, section 9: prohibition until

1808 of abolition of the importation of slaves to the United States; Article IV, section 2: return of fugitive slaves; Article I, section 8: states' militias to suppress insurrections, including slave uprisings; Article IV, section 4: Federal protection against domestic violence, again including slave uprisings; Article V: insulation of certain clauses involving slavery; Article I, sections 9 and 10: prohibition of indirect taxation of slavery.[43] So even though slaves and slavery are not referred to directly, everybody knew that certain expressions referred to them. A ready parallel can be discerned here with the emergence in recent decades of many terms in white American public discourse—"law and order," the "underclass," "welfare queens"—that are essentially coded references to blacks and black-related problems.[44] What needs to be appreciated, obviously, is that such racial cryptography goes back a long way—indeed, all the way to the founding of the republic.

Similarly, the fact that the Declaration refers to "all men" does not prove that the implicit reference was not exclusively to white men, nor is it remotely true that *white* is a modern "degenerate" term previously unemployed. Judge A. Leon Higginbotham Jr. has demonstrated that from the mid–seventeenth century onwards, blacks and whites were formally distinguished juridically, with correspondingly differentiated rights and criminal penalties.[45] And in 1790, certainly squarely within the revolutionary period, Congress made whiteness a prerequisite for naturalization. The legislators could hardly have stated more clearly the connection in their minds between race and civic virtue.[46]

So what Douglass says here is quite wrong. He seems to have relied on a naive textual formalism, focusing on what the text says to the exclusion of the standard principles of interpretation that would have given the words their actual contextual meaning. But the very banality of these rejoinders, the obvious dubiousness of Douglass's claim raise the question whether something more interesting may have been going on, especially since in 1849 he had pointed out some of these clauses himself (identified at the time by the abolitionist Wendell Phillips) and commented on how "cunning" the Constitution's framing was.[47]

One possible solution would be the "masking," the calculated two-facedness, that is part of the subversive strategy of the slave in dealings with white power.[48] Thus, in Paul Laurence Dunbar's famous poem, "We wear the mask that grins and lies / It hides our cheeks and shades our eyes / This debt we pay to human guile."[49] On this reading, Douglass was perfectly well aware that the Constitution sanctioned slavery but consciously decided to adopt the straightfaced/blackfaced literal-mindedness that, with a sophisticated "naivety," refused to see any exclusionary racial subtext in its moral guarantees, so that he could ask, in deadpan bewilderment, what had happened—if indeed all men were created equal—to the rights of black citizens. ("But Massa, dishere paper says I'se created equal ...?!") His words in 1851 (the slaveholders "are doubtless right so far as the intentions of the framers of the Constitution are concerned") point in this direction. But Douglass's anti-Garrisonian conversion, his impassioned defense of original intent in 1852 and later, seem completely genuine. Whatever he was doing, he was not playing a part. A more straightforward answer might simply be that his growing opposition to Garrisonian principles—nonresistance, political quietism, exclusive reliance on moral suasion, and disunionism ("come-outism": the demand to dissolve the union with the slaveholders)—led him to repudiate the analysis of the Constitution he associated with the upholders of these principles.[50] This would by no means be a matter of logical necessity, since the connection between principles and analysis is very loose indeed, and certainly twentieth-century black activists have had no difficulty in combining political militance with a rejection of original intent. But there are situational as well as formal logics, and given the existing politico-ideological positions of the time, this may have seemed the best strategic choice. If race and abolitionist conviction already set one outside the pale of respectability, why add to one's moral blackness by seeming to oppose the Constitution as well?

Though I think there is something to this argument, Douglass's insistence goes beyond a pragmatic adjustment to political realities. It seems that there is a genuine puzzle here, whose elucidation is useful not merely for understanding Douglass's idiosyncratic stance but, more interestingly, for the light it sheds on the general assumptions of the integrationist view. To understand his misrepresentation of the factual record and the seeming bizarreness of his arguments, we need to see Douglass as having been captured by a real insight that, given the available conceptual frameworks and the scholarship of the time, led him in dubious directions, making him distort the facts to fit the theory. We need to focus on points *c* and *d:* that recognizing blacks as both men and property would have been a contradiction, and that the Founders as natural lawyers could not have intended something wrong. These points, I suggest, are of broad significance because of what they say about the conceptual apparatus of liberalism and its blocking from sight of certain embarrassing historical truths.

Thesis 3: The "Contradiction" of Black Subordination

The idea (cited earlier as the "anomaly thesis")[51] that there is a "contradiction," an "inconsistency," an "anomaly" in the founding ideals of the republic has been widespread and has called forth much irony from critics both black and white. Samuel Johnson asked, "How is it that we hear the loudest yelps for liberty among the drivers of negroes?" and Abigail Adams wrote to her husband, John, that "it always appeared a most iniquitous scheme to me to fight ourselves for what we are daily robbing and plundering from those who have as good a right to freedom as we have."[52] The claim has also been central to the optimistic integrationist case. Douglass himself spoke, as we have seen, about the "national inconsistencies" in American practices. A hundred years later, the idea would be at the heart of Gunnar Myrdal's *An American Dilemma,* the most influential study of race in America, which describes the status of blacks as "an anomaly in the very structure of American society" and glosses the eponymous dilemma as the "everraging conflict" in the white citizenry between the general evaluations of the American creed and the specific evaluations with respect to blacks.[53] Since eliminating inconsistencies is a basic prerequisite for rational discourse, it has not seemed unreasonable for social reformers to expect that the demands of both rationality and morality will converge on the elimination of racism.

But what exactly is the putative inconsistency? It is supposedly centered on Thomas Jefferson's famous proclamation in the opening paragraph of the Declaration of Independence: "We hold these truths to be self-evident, that all men are created equal, that they are endowed by their Creator with certain unalienable Rights." Since this statement is usually taken to govern the provisions of the Constitution also, there is an apparent tension between the Declaration and the latter's (coded) acceptance of the enslavement of some men. As I have mentioned, however, Douglass's version of the inconsistency differs significantly from what most black intellectuals believe today because of his views on original intent. Douglass reads "all men" in the inclusivist color-blind sense, so that what is involved is an inconsistency between the Framers' original intent and the institution of slavery. His apparent reasoning here has been sketched earlier: natural law is committed to moral law, and universal human equality is the central principle of morality; and the Framers, as natural lawyers, would not have countenanced any violation of this principle. Most black intellectuals today, more cynical, read "all men" in the exclusivist color-coded sense, so that the inconsistency involved (attributable to what is characterized as "prejudice") is between the Framers' original intent and the moral facts of black personhood. Yet to my mind, understanding the logic that leads to Douglass's position can still be more broadly illuminating of the weaknesses in the assimilationist position.

The divergence between the two possible interpretations of the Declaration, inclusivist and exclusivist, was historically most clearly articulated in the notorious *Dred Scott* decision, in which Chief Justice Roger Taney denied Scott's petition for freedom on the grounds that the scope of the Declaration manifestly did *not* extend to blacks, who in the revolutionary period were seen as an inferior race not part of the citizenry.[54] His reasons are worth citing at length:

> It is difficult at this day to realize the state of public opinion in relation to that unfortunate race, which prevailed in the civilized and enlightened portions of the world at the time of the Declaration of Independence, and when the Constitution of the United States was formed and adopted. But the public history of every European nation displays it in a manner too plain to be mistaken.
>
> They had for more than a century before been regarded as beings of an inferior order, and altogether unfit to associate with the white race, either in social or political relations; and so far inferior, that they had no rights which the white man was bound to respect; and that the negro might justly and lawfully be reduced to slavery for his benefit. He was bought and sold, and treated as an ordinary article of merchandise and traffic, whenever a profit could be made by it. This opinion was at that time fixed and universal in the civilized portion of the white race. It was regarded as an axiom in morals as well as in politics, which no one thought of disputing, or supposed to be open to dispute....
>
> [I]f the language, as understood in that day, would embrace them, the conduct of the distinguished men who framed the Declaration of Independence would have been utterly and flagrantly inconsistent with the principles they asserted....
>
> Yet the men who framed this declaration were great men—high in literary acquirements—high in their sense of honor, and incapable of asserting principles inconsistent with those on which they were acting. They perfectly understood the meaning of the language they used, and how it would be understood by others; and they knew that it would not in any part of the civilized world be supposed to embrace the negro race, which, by common consent, had been excluded from civilized Governments and the family of nations, and doomed to slavery.[55]

Douglass was outraged by Taney's decision, seeing it as a violation of the natural law commitment to human equality (and a slander on the Framers):

> The Supreme Court of the United States is not the only power in this world. It is very great, but the Supreme Court of the Almighty is greater. Judge Taney can do many things, but he cannot perform impossibili-

ties.... He may decide, and decide again; but he cannot reverse the decision of the Most High. He cannot change the essential nature of things — making evil good, and good evil. Happily for the whole human family, their rights have been defined, declared, and decided in a court higher than the Supreme Court.... Man was born with [the right to liberty].... To decide against this right in the person of Dred Scott, or the humblest and most whip-scarred bondman in the land, is to decide against God. It is an open rebellion against God's government. It is an attempt to undo what God has done, to blot out the broad distinction instituted by the *Allwise* between men and things.[56]

And in 1861, he asserted: "By that law [of natural justice], universal, 'unchangeable and eternal,' every man is the rightful owner of his own body, and to dispossess him of this right, is, and can only be, among the highest crimes which can be committed against human nature. The only foundation for slavery is positive law against natural law."[57]

The interesting issue here is not, of course, whether Taney was morally wrong but whether his assessment of white opinion of the time and the Framers' moral perceptions is factually right. For Taney, the seeming inconsistency between Declaration and Constitution is eliminated when "all men" is read in the exclusive sense, as white, and as committing the Framers to slavery and white supremacy; for Douglass, it is eliminated when "all men" is read in the inclusive sense, as color-blind, and as committing the Framers to antislavery and anti–white supremacy. Both men relied on the premise of the honorable moral character of the Framers but they come to different conclusions. For Douglass, Taney's assessment of revolutionary white opinion was factually wrong and in any case irrelevant, since the Framers' moral natural law commitments would have precluded their endorsement of the obvious immorality of depriving self-owning men of their liberty and treating them as things. Only "positive law" and conventionalist morality could permit this.

Douglass's position here is convergent with that of the contemporary conservative constitutional scholar Harry Jaffa, also a natural law theorist and a believer in original intent.[58] So I am going to use Jaffa's more developed argument to explicate Douglass's views, since the *Dred Scott* decision is a crucial reference point for both men. In my opinion, they both misrepresent Taney, and their misrepresentation is enlightening for what it says about the restricted set of theoretical options they considered. Like Douglass, Jaffa sees the Founders as natural lawyers for whom blacks must "obviously" be men. Unlike Douglass, however, Jaffa does not deny that many clauses in the Constitution related to slavery. His is rather the most plausible version of this position: the concessions to slavery reflect a compromise with the South, a necessary evil that would eventually be eliminated, rather than a principled position resting on the restrictive interpretation of "men." He takes Taney to be endorsing a positivist thesis by which the moral status of blacks is conventionally determined. But this thesis, he argues, is clearly wrong: "That the Negro is a human being is a matter of fact and not of opinion.... Fundamental to the law of the Constitution was the fact of the Negro's personality—in short, his humanity.... That the Negro belongs to the species *Homo sapiens* is as undeniable as that any white (or yellow, red, or brown) individual belongs to this species. His rationality ... is indicative of the essence of his humanity; the color of his skin, a mere accident."[59] And the Framers, he claims, would, of course, have been equally aware of this: "For Jefferson and his contemporaries, there was no question but that the differences in natures, differences inherent in the distinctions the Bible itself draws between man and beast, had implications (as in the Bible) that were no less moral than metaphysical.... The equality of man proclaimed by the Declaration of Independence is to be understood first of all by comparison with the inequality that characterizes man's relationship with the lower orders of living beings."[60]

Jaffa therefore presents us with two alternatives: (*a*) his own interpretation of original intent as committed in the Declaration, within a natural law framework, to the morally objectivist, "obvious" truth of human equality, including black equality, and a constitutional compromise with the slave owners to save the union; and (*b*) the (alleged) Taney interpretation of original intent as committed in the Declaration, within a positivist framework, to a conventionalist moral division within the human population, whites being equal and blacks being unequal, with the proslavery clauses then being a reflection of the historical and conjunctural consensus on the moral status of blacks. Douglass's dichotomization was similar, except that, as we have seen, he denied the existence of any pro-slavery clauses.

But, as Jaffa and Douglass both point out, the Framers were natural lawyers, and natural law, from the Stoics down through the Lockean inspiration for Jefferson, is committed to human equality. It is an obvious moral and metaphysical truth that blacks are human, therefore rational, and so clearly self-owning, to be distinguished from "the lower orders of living beings." But then the Framers could *not* have had a principled position committed to white supremacy and black inferiority, and Taney's restrictive interpretation has to be a mistaken positivist one.

I suggest that Jaffa and Douglass are both wrong, and that Taney is right. For the choice is not between the jointly exhaustive alternatives of a naturalist commitment to an inclusive human equality and a positivist conventionalist moral division in the human population: this is a false dichotomization. There is a third alternative: that at least some (and maybe the majority) of the Framers were convinced of the *objective moral truth*, as *part* of natural law, of black inequality, so that excluding them from "all men" was principled rather than pragmatic. (For our purposes, it does not matter whether this naturalism was Taney's position rather than the positivism Jaffa and Douglass attribute to him, though a case for naturalism can certainly be made.) In their own eyes, the Framers would *not* then have been doing something wrong in codifying black subordination (if not necessarily slavery itself), since blacks were in fact lesser beings of a "lower order," and this had both "moral and metaphysical" implications. It was by no means merely a matter of (white) human convention and positive law.

Why do Jaffa and Douglass not consider this obvious alternative? They are both taking for granted—Jaffa with far less excuse, as a professional scholar with the advantage of a century of research to draw on—the supposed absurdity of the notion that any Enlightenment figure could ever have regarded blacks as less than human. Modernist Enlightenment liberalism operates with the (seemingly) simple category of "men," with moral egalitarianism taken as the ground floor and no formal markers to indicate differential moral/ontological standing.[61] Blacks are obviously men; *men* is a univocal homogeneous term, without qualification or degree; so once it has been established that blacks are men, all the natural law provisions must apply in full force to them also. There is supposed to be no conceptual room for the idea that if all men are equal, nonetheless some men are more equal than others. And this is what traps Douglass into concluding, against the evidence, that the Framers must have meant the term inclusively.

The feminists' exposure of the gender specificity of these "men" is by now a familiar story.[62] But the facially raceless appearance of the category better conceals its *racial* specificity. Yet this claim of racial neutrality is quite false. The classic contractarians, I suggest, were really expounding a *racial contractarianism*, wherein racial exclusion is not a matter of contingent prejudice but part of the architecture of the theory. The modern natural law tradition that provides the normative background for liberalism evolved in a period of European encroachment on the rest of the world and was shaped accordingly. And the prerequisites for being a man in the full rational sense that entitles one to natural law protection were constructed so as to exclude non-Europeans. Thus "men" is by no means an unambiguously inclusive category, but one that is internally divided, in tacit contrast to "savages." A conceptual space opens up in European thought for entities who are humanoid but not fully human, men who are not men — seen variously as beasts in human form, lesser humans of a different species and a different genesis, or admitted yet inferior members of the same species — but in all cases subpersons rather than persons. *And for these beings, a different set of normative rules applies; natural law speaks differently.*

This reasoning should be less surprising when one recognizes that there is a precedent in the vaunted legacy of the ancient world. It is a familiar fact that Aristotle thought that some men were biologically destined to be slaves (though there were epistemic problems in identifying them), but as Anthony Pagden has pointed out, even the egalitarian Cicero tied full humanity to cultural membership in the Roman Empire.[63] The modern period brought race into existence as the infallible epistemic marker that conveniently linked inferior biology with inferior culture, thereby dividing the population covered by the natural law framework into persons and subpersons. The result is a dichotomized racial logic in most of the classic contractarian texts. In the nonmainstream prudential contract of Hobbes's *Leviathan,* Native Americans are the only examples cited of the real-life, literal state of nature, Europeans being sufficiently rational to institute the absolutist sovereign necessary to avoid the bestial state of war.[64] And in the mainstream morally objectivist contract, whether Lockean or Kantian, there is a racial partitioning in different peoples' ability to perceive the prescriptions of natural law. Locke's unEnlightened Native Americans are not sufficiently "industrious and rational" to appropriate and add value to the land God has given them, unlike hardworking day laborers in England;[65] so their later expropriation by European settlers is clearly justifiable. Kant, the preeminent Enlightenment theorist of personhood and the founder of the modern concept of race, was thus in a sense, fittingly, the preeminent theorist of subpersonhood also. He mapped a natural racial hierarchy of degrees of human rationality and moral educability, in which it turns out that Native Americans are at the bottom, being completely impervious to such education, whereas blacks, one rung above, have innate abilities no more extensive than would equip them for slavery or servanthood.[66] Finally, Emer de Vattel, the natural law theorist whose work was to provide the authoritative juristic framework for international relations, explicitly endorsed the moral rightness of the civilized taking possession of "lands which the savages have no special need of and are making no present and continuous use of," thereby giving general normative backing to the process of European expansionism and settlement.[67]

So if the leading Enlightenment theorists of the age had no difficulty in racing and partitioning personhood, felt no embarrassment in reconciling an ostensibly general commitment to universal human equality with non-white subordination, why should the Framers have been any more conceptually discommoded? Indeed, one of the ironies of Douglass's complaints about white moral blindness is the myopia arising from his own (at least partial) identification with the white West. In protesting his exclusion from full American citizenship, he failed to see that the same Jeffersonian Declaration of Independence he was citing as evidence of *his* personhood distinguishes the "men" in whose ranks he wanted to be included from the "merciless Indian Savages," who are clearly relegated to a separate category. Douglass satirized the ironies and contradictions of white doublethink, insisting that he was part of the human community and that this country was legitimately his also, while failing to recognize that to some extent he was practicing the same exclusionary logic as they were.[68]

Once one recognizes that such a category exists, then, the whole notion of a contradiction/inconsistency/anomaly becomes much fuzzier and more problematic. And this will have implications not merely for Douglass's peculiar version of the "inconsistency" (which absolves the Framers) but also for the general claim that there is a deep "American dilemma" involving race, a cognitive dissonance between norms for blacks and whites. The assimilationist school, even when more negative about the Framers than Douglass, has generally conceptualized race within the framework of prejudice, bigotry, and attitudes and practices seen as deviations from a raceless democratic ideal taken to be central to the European tradition. What I have argued is that to frame the matter in terms of a "deviation" is misleading. I am suggesting that we need to see European expansionism as rewriting that tradition, reshaping those ideals, and bringing into existence in America a *new kind* of political formation, a racial polity that is misleadingly conceptualized within orthodox categories. The division of the human population generates what could be regarded as a racial liberalism and a *Herrenvolk* ethics, intellectual systems that are structured precisely around the differential treatment of the nonwhite population and conceptually shaped accordingly. It is a matter not of black subordination coming into straightforward and clear-cut conflict with abstract raceless normative principles but rather of encountering principles that have themselves historically been rewritten by race, so that white moral consciousness is used to negotiating and accommodating differentiated treatment.

Morality is then racialized. Contemporary naturalists such as Ronald Dworkin argue, against positivists, that although it is certainly logically possible for any set of formally valid laws to be issued as commands, in practice a background sense of justice and fairness plays a role in determining what laws will become acceptable to the population. Thus he designates as "principles" those moral appeals that are part of the discursive moral logic of the system and that are crucial to decision making.[69] So it is not a matter of crass power politics, with the simple imposition of the will of the stronger. Rather, there is a genuine internal moral logic present, which will assert itself like a normative lodestone, guiding judgments of correctness.

And this set of background principles, this deeply "felt" sense of what is right and wrong, will in a racial polity be racially normed. The "original intent" that is both morally and causally important will, as I have suggested, be the majoritarian white intent that historically and currently has been committed to white domination, originally more openly proclaimed, now more usually concealed under the cloak of an ostensibly neutral baseline that is not to be tampered with. What is obfuscated in the original documents is made clear in the Taney decision, so that this undeservedly calumniated figure is really being excoriated for his plain speaking, for spelling out what is hidden by constitutional circumlocution and racial cryptography. As Donald Lively underlines, the decision's "virtual disappearance from most contemporary constitutional law case books" conceals the embarrassing reality that it was "a fair reflection of geographically unqualified values and attitudes," comporting "not only with the imperatives of slavery but also with the priorities of general society which by law had pervasively and overtly expressed its racism."[70] Similarly, while Don Fehrenbacher points out the many mistakes in the decision, he emphasizes nonetheless that "the racial theory underlying his opinion was majoritarian.... [A]lthough the principal conclusions of Taney's opinion were soon wiped away by the Civil War and subsequent constitutional amendments, the spirit of the opinion survived for a century in the racial sequel to emancipation."[71] Taney was wrong on the details but right on the principle. His central underlying rationale is basically entirely correct: blacks were seen as an inferior race who could—normatively, legitimately, morally—be subordinated by the white majority.[72] Taney is the indiscreet speaker who blurts out in public what is supposed to be mentioned only in private: that the polity is a racial one. What accounts for his banishment from case history is not his falsehoods but his truth.

Douglass's wrath is therefore misdirected, and his (and Jaffa's) claims of original revolutionary racelessness are unfounded. What is involved is not a degeneration from an original, all-encompassing, colorless humanism to a novel nineteenth-century racism but rather a shift from a racial "common sense" without scientific backing, and in uneasy tension with lingering Enlightenment environmentalism, to a gradually hardening, scientifically rationalized racism. George Fredrickson characterizes the former period as one of "proto-racism" rather than racism proper, but he concedes that this is a semantic stipulation.[73] In the broader sense useful for our purposes, racism—the conviction of the inferiority of nonwhites—was already widespread in the white population and was seen as an objective moral/ political/metaphysical truth. Obviously, if there had not been some degree of bad conscience about slavery, it would not have been necessary to resort to circumlocution in the Constitution. And undoubtedly the Framers represented a range of positions, and some were genuinely concerned about what they were doing. Jefferson's *Notes on the State of Virginia* would advance black inferiority "as a suspicion only" and leave room for nonbiological explanations.[74] But as indicated, the view of blacks' inferiority, theologically or culturally if not biologically explained, and the conviction that they were "a permanently alien and unassimilable element of the population,"[75] had been around for more than a century by the time of the Philadelphia congress and was already reflected in prerevolutionary practices of discrimination.[76] As Reginald Horsman has argued, the notion of an Anglo-Saxonist "manifest destiny," by which race was the basis of the nation, became central to the conception of the American polity.[77] Blacks and Indians were seen as lacking the civic virtues requisite to be good citizens of the new republic, so that fitness for entry into the realm of the political was explicitly racially normed.[78]

Thus, as Fredrickson concludes elsewhere, natural rights were codified in a white social contract from which slaves were excluded, the Declaration, *pace* Douglass, being not universalistic but intended "more to assert the right of a particular 'homogeneous' community to self-determination than to establish a haven of freedom and equality for all types and varieties of people.... [A]ll nonwhites were, from the beginnings of nationhood, commonly regarded as 'aliens' of the unassimilable kind."[79] Majoritarian original intent, though somewhat divided on the issue of slavery itself, was racial, committed to white domination, and by Douglass's time had hardened with the rise of racist theory to a point at which the inequality of races was scientifically rationalized. This would be true for the rest of the century: across the political spectrum—liberals and conservatives, abolitionists and antiabolitionists—and across the country—North and South—virtually all whites would assume black inferiority, whatever their differences as to its implications.[80] Thus one could speak of a national "consensus in favor of white supremacy, although at times the proper mechanism to ensure white domination might be in dispute."[81] If there was controversy over whether slavery was wrong, there was no controversy over the political axiom that, emancipated or not, blacks were not to be social equals.

Thesis 4: Optimism about Black Inclusion

Once one faces this fact, the whole concept of a "contradiction" or "inconsistency" becomes much more dubious. If the United States was intended to be and is basically a nonracial liberal democracy in which racism is a "deviation" from the ideal norm, since the Framers' and the white majority's original intent was to include all races, then there is indeed a clear internal contradiction with which one can work. But if the United States was intended to be and is in some ways still a white republic (Saxton), a *Herrenvolk* democracy (van den Berghe), a caste society (Myrdal), a white supremacist state (Fredrickson),[82] in which the Framers' and the white majority's original intent was to privilege whites, then if there is a contradiction, it is of quite a different sort, an external contradiction between the system as a whole and the facts of black personhood. The socioeconomic changes that would have to be made are much more radical, and the obstacles to be overcome in the white psyche are much more formidable, since the white citizenry have historically benefited from and been cognitively and affectively molded by their entitlement to differential treatment. This is in fact what whiteness comes to *mean,* so that it is embedded at the deepest level of one's identity, locating one in the superior tier of this new type of polis, not to be found in the classical taxonomies of the Old World. The category of "prejudice" is inadequate to capture this relation, since what is really involved is a system for which racially determined structural advantage and handicap are foundational. Douglass, as an adherent of the "anomaly" view, took the polity to be essentially nonracial. For the alternative perspective (cited previously as the "symbiosis thesis"),[83] race is built in to the structure of the polity. So for white Americans with these racial views, there is no real "American dilemma," and the assumption that there is one shows that the nature of the polity has been misunderstood.[84]

The symbiosis view (according to which liberalism for whites and racism for blacks are in symbiosis rather than contradiction) has traditionally been associated with separatist prescriptions and sometimes also with a biologistic understanding of race. But neither of these associations is conceptually necessary. Race can be seen as "constructed" but nonetheless real. (The inference that the nonbiological character of race implies its unreality has recently earned its own pejorative: "vulgar anti-essentialism.")[85] And symbiosis theorists can still advocate integration as an ideal, while being far less optimistic about its likelihood. The defining feature of this alternative view is simply what Gary Peller calls its "race-consciousness," its emphasis, in defiance of the official myth of race neutrality and a "color-blind" Constitution, that race has been central to the makeup of the American polity, and that this fact needs to be faced in any viable set of proposals for reform.[86]

Separatists have always had a much keener appreciation of these realities than assimilationists, and if their own resulting prescriptions have not always been realistic, one has to bear in mind the restricted menu of available options. From this perspective, white racial privilege—whether or not it is termed "white supremacy"—is really the fundamental overarching political category, with black slavery being just one form of nonwhite disadvantage. Douglass and many other black abolitionists mistakenly identified all white moral opposition to slavery with a white moral commitment to black equality, and assumed that after emancipation racism would soon wither away. But one can oppose slavery as wrong while still being convinced of black inferiority, and one can recognize slavery as unfair while denying that other systems of racial disadvantage are unfair or, indeed, without conceding that they *are* systems of disadvantage. The "contradiction," if there is one, becomes much more easily negotiable. A transcendence of the traditional terms of the debate (assimilationist/separatist) would incorporate the separatist insight of the centrality of race to critique the assimilationist dream of integration of the "races" as they are into *existing* America. Since that "America" has been constructed precisely on racial exclusion, transformation of the polity would require the genuine transcendence of race, not through an evasive "color-blindness" that encodes and perpetuates white privilege without naming it but through the dismantling of the objective structures and subjective psychology of racial domination and subordination.

So the criticism is not that Douglass was so impressed by the power of moral suasion that he thought it sufficient to overcome the vested interests that whites had in the racial structure. (After all, he broke with the Garrisonians precisely because he realized that political activism would also be necessary. And he is, of course, the author of the speech on West Indian emancipation that famously points out, "Power concedes nothing without a demand. It never did and it never will.")[87] Rather, the criticism is that he failed to fully recognize how deeply race and racial self-interest had entered into the creation of the polity and its citizens' identities, so that he would later underestimate and be astonished by the extent of white resistance to racial equality. Like many others of the period, Douglass tied color prejudice so tightly to slavery—recall his mistaken claim that "race" did not become a significant category until the mid–nineteenth century—that he assumed that after Emancipation it would quickly disappear.[88] George Fredrickson comments on the widespread failure of blacks to perceive "that more than two hundred years of slavery and discrimination had planted the notion of black 'otherness' and inferiority so deeply into the white psyche that liberation of blacks from bondage could not remove it." The polity was predicated on a white race consciousness that "maintained and reinforced the positive self-image and status pretensions of white Americans" vis-à-vis inferior blacks."[89]

Douglass hints that race may become more deep-rooted and autonomous, shaping white psychology in such a way as to make black equality threatening to white self-respect. "My *crime* is," he says disgustedly at one point, "that I have assumed to be a man, entitled to all the rights, privileges and dignity, which belong to human nature."[90] And elsewhere: "Properly speaking, *prejudice against color* does not exist in this country.... While we are servants, we are never offensive to the whites.... In these conditions, we are thought to be in our place; and to aspire to anything above them, is to contradict the established views of the community—to get out of our sphere, and commit the provoking sin of *impudence*."[91] But these insights are scattered and not integrated into any larger theory. Had he followed them up and systematized them, they might have led to a more realistic sense of race as a global system of self-definition with respect to a nonwhite Other that could survive the demise of slavery. But for Douglass, the Constitution, original intent, and the Enlightenment polity were all color-blind. How, then, could it not soon become obvious to whites, with their Enlightenment rationality, that blacks, like themselves, were self-owning Lockean persons? A leading official of the Republican Party after the war, he became in later life a strong opponent of independent black political action, in keeping with his faith in a raceless Constitution that, the very year after his death in 1895, would accommodate the *Plessy* v. *Ferguson* decision that formally legitimated "separate but equal."

Douglass's idealism and misconception of the nature of the polity thus discounted or at least seriously undercounted what W. E. B. Du Bois later termed "the wages of whiteness,"[92] the multidimensional payoff from whiteness—economic, juridico-political, social, cultural, somatic, "ontological"—in a white-supremacist system.[93] (Whites themselves offer a more realistic accounting. Andrew Hacker routinely asks his white students how much compensation they would require to agree to be turned into blacks; the standard response is $1 million a year for life.) This investment in whiteness, whether individually (oneself and one's children) or collectively (group interests), constitutes a formidable barrier to be overcome by morality-based accounts of social change.[94] Moreover, apart from the resistance arising from straight interest-based motivation, there are cognitive problems inherent in the demonstration of the "contradiction," problems that would become manifest in the disappointments of the aftermath of the victories over de jure segregation in the 1950s and 1960s. Twentieth-century civil rights activists, following in Douglass's footsteps, have in some respects recapitulated his stumbles.

Proponents of the anomaly thesis often seem to be assuming the following simple model: Whites believe in a moral code, M; there is a clear contradiction between the prescriptions of this code and the treatment of blacks; so whites can be enlightened to recognize this contradiction. But to begin with, insofar as moral prescription arises out of a combination of normative commitment and *factual* assessment, certain empirical claims about the treatment of blacks have to be accepted before the existence of a contradiction is conceded. So it is not a straightforward matter of the implications of the moral code M, but rather of the implications of M in conjunction with empirical claims, of $M + E$. If one's model of discrimination is slavery and Jim Crow, if one's conceptualization of white domination is based on the plantation and the formal demarcations of "White" and "Colored" signs, one will find it much more difficult to "see" these realities in the present period. When they are no longer so empirically visible, they require theoretical labor. Indeed, the same dominant American creed being appealed to has descriptive as well as normative implications, shaping people's consciousness with a naive but hugely influential individualist folk sociology, according to which it is basically up to the individual to succeed or fail. There is little grasp of the global workings of a class and racial system, especially when whites' education largely deprives them of a historical appreciation of the full extent of black subordination and imprints on their minds a conceptual framework (the United States as a nonracial liberal democracy) refractory to an understanding of these realities.

Thus most whites, even apart from motivational factors, will be cognitively disadvantaged both experientially, through their segregated sheltering in a white life-world distant from the hard empirical facts, and discursively, by the theoretical framework into which they have been socialized. A few high-profile black success stories (a Colin Powell, an Oprah Winfrey, a Michael Jordan) will for many whites be more cognitively salient, sticking in the mind as evidence of the diminution or nonexistence of racial barriers for those willing to work hard. The fate of their more representative black brothers and sisters will then be explained otherwise than through race. Many very respectable, apparently nonracist theories advanced to account for continuing black problems—variants of the "culture of poverty," the claim of too much dependence on Big Government, black clinging to the "myth of victimization"—are made even more respectable by their endorsement by some black conservatives. Whites can (and do) say to themselves and to others that they have never owned slaves, they have never oppressed anybody; all of that sorry business is the ancient and dead past, whatever compensation was required was made years ago, and it is time to move on. Reynolds Farley summarizes the situation:

> The idea of making special investments in blacks so that they could be brought to the starting line of a fair race is now dormant or dead, and affirmative action increasingly has come to imply reverse discrimination.... [I]f whites ever felt any guilt about their treatment of blacks and a need to make recompense, the civil rights revolution relieved them of it. Changes in the law seemingly removed all barriers to equal opportunities for blacks, thereby giving whites moral absolution and a certainty that discrimination, if it ever were directed against blacks, was a practice of the distant past.... [W]hites realize that blacks have worse jobs, lower incomes, and less desirable housing, but racial discrimination is not seen as the primary cause of these inequities. Lack of motivation and lack of ability are cited by whites as the explanation for the status of blacks. Whites, in general, believe that opportunities are open to blacks.[95]

As a result, the white population are able to think of themselves as innocent, since the notion that they are collectively the group beneficiaries of a system of domination is alien to the individualist framework that writes race out of the polity.[96] One then demonstrates one's antiracist commitments through individual acts of sympathy and friendship, which, however morally praiseworthy and well intentioned, do not address the legacy of structural disadvantage.[97]

So even when whites do *not* have racist views, the "contradiction" can easily be negotiated around rather than activated, since auxiliary factual claims need to be accepted for a contradiction to be perceived in the first place. But the second point, of course, is that the picture of an abstract moral code, M, prescribing black equality, is questionable to begin with. In the years immediately after the appearance of Myrdal's book, several sociologists did empirical testing of his thesis that the supposed contradiction would generate tensions leading to a favorable resolution, and what they found was that this notion was naive because it ignored the many alternative mechanisms for reducing cognitive dissonance on the issue.[98] People may shift back and forth between the abstract code and versions customized for local realities. Or, as I argued in Chapter 7, one may suggest that the abstract code M never really existed in the first place, being reshaped by race from the beginning into *RM*—a racial morality, a *Herrenvolk* ethics, a sense of white right—in which there are elaborate internal conceptual mechanisms to sidestep apparent inconsistencies, cognitive schemas for generating racially concrete instantiations of general abstractions, and empathic buffers to mute the impact of black suffering. "It is possible to assert, in contrast to Myrdal's profile of American values, that racism is not a 'lower' and 'local' set of attitudes, but rather a complex value orientation equal in every respect (except that of a humanistic morality) to that of the [ostensible] American creed," says Stanford Lyman.[99] And in view of the long-enduring character of this "contradiction," in view of the hundreds of years whites have lived with it, would the opposite not be far more surprising? In the evolution of the American polity, whiteness as entitlement to differential privilege itself becomes property, so that a line of normative consistency can be traced out by which, through the various shifts in race relations, this baseline of differential white privilege is maintained, and norms for action and inaction are constructed accordingly to guarantee its protection.[100]

Morality and racism, then, do not collide as separate externals; rather, they interpenetrate each another. Even under slavery and Jim Crow, a racial moral economy was able largely to reconcile the American creed with formal black subordination. How much easier will this reconciliation be now that such subordination has apparently been eradicated by a color-blind Constitution? The optimistic integrationist position would then have to face not the scenario (problematic enough in itself) of an ideal morality set in clear opposition to (and expected to triumph over) interest-based motivation, but the worst-case outcome: perceived group interest and a sensed moral entitlement converge on the preservation of the existing racial system.

This more pessimistic but arguably more realistic analysis is supported by the historical record. The three great moments of possibility for transforming the republic were the Founding, postbellum Reconstruction, and the ending of Jim Crow. All three instances were opportunities to write blacks fully into the polity and end its racial nature. And all three were missed, the first clearly and completely, through the constitutional sanctioning of slavery, the second and third partially, through constitutional and juridical change unsupported by majoritarian white moral transformation and commitment to full black equality. The outcome was that legal advances were later reversed; the Fourteenth and Fifteenth amendments remained dead letters for a century; and post-*Brown* antidiscrimination, desegregation and affirmative action law, after the high point of *Griggs* v.

Duke Power Company, (1971)[101] is gradually being whittled away through a series of negative Supreme Court decisions in response to white backlash. "Progress peaked in the 1970s," concludes Julius Chambers. "In the 1990s, civil rights groups and their supporters are committing most of their resources simply to hold the line."[102]

Moreover, "materialist" explanations for such progress as has been made further undermine the case for a contradiction-driven moral dynamic as the hoped-for primary causal agent. Derrick Bell's interest-convergence thesis is the best-known contemporary exemplar of the view that major changes in blacks' racial status have come about largely through contingent convergence with white agendas.[103] The emancipation of the slaves eventuated out of sectional conflict over the future development of the country and the need to assert federal authority over the breakaway South, whereas global Cold War competition with the Soviet Union has sometimes been cited as a major factor in federal support for an end to de jure segregation.[104] Undoubtedly many white Americans were morally disturbed by slavery, but as I earlier pointed out, repudiation of slavery by no means necessarily implied a commitment to black equality. If there had been a national change of heart on the status of blacks, a genuine radical moral transformation, why would the country have permitted the postbellum black codes; the Hayes-Tilden Compromise, which essentially left blacks to the mercies of their former owners; the disappearance of the franchise; the institutionalization of Jim Crow; the thousands of unpunished lynchings? Or if *Brown* had genuinely signaled the desire, once and for all, to realize the supposed color-blind ideals, why should there have been "massive resistance" to desegregation, opposition to opening up the employment market, indifference to the fate of the black underclass when — with the postwar boom over — it became obvious that further black gains would mean white losses?

Those who take the anomaly view, of which Douglass's position is a variant, have the constant problem of devising ad hoc explanations to account for this pattern of advance and retreat. At each crucial juncture, one has to cite particular circumstances to explain the nonfulfillment of the constitutional ideal, the discrepancy between what is written down on paper and how it is interpreted, between what is said and what is enforced. Once one starts instead from the assumption that the United States has historically been, and in some ways continues to be, a racial polity, a political system predicated on nonwhite subordination, then the pattern of promise and betrayal of black liberation can be explained with an elegance and simplicity impossible for the anomalists. *The original and continuing intent has been to establish and maintain white privilege. Some manifestations of this privilege are given up while the crucial ones are retained, and progress comes largely through contingent convergence of white elite or majoritarian interests with black interests rather than independent white moral awakening.* The shifting meaning of the Constitution is then really determined by the white majority. Thus while constitutional reform is not unimportant, it is ultimately subject to a racialized interpretive logic by which federal action or inaction is determined by the assumption that the status quo of historic white privilege is neutral rather than the unfair legacy of the racial polity.[105] In Donald Lively's summary: "The jurisprudence of race over two centuries has consistently frustrated initiatives and theories that might animate the Constitution in a way that would significantly account for minority interests.... [E]qual protection [for blacks] over the course of its existence has not amounted to much more than cultural norms will allow."[106] Material changes may ultimately alter the situation—for example, the impending demographic shift to a nonwhite majority, a possible labor shortage in the coming years,[107] the increasing social costs of racism, or a transformative political project that unites nonwhites and those whites whose benefit from white supremacy is more marginal—but the role of detached moral enlightenment is unfortunately limited, and can hardly be otherwise given how racially colored the original Enlightenment was. Douglass's faith in the official institutions and ideals was misplaced, because those institutions and ideals were not race-neutral to begin with. The John Locke he invoked to proclaim his self-ownership was, after all, the same John Locke who was an investor in the Atlantic slave trade and author of the Carolina Constitution, which—in seeming contradiction to his later prescriptions in the *Second Treatise*—enshrined hereditary slavery.[108] He would have been able to explain to Douglass the hard truth that in the eyes of a racial liberalism, he was *not* fully self-owning.

I began this chapter by extracting four essential theses from Douglass's speech: that natural law is the appropriate framework for examining these moral and jurisprudential issues; that the original intent of the Framers is important, and that this intent was antislavery and anti–white supremacy; that there is an inconsistency between the actuality and the founding principles of the American polity which can be used by those agitating for change; and that therefore there are grounds for hope that blacks will eventually be accepted as full citizens. The burden of my argument is that all of these claims are false or at least need to be seriously qualified. A natural law framework hinders our understanding of the sociohistoric shaping of the law and of people's conceptions of the right. The original intent of the Framers is dubiously antislavery, is certainly not anti–white supremacy, should not be morally decisive for us, and is in any case less important as an independent causal factor than as a reflection of the white population's majoritarian racial intent. The notion of an internal inconsistency between the principles and the reality of the American polity evaporates once that polity is conceptualized, accurately, as historically a racial one, though there is an *external* inconsistency between these principles and the reality of black personhood. But whether this inconsistency can be resolved will depend on largely "material" politico-economic factors, not on an ideal juristic constitutional logic. So given the unfavorable political climate of our time, there is, at least for the near future, no reason for great optimism about the inclusion of the black population as a whole. Douglass was obviously mistaken about his own time, and more than a century after his death his prognosis has yet to be fulfilled. In short, everything Douglass said was wrong.

Why, then, should we continue to value this speech? Because aside from being a dazzling piece of oratory, it can still inspire us by its courage, moral outrage, and political intransigence. Douglass saw, correctly, that July Fourth belonged to white Americans rather than to all Americans, and his anger at this appropriation continues to resound with us. What he did not see was how old and foundational this exclusionary ownership was, the white property of differential rights at the heart of the white property-owning polity that justifies its racial architecture and shapes the moral consciousness and sense of entitlement of its white citizens. What he did not see was that the very principles to which he was appealing had themselves been precoded by race. So one can reject his analysis and be skeptical about the foundations of his optimism while still applauding his conviction and being awed by his resolution. His political illusions about white original intent are less important than his political affirmations of his own black will, the will he was not supposed to have. He stood up — this black slave who had become a black man, this piece of property who had stolen himself, this person who had repudiated his official subpersonhood — he stood up, defying white power's original and continuing intent to subordinate him, and asserted his own human intent to be free. Frederick Douglass stood up for all of us. In the end that is what counts, and that is the example we need to follow in laying equal claim to the Fourth of July.

Notes

1. Non-Cartesian *Sums*:
Philosophy and the African-American Experience

1. At that time, Leonard Harris, ed., *Philosophy Born of Struggle: Anthology of Afro-American Philosophy from 1917* (Dubuque, Iowa: Kendall/Hunt, 1983) was the main available source. Since then, John Pittman's edited special triple issue of *Philosophical Forum* 24, nos. 1–3 (Fall 1992–Spring 1993), has been issued as a book: John Pittman, ed., *African-American Perspectives and Philosophical Traditions* (New York: Routledge, 1996). Various other collections (of varying degrees of accessibility and generality) have also appeared. See, for example, Howard McGary and Bill E. Lawson, *Between Slavery and Freedom: Philosophy and American Slavery* (Bloomington: Indiana University Press, 1992); Bill Lawson, ed., *The Underclass Question* (Philadelphia: Temple University Press, 1992); Kwame Anthony Appiah, *In My Father's House: Africa in the Philosophy of Culture* (New York: Oxford University Press, 1992); Fred Lee Hord (Mzee Lasana Okpara) and Jonathan Scott Lee, eds., *I Am Because We Are: Readings in Black Philosophy* (Amherst: University of Massachusetts Press, 1995); Lucius T. Outlaw Jr., *On Race and Philosophy* (New York: Routledge, 1996); Lewis R. Gordon, ed., *Existence in Black: An Anthology of Black Existential Philosophy* (New York: Routledge, 1997). Other collections are also scheduled to appear, and this listing is not meant to be exhaustive.

2. The total population is also still very small—only about 1 percent of North American philosophers.

3. For some thoughts on this subject, see Howard McGary Jr., "Philosophy and Diversity: The Inclusion of African and African-American Materials," and Charles L. Griswold Jr., "Attracting Blacks to Philosophy," *APA Newsletter on Feminism and Philosophy* 92, no. 1 (1993), 51–55, 55–59.

4. The characterization comes from David Hoekema, former editor of *APA Proceedings and Addresses*.

5. Thomas Wartenberg, "Teaching Women Philosophy," *Teaching Philosophy* 11 (1988), 15–24.

6. See, for example, Mary Briody Mahowald, ed., *Philosophy of Woman: An Anthology of Classic and Current Concepts*, 2d ed. (1978; Indianapolis: Hackett, 1983); Susan Moller Okin, *Women in Western Political Thought* (Princeton: Princeton University Press, 1979); Diana H. Coole, *Women in Political Theory: From Ancient Misogyny to Contemporary Feminism* (Boulder, Colo.: Lynne Rienner, 1988).

7. Further research since the initial draft of this article has made me more cautious about the truth of this statement. The European idea of "wildness," which evolved from the medieval concept of the "Wild Man" to become, in the Age of Discovery, a *general* trope for representing the "uncivilized savages" of the nonwhite world being subjugated by European colonialism, may require more examination as a conceptual precursor of racism, in which case (depending in part on how one defines the term) racism *is* more theoretically central to the tradition than it may

first appear. See Edward Dudley and Maximillian E. Novak, eds., *The Wild Man Within: An Image in Western Thought from the Renaissance to Romanticism* (Pittsburgh: University of Pittsburgh Press, 1972). Note that all of the classic social contract theorists—Hobbes, Locke, Rousseau, Kant—take it for granted that Native Americans have no civilization, deeming them to be in a "state of nature" rather than part of civil society.

8. Here are some of the most frequently cited passages: Aristotle's views on "natural slaves" in the *Politics*, not, of course, aimed at Africans but ideologically very important for the ammunition that they gave both to Spanish colonizers in justifying their treatment of Native Americans and later to southern antiabolitionists in the nineteenth-century U.S. debates on slavery; David Hume's footnote in his essay "Of National Characters" judging that "the negroes, and in general all the other species of men" are "naturally inferior to the whites"; Immanuel Kant's comment in *Observations on the Feeling of the Beautiful and Sublime* that "a clear proof that what [a Negro] said was stupid" was that "this fellow was quite black from head to foot"; John Stuart Mill's procolonialist exclusion in *On Liberty* of "barbarians," "those backward states of society in which the race itself may be considered as in its nonage," from the class of human beings for whom "despotism" was not legitimate. Some examples from figures less central to the analytic tradition are G. W. F. Hegel's contemptuous description of sub-Saharan Africa in the Introduction to *The Philosophy of History;* Karl Marx and Frederick Engels's occasional remarks, usually in the correspondence rather than the theoretical works, about "niggers," and their frequent defense of European colonialism and civilization against "barbarian nations"; and, somewhat more obscure, Voltaire's endorsement in "The People of America" of polygenesis, the view that blacks were a separate species. Doubtless an industrious researcher could turn up a lot more embarrassing material, but in philosophy it is not comparable in volume or salience to the writings about women and could not plausibly be argued to be a prime deterrent of black philosophical interest. (For two excellent secondary sources, to which I am indebted for most of these references, see Thomas F. Gossett's *Race: The History of an Idea in America* [1963; New York: Schocken, 1965], and Winthrop D. Jordan, *White over Black: American Attitudes toward the Negro, 1550–1812* [1968; New York: Norton, 1977]. For an analysis, see chap. 2, "A Genealogy of Modern Racism," of Cornel West's *Prophesy Deliverance!: An Afro-American Revolutionary Christianity* [Philadelphia: Westminster Press, 1982], 47–65.) Since misunderstanding of my claim is possible here, I should expressly say that I am neither taking the historical significance of a passage to be in proportion to its length (because of the stature of Aristotle and Hume, their comments had tremendous authority and impact) nor implying that most philosophers' taciturnity on this subject means that they were *not* racist. I merely wish to show the disanalogies within philosophy between antiwoman and antiblack prejudice; the latter is manifested more in strategic silences and inconsistencies than in explicitly racist theorizing. (But see n. 7 for a qualification of this claim.)

Emmanuel Chukwudi Eze's edited volume, *Race and the Enlightenment: A Reader* (Cambridge, Mass.: Blackwell, 1997), brings together statements on race by Hume, Kant, and Hegel, as well as by some nonphilosophers. I would argue that his book vindicates my point in that only three important philosophers are excerpted, and though there is some remarkably revealing material from Kant, it is not in the moral and political works the average student is likely to encounter. The real source of the problem (minority disinterest) is not that these theorists are routinely overtly racist in their work but that since their tacit reference when they write about "people" is usually to whites, their theories are so structured as to exclude the distinctive and radically different experience of those, particularly blacks, who will *not* have been treated simply as people.

9. David Brion Davis, *The Problem of Slavery in Western Culture* (1966; New York: Oxford University Press, 1988), 108–9.

10. See, for example, Lorenne M. G. Clark, "Women and Locke: Who Owns the Apples in the Garden of Eden?" in *The Sexism of Social and Political Theory: Women and Reproduction from Plato to Nietzsche*, ed. Lorenne M. G. Clark and Lynda Lange (Toronto: University of Toronto Press, 1979), 16–40.

11. John Rawls, *A Theory of Justice* (Cambridge: Harvard University Press, 1971); Robert Nozick, *Anarchy, State, and Utopia* (New York: Basic Books, 1974).

12. See, for example, the special issue of *Teaching Philosophy* on multiculturalism in philosophy, 14, no. 2 (June 1991).

13. David Walker, *Appeal...to the Coloured Citizens of the World...*, 3d ed. (1830; Baltimore: Black Classic Press, 1993); C. L. R. James, *The Black Jacobins: Toussaint L'Ouverture and the San Domingo Revolution*, 2d ed. (1938; New York: Vintage, 1963). I should emphasize that I do *not* mean to endorse the scholarly opinion widely held at the turn of the century, and since discredited, that African culture was completely erased by the experience of slavery, so that the black mind was a tabula rasa to be written upon by the white pen. For a classic critique, see Melville J. Herskovits, *The Myth of the Negro Past* (1941; Boston: Beacon, 1990).

14. Davis, *Problem of Slavery,* pp. 223, 248.

15. Ralph Ellison, *Invisible Man* (1952; New York: Vintage, 1995).

16. Ibid., 3–4. Cf. W. E. B. Du Bois's famous image, in his 1940 autobiography, *Dusk of Dawn*, of blacks trying, as if through a "thick sheet of invisible but horribly tangible plate glass," to communicate their oppression to an indifferent white world: "They get excited; they talk louder; they gesticulate.... [But the passers-by] laugh and pass on.... Then the people within may become hysterical.... It is hard under such circumstances to be philosophical and calm, and to think through a method of approach and accommodation between castes. The entombed find themselves ... trying to make the outer world understand their essential and common humanity": W. E. B. Du Bois, "The Concept of Race," in Hord and Lee, *I Am Because We Are*, 259–60.

17. Ellison, *Invisible Man*; Richard Wright, *Native Son* (New York: Harper, 1940); James Baldwin, *Nobody Knows My Name: More Notes of a Native Son* (1961; New York: Vintage International, 1993); John A. Williams, *The Man Who Cried I Am* (Boston: Little, Brown, 1967); bell hooks, *Ain't I a Woman: Black Women and Feminism* (Boston: South End Press, 1981).

18. Gordon, Introduction to *Existence in Black*, 1–9.

19. W. E. B. Du Bois, *The Souls of Black Folk* (1903; New York: New American Library, 1969), 45.

20. Robert Birt, "Existence, Identity, and Liberation," in Gordon, *Existence in Black,* 207.

21. John S. Mbiti, *African Religions and Philosophy,* 2d ed. (Oxford: Heinemann, 1989), 141; cited in Hord and Lee, *I Am Because We Are,* 8.

22. Lewis R. Gordon, *Fanon and the Crisis of European Man: An Essay on Philosophy and the Human Sciences* (New York: Routledge, 1995), 9–10, 24, 39.

23. See Adrian Piper, "Passing for White, Passing for Black," in *Passing and the Fictions of Identity,* ed. Elaine K. Ginsberg (Durham, N.C.: Duke University Press, 1996), 234–69.

24. Naomi Zack, *Race and Mixed Race* (Philadelphia: Temple University Press, 1993); Naomi Zack, "Race, Life, Death, Identity, Tragedy, and Good Faith," in Gordon, *Existence in Black,* 99–109.

25. Zack, "Race, Life, Death," 100, 105.

26. Appiah, *In My Father's House,* and, more recently, "Race, Culture, Identity: Misunderstood Connections," in K. Anthony Appiah and Amy Gutmann, *Color Conscious: The Political Morality of Race* (Princeton: Princeton University Press, 1996), 30–105.

27. Appiah, "Race, Culture, Identity," 92, 97, 99.

28. Outlaw, *On Race and Philosophy.*

29. Immanuel Kant, *Groundwork of the Metaphysic of Morals,* trans. H. J. Paton (1948; New York: Harper Torchbooks, 1964).

30. Samuel Clemens, *Adventures of Huckleberry Finn,* Norton Critical Edition, 2d ed., ed. Sculley Bradley et al. (1962; New York: Norton, 1977), 175.

31. William Faulkner, *Intruder in the Dust* (1948; New York: Vintage International, 1991).

32. Richard Wright, "The Ethics of Living Jim Crow" (1937), in *Bearing Witness: Selections from African-American Autobiography in the Twentieth Century,* ed. Henry Louis Gates Jr. (New York: Pantheon, 1991), 39–51.

33. Lewis R. Gordon, "Existential Dynamics of Theorizing Black Invisibility," in Gordon, *Existence in Black,* 72–75. See also Gordon, *Fanon,* and Lewis R. Gordon, *Bad Faith and Antiblack Racism* (Atlantic Highlands, N.J.: Humanities Press, 1995), esp. chaps. 7 and 14.

34. Joy Ann James, "Black Feminism: Liberation Limbos and Existence in Gray," in Gordon, *Existence in Black,* 215.

35. Hord and Lee, Introduction to *I Am Because We Are,* 5.

36. See, for example, Bernard Boxill, *Blacks and Social Justice,* rev. ed. (1984; Lanham, Md.: Rowman & Littlefield, 1992); Bernard Boxill, "Two Traditions in African American Political Philosophy," in Pittman, *African-American Perspectives,* 119–35; McGary and Lawson, *Between Slavery and Freedom;* Lawson, *Underclass Question;* Bill Lawson and Frank Kirkland, eds., *Frederick Douglass: Philosopher* (Cambridge, Mass.: Blackwell, forthcoming).

37. Henry Louis Gates Jr., "Writing 'Race' and the Difference It Makes," Introduction to *"Race," Writing, and Difference,* ed. Gates (Chicago: University of Chicago Press, 1986).

38. See, for example, Toni Morrison's claim that white American literature is shaped by an unacknowledged response to "a dark, abiding, signing Africanist presence": *Playing in the Dark: Whiteness and the Literary Imagination* (Cambridge: Harvard University Press, 1992).

2. Alternative Epistemologies

1. For some discussions, see, for example, Lorraine B. Code, "Is the Sex of the Knower Epistemologically Significant?" *Metaphilosophy* 12 (1981), 267–76; Alan Soble, "Feminist Epistemology and Women Scientists," *Metaphilosophy* 14 (1983), 291–307; Sandra Harding and Merrill B. Hintikka, eds., *Discovering Reality: Feminist Perspectives on Epistemology, Metaphysics, Methodology, and Philosophy of Science* (Dordrecht: D. Reidel, 1983), esp. the essays by Jane Flax, Nancy Hartsock, and Sandra Harding; Alison M. Jaggar, *Feminist Politics and Human Nature* (Totowa, N.J.: Rowman & Allanheld, 1983), esp. chap. 11; Jean Grimshaw, *Philosophy and Feminist Thinking* (Minneapolis: University of Minnesota Press, 1986); Sandra Harding, *The Science Question in Feminism* (Ithaca: Cornell University Press, 1986); Marsha Hanen and Kai Nielsen, eds., *Science, Morality, and Feminist Theory, suppl. to Canadian Journal of Philosophy* 13 (1987). For a good overview, see Linda Alcoff and Elizabeth Potter, eds., *Feminist Epistemologies* (New York: Routledge, 1993).

2. See, for example, Leonard Harris, ed., *Philosophy Born of Struggle: Anthology of Afro-American Philosophy from 1917* (Dubuque, Iowa: Kendall/Hunt, 1983); Howard McGary Jr., "Teaching Black Philosophy," *Teaching Philosophy* 7 (1984), 129–37. (Happily, much more material is now available; see the sources listed in chap. 1, n. 1.)

3. In his 1986 statistical profile of the American Philosophical Association (APA) membership, compiled from responses on renewal notices, David Hoekema reports that of the 2,961 philosophers who responded (a 48 percent response rate), only 35 identified themselves as black. He emphasizes that a substantial number of people (719) failed to answer the question on minority status, but the figure seems significant nonetheless. Of those 35, only 3 were women. See *Proceedings and Addresses of the APA* 59 (1986), 717–23. Similarly, an APA survey on member departments yielded the information that in 1985 blacks earned only 1 percent of the Ph.D.'s in philosophy, by comparison with 3.3% rate for Ph.D.'s generally. See *Proceedings and Addresses of the APA* 61 (1987), 357–60. As with any other complex social phenomenon, racism is sustained by a plurality of causes. Thus a past history of racist practices (like the response given to the black philosopher Broadus Butler in 1952 when he applied for a job at a "white" university: "Why don't you go where you will be among your own kind?"—cited in Harris, *Philosophy Born of Struggle*, ix) obviously has a "bleaching" effect on the discipline that tends to perpetuate itself in other ways, since traditional philosophy in the academy—the ivory tower's ivory tower—then seems completely remote from black concerns and interests, and thus fails to attract potential graduate students. It is clearly significant that both McGary's and Harris's bibliographies have so few listings for philosophy journals and

that many of the most prominent black thinkers cited are not academic philosophers, at least as narrowly defined. (Since this chapter was written, the profile of blacks in the profession has improved significantly, as indicated by the number of books and anthologies published and forthcoming, the formal recognition of Africana philosophy, the launching in 1991 of the *APA Newsletter on Philosophy and the Black Experience,* and the establishment of the *Journal of Africana Philosophy.* Obviously, a tremendous distance still remains to be covered, both in numbers—blacks constitute only about 1% of North American philosophers—and in influence on the content of the discipline.)

4. The classic example of such an interpretation is, of course, George Lukacs's *History and Class Consciousness,* trans. Rodney Livingstone (1968; Cambridge: MIT Press, 1971). See esp. "Reification and the Consciousness of the Proletariat," 83–222.

5. See Jaggar, *Feminist Politics,* chap. 11.

6. David Hume, *A Treatise of Human Nature,* ed. L. A. Selby-Bigge (Oxford: Clarendon, 1888), 216, 269.

7. Soble, "Feminist Epistemology," 294.

8. Jaggar, *Feminist Politics,* 366–67.

9. Harding, *Science Question,* 179–82.

10. Abiola Irele, Introduction to Paulin J. Hountondji, *African Philosophy: Myth and Reality,* trans. Henri Evans and Jonathan Ree (1976; Bloomington: Indiana University Press, 1983), 18.

11. Harding, *Science Question,* 179.

12. Irele, *African Philosophy,* 21.

13. Steven Rose, Leon J. Kamin, and R. C. Lewontin, *Not in Our Genes: Biology, Ideology, and Human Nature* (Harmondsworth: Penguin, 1984), chap. 6.

14. See Code, "Is the Sex," 270–71, and Rose et al., *Not in Our Genes,* chap. 6.

15. Harding, *Science Question,* chap. 6.

16. For a detailed account of such an interpretation, see Russell Keat and John Urry, *Social Theory as Science,* 2d ed. (1975; London: Routledge & Kegan Paul, 1982).

17. See the discussions in Jarrett Leplin, ed., *Scientific Realism* (Berkeley: University of California Press, 1984).

18. See, for example, Barry Barnes, *Scientific Knowledge and Sociological Theory* (London: Routledge & Kegan Paul, 1974), and David Bloor, *Knowledge and Social Imagery* (London: Routledge & Kegan Paul, 1976).

19. Karl Marx, *Capital,* vol. 1 (New York: International Publishers, 1967), 59–60.

20. Jaggar, *Feminist Politics,* 6, 370.

21. Jon Elster, "Belief, Bias, and Ideology," in *Rationality and Relativism,* ed. Martin Hollis and Steven Lukes (Cambridge: MIT Press, 1982), 131.

22. Soble, "Feminist Epistemology," 302.

23. Karl Marx and Frederick Engels, *Collected Works,* vol. 3 (New York: International Publishers, 1975), 186.

24. Joseph McCarney, "Recent Interpretations of Ideology," *Economy and Society* 14 (1985), 89–90.

25. Jon Elster, *Making Sense of Marx* (New York: Cambridge University Press, 1985).

26. Bhikhu Parekh, *Marx's Theory of Ideology* (Baltimore: Johns Hopkins University Press, 1982), 18–19.

27. Sandra Harding, "Ascetic Intellectual Opportunities: Reply to Alison Wylie," in Hanen and Nielsen, *Science, Morality, and Feminist Theory*, 77.

28. Ralph Ellison, *Invisible Man* (1952; New York: Vintage, 1995), 16.

29. Elster discusses "hot" and "cold" mechanisms of cognitive distortion in *Making Sense of Marx*, 18–22.

30. Ibid., 19.

31. Marx, *Capital*, 1:176, 539–40.

32. See, for example, G. A. Cohen, "The Structure of Proletarian Unfreedom," *Philosophy and Public Affairs* 12 (1983), 3–33.

33. Elster, *Making Sense of Marx*, 474.

34. W. H. Newton-Smith, *The Rationality of Science* (Boston: Routledge & Kegan Paul, 1981), 253.

35. See the discussion of Warren Schmaus, "Reasons, Causes, and the 'Strong Programme' in the Sociology of Knowledge," *Philosophy of the Social Sciences* 15 (1985), 189–96.

36. Hilary Kornblith, ed., *Naturalizing Epistemology* (Cambridge: MIT Press, 1987), 1.

37. David-Hillel Ruben, *Marxism and Materialism: A Study in Marxist Theory of Knowledge*, 2d ed. (1977; Atlantic Highlands, N.J.: Humanities Press, 1979), 109.

38. Lorraine Code, "Second Persons," in Hanen and Nielsen, *Science, Morality and Feminist Theory*, 374–75, 377–78.

39. Richard Nisbett and Lee Ross, *Human Inference: Strategies and Shortcomings of Social Judgment* (Englewood Cliffs, N.J.: Prentice-Hall, 1983), 28–29.

40. John McMurtry, *The Structure of Marx's World-View* (Princeton: Princeton University Press, 1978), chap. 6.

41. Arthur Brittan and Mary Maynard, *Sexism, Racism, and Oppression* (Oxford: Basil Blackwell, 1984), 183.

42. Nisbett and Ross, *Human Inference*, 31.

43. William Ryan, *Blaming the Victim*, 2d ed. (1972; New York: Vintage, 1976).

44. For a good discussion, see Frank Cunningham, *Democratic Theory and Socialism* (New York: Cambridge University Press, 1987), chap. 9.

45. Jaggar, *Feminist Politics*, 307–17.

46. Sandra Harding, "Why Has the Sex/Gender System Become Visible Only Now?", in Harding and Hintikka, *Discovering Reality*, 311–24.

47. For some discussions, see, for example, Cedric J. Robinson, *Black Marxism: The Making of the Black Radical Tradition* (London: Zed, 1983); Manning Marable, "Black Studies: Marxism and the Black Intellectual Tradition," in *The Left Academy: Marxist Scholarship on American Campuses*, vol. 3, ed. Bertell Ollman and Edward Vernoff (New York: Praeger, 1986), 35–66; Bernard R. Boxill, "The Race-Class Questions," and Lucius T. Outlaw Jr., "Race and Class in the Theory and Practice of Emancipatory Social Transformation," both in Harris, *Philosophy Born of Struggle*, 107–16 and 117–29.

48. Ronaldo Munck, *The Difficult Dialogue: Marxism and Nationalism* (London: Zed, 1986), 2. See also Ephraim Nimni, "Marxism and Nationalism," in *Marxist So-*

ciology Revisited: Critical Assessments, ed. Martin Shaw (London: Macmillan, 1985), 99–142.

49. See Nimni, "Marxism and Nationalism," and Munck, *Difficult Dialogue,* chap. 1.

50. Robinson, *Black Marxism,* 451.

51. Orlando Patterson, *Slavery and Social Death: A Comparative Study* (Cambridge: Harvard University Press, 1982), 5–7.

52. Alison Wylie, "The Philosophy of Ambivalence: Sandra Harding on *The Science Question in Feminism,"* in Hanen and Nielsen, *Science, Morality, and Feminist Theory,* 65.

53. See, for example, Cary Nelson and Lawrence Grossberg, eds., *Marxism and the Interpretation of Culture* (Urbana: University of Illinois Press, 1988), where several articles seem to take this connection for granted.

54. Jaggar, *Feminist Politics,* 384.

55. Grimshaw, *Philosophy and Feminist Thinking,* 84–85.

56. See Soble, "Feminist Epistemology."

57. See, for example, Angela Davis, *Women, Race, and Class* (New York: Random House, 1981), esp. chap. 11, which discusses Susan Brownmiller's *Against Our Will: Men, Women, and Rape* (New York: Simon & Schuster, 1975); bell hooks, *Ain't I a Woman: Black Women and Feminism* (Boston: South End Press, 1981); Gloria T. Hull, Patricia Bell Scott, and Barbara Smith, eds., *All the Women Are White, All the Blacks Are Men, But Some of Us Are Brave: Black Women's Studies* (Old Westbury, N.Y.: Feminist Press, 1982). For more recent work, see Patricia Hill Collins, *Black Feminist Thought: Knowledge, Consciousness, and the Politics of Empowerment* (1990; New York: Routledge, 1991).

3. "But What Are You *Really?*" The Metaphysics of Race

1. As simply illustrated, for example, by the title— *Being and Race*—of novelist Charles Johnson's book on recent black American fiction. Charles Johnson, *Being and Race: Black Writing since 1970* (Bloomington: Indiana University Press, 1988).

2. See, for example, Howard McGary and Bill E. Lawson, *Between Slavery and Freedom: Philosophy and American Slavery* (Bloomington: Indiana University Press, 1992); Kwame Anthony Appiah, *In My Father's House: Africa in the Philosophy of Culture* (New York: Oxford University Press, 1992); Naomi Zack, *Race and Mixed Race* (Philadelphia: Temple University Press, 1993); Naomi Zack, ed., *American Mixed Race: The Culture of Microdiversity* (Lanham, Md.: Rowman and Littlefield, 1995); Lewis R. Gordon, *Bad Faith and Antiblack Racism* (Atlantic Highlands, N.J.: Humanities Press, 1995); John Pittman, ed., *African-American Perspectives and Philosophical Traditions* (New York: Routledge, 1996); Lucius T. Outlaw Jr., *On Race and Philosophy* (New York: Routledge, 1996); Lewis R. Gordon, ed., *Existence in Black: An Anthology of Black Existential Philosophy* (New York: Routledge, 1997).

3. "Ideal" here, of course, has no moral connotations, just meaning "model," a system that has the virtue of being well designed to carry out its designated end. In that spirit, one could speak about an ideal concentration camp or an ideal instrument of torture.

4. Physical and aesthetic criteria may also be employed and have certainly been of great historical significance. As late as the 1936 Berlin Olympics, for example, Hitler's intention was that Aryan superiority be demonstrated by German domination of the games (an intention defeated by the four gold medals of the black American sprinter Jesse Owens). But in a modern technological society, achievements of strength and speed become increasingly less important, so that the subordinate races may be granted a higher standing on this dimension, indeed as a positive indicator of their closer proximity to the animal kingdom. See, for example, John M. Hoberman, *Darwin's Athletes: How Sport Has Damaged Black America and Preserved the Myth of Race* (Boston: Houghton-Mifflin, 1997).

5. Andrew Hacker, *Two Nations: Black and White, Separate, Hostile, Unequal* (New York: Charles Scribner's Sons, 1992); Derrick Bell, *Faces at the Bottom of the Well: The Permanence of Racism* (New York: Basic Books, 1992); Douglas S. Massey and Nancy A. Denton, *American Apartheid: Segregation and the Making of the Underclass* (Cambridge: Harvard University Press, 1993); Donald R. Kinder and Lynn M. Sanders, *Divided by Color: Racial Politics and Democratic Ideals* (Chicago: University of Chicago Press, 1996).

6. See the very useful discussion in Appiah, *In My Father's House,* chap. 1.

7. Ibid., 13. In part, the issue is simply about how we're going to use words and the fuzziness of *racism* as a term. Certainly, it could be argued that *any* differentiation in presumed moral, intellectual, characterological, or spiritual traits among human "racial" groups counts as racism, even if R1s' greater intelligence is supposed to be counterbalanced by R2s' deeper spiritual capacity (as in nineteenth-century romantic racialism, for example). The issue does not usually arise because most racists have judged their group to be superior on all the important dimensions of appraisal, or at least those seen as characteristically mental and thus paradigmatically human. (As earlier noted, physical ability in the inferior race—strength, speed, reflexes, natural rhythm—is less threatening.) But certainly it is possible to imagine a group being stigmatized as more intelligent but of dubious character: think of some traditional racist representations of Jews, for example.

8. See, for example, F. James Davis, *Who Is Black? One Nation's Definition* (University Park, Pa.: Pennsylvania State University Press, 1991).

9. David O. Brink, *Moral Realism and the Foundations of Ethics* (New York: Cambridge University Press, 1989), 19–20.

10. Michael Omi and Howard Winant, *Racial Formation in the United States: From the 1960s to the 1980s* (New York: Routledge and Kegan Paul, 1986); Theodore W. Allen, *The Invention of the White Race,* vol. 1, *Racial Oppression and Social Control* (New York: Verso, 1994); Ian F. Haney López, "The Social Construction of Race," in *Critical Race Theory: The Cutting Edge,* ed. Richard Delgado (Philadelphia: Temple University Press, 1995), 191–203; Ian F. Haney López, *White by Law: The Legal Construction of Race* (New York: New York University Press, 1996).

11. See, for example, Frank B. Livingstone, "On the Nonexistence of Human Races" (1962), rpt. in *The "Racial" Economy of Science: Toward a Democratic Future,* ed. Sandra Harding (Bloomington: Indiana University Press, 1993), 133–41, and the special issue of *Discovery,* November 1994, "Race: What Is It Good For?"

12. See, for example, David Roediger, *The Wages of Whiteness: Race and the Making of the American Working Class* (New York: Verso, 1991).

13. See, for example, many of the essays in Dominick LaCapra, ed., *The Bounds of Race: Perspectives on Hegemony and Resistance* (Ithaca: Cornell University Press, 1991).

14. I will later argue, however, that in some circumstances individual choice *does* make a difference, though certain "objective" prerequisites have to be met first.

15. J. L. Mackie, *Ethics: Inventing Right and Wrong* (Harmondsworth, Middlesex: Penguin, 1977).

16. John Locke, *An Essay Concerning Human Understanding,* ed. Roger Woolhouse (New York: Penguin, 1997), 302–14.

17. Marvin Harris, *Patterns of Race in the Americas* (New York: W. W. Norton, 1964).

18. In a course on African-American philosophy I taught some years ago, it became clear to me that my black students saw this as a testimony to the superior strength of blackness. In other words, "black blood" was viewed as a kind of super-concentrated solution, any drops of which would remain triumphantly undiluted even by gallons upon gallons of the feebler white stuff. What had been intended as a stigma, "pollution," had been inverted, redefined as "power."

19. George M. Fredrickson, *White Supremacy: A Comparative Study in American and South African History* (New York: Oxford University Press, 1981), 96–97.

20. For example, Charles W. Chesnutt, *The House Behind the Cedars* (1900; New York: Penguin, 1993); James Weldon Johnson, *The Autobiography of an Ex-Colored Man* (1912; New York: Penguin, 1990); Nella Larsen, *Passing,* in *Quicksand and Passing,* ed. Deborah E. McDowell (1928, 1929; New Brunswick, N.J.: Rutgers University Press, 1986); Langston Hughes, "Passing," in *The Ways of White Folks* (1933; New York: Vintage Classics, 1990), 51–55; and the whole "tragic mulatto" literature, some of it made into films, e.g., *Pinky* (1949), and *Imitation of Life* (1934, 1959).

21. Walter White, *A Man Called White: The Autobiography of Walter White* (Bloomington: Indiana University Press, 1948).

22. For a fascinating account of Broyard's life of deception, see Henry Louis Gates Jr., "White Like Me," *New Yorker,* June 17, 1996, 66–81.

23. And it poses the following puzzle: consider two individuals of different temperaments who both pass successfully over the course of their lifetimes, but with one person having experienced apprehension all throughout the masquerade while the other, more self-confident, never gave the possibility of discovery a moment's thought. Would their achievement/nonachievement of whiteness then turn on this phenomenological difference?

24. Mark Twain, *Pudd'nhead Wilson* (New York: Bantam Classic, 1981).

25. Gregory Howard Williams, *Life on the Color Line: The True Story of a White Boy Who Discovered He was Black* (New York: Dutton, 1995).

26. George Schuyler, *Black No More: Being an Account of the Strange and Wonderful Workings of Science in the Land of the Free,* A.D. *1933–1940* (1931; Boston: Northeastern University Press, 1989). Schuyler was one of the leading lights of the Harlem Renaissance.

27. Norman Mailer, "The White Negro: Superficial Reflections on the Hipster," in Mailer, *Advertisements for Myself* (New York: G. P. Putnam's Sons, 1959), 337–58.

28. John Howard Griffin, *Black Like Me,* thirty-fifth anniversary edition (1961; New York: Signet, 1996). The jacket copy claims sales of ten million copies.

29. See, for example, Kathy Russell, Midge Wilson, and Ronald Hall, *The Color Complex: The Politics of Skin Color Among African Americans* (New York: Harcourt Brace Jovanovich, 1992).

30. For a collection of writings on the subject, see Zack, ed., *American Mixed Race.* Linda Alcoff gives a personal and philosophical exploration of the issue in her "Mestizo Identity," ibid., 257–78.

31. Davis, *Who Is Black?,* 136–37.

32. Naomi Zack, "An Autobiographical View of Mixed Race and Deracination," *APA Newsletter on the Black Experience* 91, no. 1 (1992), 9.

4. Dark Ontologies: Blacks, Jews, and White Supremacy

1. Kant's place in the history of ethics has, of course, long been secure. He is "arguably the most important moral philosopher in the modern period": Roger J. Sullivan, *Immanuel Kant's Moral Theory* (New York: Cambridge University Press, 1989), xiii. His dramatic rise in stature in Anglo-American *political* theory is more recent, originally stimulated by the Kantian themes in the book usually credited with reviving postwar Western political philosophy, John Rawls's *A Theory of Justice* (Cambridge: Harvard University Press, 1971). We can track the trajectory over the past quarter-century by comparing Hans Reiss's Introduction to his first edition (1968) of Kant's political writings with his Postscript to the second edition (1989): "Kant, at least in English-speaking countries, is not generally considered to be a political philosopher of note"; "Kant's standing as a political thinker has been substantially enhanced in the English-speaking world since this volume went to the printers just over two decades ago. More and more scholars are willing to rank him among the leading figures in the history of political thought": Hans Reiss, ed., *Kant: Political Writings,* 2d ed., trans. H. B. Nisbet (1970; New York: Cambridge University Press, 1991), 3, 250.

2. An anthology of articles, with illustrations from the exhibition, accompanies it: *Bridges and Boundaries: African Americans and American Jews,* ed. Jack Salzman with Adina Back and Gretchen Sullivan Sorin (New York: George Braziller/Jewish Museum, 1992). See also Paul Berman, ed., *Blacks and Jews: Alliances and Arguments* (New York: Delacorte, 1994). An older but still valuable collection is Nat Hentoff, ed., *Black Anti-Semitism and Jewish Racism* (New York: Richard W. Baron, 1969). Some of the articles in the Salzman anthology date back to the 1940s, demonstrating how longstanding the issue really is. See, for example, Kenneth B. Clark, "Candor about Negro-Jewish Relations" (1946), in Salzman, *Bridges and Boundaries,* 91–98.

3. "Kant has rightly been called the philosopher of the French Revolution" (Reiss, *Kant,* 3), though paradoxically he rejected the right to revolution (ibid., Postscript, sec. VII).

4. Sullivan, *Kant's Moral Theory,* 197.

5. Immanuel Kant, *Groundwork of the Metaphysic of Morals,* trans. H. J. Paton (1948; New York: Harper & Row, 1964); Immanuel Kant, *The Metaphysics of Morals,* trans. Mary Gregor (New York: Cambridge University Press, 1991). One needs to distinguish "ideal Kantianism" from Kant's own views, since, as Reiss reminds us, Kant had "a very narrow conception ... of what kind of individuals can be expected to achieve maturity and autonomy of political judgment," a conception that in fact excludes the majority of the population (Reiss, *Kant,* 257). For Kant's relegation of women to the status of "passive citizens," see Susan Mendus, "Kant: 'An Honest but Narrow-Minded Bourgeois'?" in *Essays on Kant's Political Philosophy,* ed. Howard Lloyd Williams (Chicago: University of Chicago Press, 1992), 166–90.

6. *The Philosophy and Opinions of Marcus Garvey,* ed. Amy Jacques-Garvey, 2 vols. (1923–25; New York: Atheneum, 1992); E. David Cronon, *Black Moses: The Story of Marcus Garvey and the Universal Negro Improvement Association,* 2d ed. (1955; Madison: University of Wisconsin Press, 1969); John Henrik Clarke, ed., *Marcus Garvey and the Vision of Africa* (New York: Vintage, 1974); Rupert Lewis and Patrick Bryan, eds., *Garvey: His Work and Impact* (Kingston, Jamaica: ISER, University of the West Indies, 1988).

7. Rex Nettleford, "Garvey's Legacy: Some Perspectives," in Lewis and Bryan, *Garvey,* 312.

8. V. G. Kiernan, *The Lords of Human Kind: Black Man, Yellow Man, and White Man in an Age of Empire* (1969; New York: Columbia University Press, 1986).

9. C. Vann Woodward, *The Strange Career of Jim Crow,* 3d ed. (1955; New York: Oxford University Press, 1974); George M. Fredrickson, *White Supremacy: A Comparative Study in American and South African History* (New York: Oxford University Press, 1981).

10. Edward W. Said, *Culture and Imperialism* (New York: Knopf, 1993), 8.

11. Frantz Fanon, *The Wretched of the Earth,* trans. Constance Farrington (1961; New York: Grove Press, 1968).

12. Stephen Jay Gould, *The Mismeasure of Man* (New York: Norton, 1981).

13. For a discussion of the enterprise of "naturalizing" ethics, see Alvin I. Goldman, "Ethics and Cognitive Science," *Ethics* 103 (1993), 337–60.

14. Philip D. Curtin, Introduction to *Imperialism* (New York: Walker, 1971), xiii; Pierre L. van den Berghe, *Race and Racism: A Comparative Perspective,* 2d ed. (1967; New York: Wiley, 1978).

15. Van den Berghe, *Race and Racism,* 18. The "democracy" is, of course, further qualified by exclusions of gender. Note that van den Berghe has political sympathies with sociobiology, which I do not share, and which I believe can be detached from the useful notion of a "*Herrenvolk.*" For me, this is a sociopolitical category rather than a natural one.

16. The judgment of the German anthropologist Wilhelm Mühlmann, *Geschichte der Anthropologie* (Frankfurt am Main, 1968), 57, quoted in Léon Poliakov, "Racism from the Enlightenment to the Age of Imperialism," in *Racism and Colonialism,* ed. Robert Ross (The Hague: Martinus Nijhoff, 1982), 59.

17. Immanuel Kant, *Observations on the Feeling of the Beautiful and Sublime,* trans. John T. Goldthwait (Berkeley: University of California Press, 1960), 111–13.

18. David Theo Goldberg, *Racist Culture: Philosophy and the Politics of Meaning* (Cambridge, Mass.: Blackwell, 1993), 32, 241, n. 45.

19. Immanuel Kant, "On the Different Races of Man," in *Race and the Enlightenment: A Reader,* ed. Emmanuel Chukwudi Eze (Cambridge, Mass.: Blackwell, 1997), 38–48. See also the other selections from Kant's writings excerpted ibid, 49–70.

20. George L. Mosse, *Toward the Final Solution: A History of European Racism* (1978; Madison: University of Wisconsin Press, 1985), 31. See also Kant's 1785 "Bestimmung des Begriffs einer Menschenrasse," in *Gesammelte Schriften,* Ausgabe der Königlichen Preussischen Akademie, vol. 8 (Berlin: Walter de Gruyter, 1923), 89–106.

21. Emmanuel Eze, "The Color of Reason: The Idea of 'Race' in Kant's Anthropology," in *Anthropology and the German Enlightenment: Perspectives on Humanity,* ed. Katherine M. Faull (Lewisburg, Pa.: Bucknell University Press, 1995), 196–237. Eze cites an earlier essay by Christian Neugebauer, "The Racism of Kant and Hegel," in *Sage Philosophy: Indigenous Thinkers and Modern Debate on African Philosophy,* ed. H. Odera Oruka (Leiden: E. J. Brill, 1990), 259–72. One of Neugebauer's main sources is a German compilation by E. Henscheid, *Der Neger* (Frankfurt am Main, 1985).

22. Eze, "Color of Reason," 209–19, 217.

23. This is not to say that Kant would necessarily have endorsed all the practices of European domination. In one passage of *The Metaphysics of Morals,* for example, he characterizes as a "vacuum" those lands "uninhabited by civilized people" but peopled rather by "savages" (American Indians, Hottentots, the inhabitants of New Holland) not in "a rightful condition." But though he understands the temptation for Europeans "to found colonies" by force or fraud and thus "establish a civil union with them," thereby fulfilling "the end of creation," he explicitly repudiates "this veil of injustice (Jesuitism), which would sanction any means to good ends" (*Metaphysics of Morals,* 86–87). So the question of the extent to which Kant could be categorized as a "*Herrenvolk* Kantian" is too complex to be resolved here and would require a systematic survey of his writings that confronted rather than ignored and evaded the role race plays in his moral/political theory and philosophy of history. A defender might argue that his polarized moral universe, divided simply between persons and nonpersons, leaves no conceptual room for subpersons, and that as long as a basement level of rationality has been achieved, nonwhites would count as full persons. But the racial hierarchy cited above raises questions. Feminists have long pointed out that the introduction of the "active citizen/passive citizen" distinction shows how easily the formal commitment to respect for all persons can be deprived of content; see Mendus, "Kant" (n. 5 above). The characteristics Kant lists as typical of passive citizens — lack of civil personality, dependence on the will of others, inequality (e.g., *Metaphysics of Morals,* 126) — would certainly all have been seen as completely applicable to the status of blacks in the New World.

24. Reference throughout, of course, is to European Jews. Lewis Gordon points out to me that the traditional framing of the issue ("blacks and Jews") ignores the

existence of those Jews who are black. See, for example, Howard Brotz, *The Black Jews of Harlem: Negro Nationalism and the Dilemma of Negro Leadership* (1964; New York: Schocken, 1970).

25. Richard Nisbett and Lee Ross, *Human Inference: Strategies and Shortcomings of Social Judgment* (Englewood Cliffs, N.J.: Prentice-Hall, 1980). See also the opening chapters of Paul Thagard's *Conceptual Revolutions* (Princeton: Princeton University Press, 1992), in which he emphasizes the importance of conceptual change in belief revision.

26. Mosse, *Toward the Final Solution,* ix, 231.

27. Léon Poliakov, *The Aryan Myth: A History of Racist and Nationalist Ideas in Europe,* trans. Edmund Howard (1971; New York: Basic Books, 1974), 5.

28. Theodore W. Allen, *The Invention of the White Race,* vol. 1, *Racial Oppression and Social Control* (New York: Verso, 1994).

29. In the famous judgment of Frank B. Livingstone, "There are no races, there are only clines [continuously varying phenotypical traits]": "On the Nonexistence of Human Races," in *The "Racial" Economy of Science: Toward a Democratic Future,* ed. Sandra Harding (Bloomington: Indiana University Press, 1993), 133–41.

30. For a discussion, see, for example, Cornel West, "A Genealogy of Modern Racism," in *Prophesy Deliverance!: An Afro-American Revolutionary Christianity* (Philadelphia: Westminster Press, 1982), 47–65, and Lucius T. Outlaw Jr., *On Race and Philosophy* (New York: Routledge, 1996), esp. chaps. 7 and 8.

31. David Hume, footnote to the 1753–54 edition of his essay "Of National Characters," first published in 1748, included in Eze, *Race and the Enlightenment,* 30–33. Voltaire, "The People of America," quoted in Thomas F. Gossett, *Race: The History of an Idea in America* (1963; New York: Schocken, 1965), 44–45. G. W. F. Hegel, Introduction to *The Philosophy of History,* trans. John Sibree (New York: Dover, 1956), 91–99, and in Eze, *Race and the Enlightenment,* 109–53.

32. Martin Bernal, *Black Athena: The Afroasiatic Roots of Classical Civilization,* vol. 1, *The Fabrication of Ancient Greece, 1785–1985* (New Brunswick, N.J.: Rutgers University Press, 1987).

33. See, for example, Winthrop D. Jordan, *White over Black: American Attitudes toward the Negro, 1550–1812* (1968; New York: Norton, 1977).

34. Ibid. Joel Kovel, *White Racism: A Psychohistory* (1970; New York: Columbia University Press, 1984).

35. Jan Nederveen Pieterse, *White on Black: Images of Africa and Blacks in Western Popular Culture* (New Haven: Yale University Press, 1992). Those more sympathetic to politico-economic explanations, however, such as Pieterse himself, argue that there are clear temporal shifts in the Western iconography of blacks, and that universally negative images come to prevail only after a certain period (the rise of the Atlantic slave trade).

36. Oliver Cox, *Caste, Class, and Race* (New York: Modern Reader, 1948); Cedric J. Robinson, *Black Marxism: The Making of the Black Radical Tradition* (London: Zed, 1983); David Roediger, *The Wages of Whiteness: Race and the Making of the American Working Class* (New York: Verso, 1991).

37. Kirkpatrick Sale, *The Conquest of Paradise: Christopher Columbus and the Columbian Legacy* (New York: Knopf, 1990); David E. Stannard, *American Holocaust: The Conquest of the New World* (New York: Oxford University Press, 1992).

38. Kiernan, *Lords of Human Kind.*

39. Jordan, *White over Black,* 254.

40. Mosse, *Toward the Final Solution,* 14.

41. Salzman, *Bridges and Boundaries,* 183–85.

42. For example, Nathan Glazer and Daniel Patrick Moynihan, *Beyond the Melting Pot,* 2d ed. (Cambridge: MIT Press, 1970). For a critique, see Stephen Steinberg, *The Ethnic Myth: Race, Ethnicity, and Class in America,* rev. ed. (Boston: Beacon, 1989), and *Turning Back: The Retreat from Racial Justice in American Thought and Policy* (Boston: Beacon, 1995).

43. Douglas S. Massey and Nancy A. Denton, *American Apartheid: Segregation and the Making of the Underclass* (Cambridge: Harvard University Press, 1993).

44. Laurence Mordekhai Thomas, *Vessels of Evil: American Slavery and the Holocaust* (Philadelphia: Temple University Press, 1993).

45. Apart from the authors actually cited, these points have been derived variously from the three anthologies mentioned earlier — Hentoff, *Black Anti-Semitism and Jewish Racism;* Salzman, *Bridges and Boundaries;* Berman, *Blacks and Jews* (esp. Julius Lester, "The Lives People Live," 164–77) — and my own thoughts on the matter.

46. Cronon, *Black Moses.*

47. Bruce Wright, *Black Robes, White Justice* (New York: Lyle Stuart, 1987), 53.

48. See, for example, Sander L. Gilman, *Smart Jews: The Construction of the Image of Jewish Superior Intelligence* (Lincoln: University of Nebraska Press, 1996).

49. Between 1972 and 1989, the average household income of Jewish Americans was 1.55 times the U.S. national average. Blacks, by contrast, were near the bottom, at 0.68 of the national average. National Opinion Research Center, *Cumulative General Social Survey, 1972–1989,* cited in Christopher Jencks, *Rethinking Social Policy: Race, Poverty, and the Underclass* (Cambridge: Harvard University Press, 1992), 28.

50. Laurence Thomas, "Group Autonomy and Narrative Identity: Blacks and Jews," in Berman, *Blacks and Jews,* 286–303.

51. In a personal conversation, however, Roger Gottlieb has argued that the narrative structure of the multiple Academy Award–winning *Schindler's List* (1993) tacitly testifies to the power of continuing anti-Semitism in that the focus is on the morally agonized German, whereas the Jews whose story it should really be are basically a backdrop.

52. I am indebted to my colleague Sandra Bartky for reminding me of this.

53. Donald Bogle, *Toms, Coons, Mulattoes, Mammies and Bucks: An Interpretive History of Blacks in American Films,* rev. ed. (New York: Continuum, 1989). See also, more recently, Daniel Bernardi, ed., *The Birth of Whiteness: Race and the Emergence of U.S. Cinema* (New Brunswick, N.J.: Rutgers University Press, 1996), and Michael Rogin, *Blackface, White Noise: Jewish Immigrants in the Hollywood Melting Pot* (Berkeley: University of California Press, 1996).

54. Richard J. Herrnstein and Charles Murray, *The Bell Curve: Intelligence and Class Structure in American Life* (New York: Free Press, 1994), endorses a basically hereditarian analysis of the well-documented fact that the average score for blacks on IQ tests is about one standard deviation (15 points) below the average score for whites. Note also — with respect to point 9 of the "differences" between blacks and Jews — the authors' observation (275) that "Jews — specifically, Ashkenazi Jews of European origins — test higher than any other ethnic group." For a critique of *The Bell Curve*, see Russell Jacoby and Naomi Glauberman, eds., *The Bell Curve Debate: History, Documents, Opinions* (New York: Random House, 1995).

55. Mosse, *Toward the Final Solution*, 235–36.

56. Kant, *Metaphysics of Morals*, 230–31.

57. See, for example, Bernard R. Boxill, "Self-Respect and Protest," in *Philosophy Born of Struggle: Anthology of Afro-American Philosophy from 1917*, ed. Leonard Harris (Dubuque, Iowa: Kendall/Hunt, 1983), 190–98, and Michele M. Moody-Adams, "Race, Class, and the Social Construction of Self-Respect," in *African-American Perspectives and Philosophical Traditions*, ed. John Pittman (New York: Routledge, 1996), 251–66.

58. Noel Ignatiev, *How the Irish Became White* (New York: Routledge, 1995); Karen Brodkin Sacks, "How Did Jews Become White Folks?" in *Race,* ed. Steven Gregory and Roger Sanjek (New Brunswick, N.J.: Rutgers University Press, 1994), 78–102.

59. Cornel West, "On Black-Jewish Relations," in West, *Race Matters* (Boston: Beacon, 1993), 101–16.

60. See Rogin, *Blackface, White Noise*.

61. Fredric Jameson, *Postmodernism, or, The Cultural Logic of Late Capitalism* (Durham, N.C.: Duke University Press, 1991), 38.

62. Gary K. Okihiro, *Margins and Mainstreams: Asians in American History and Culture* (Seattle: University of Washington Press, 1994), 120, and, more generally, chap. 5, "Perils of the Body and Mind."

63. Gary B. Nash and Richard Weiss, eds., *The Great Fear: Race in the Mind of America* (New York: Holt, Rinehart & Winston, 1970).

64. Lothrop Stoddard, *The Rising Tide of Color against White World-Supremacy* (New York: Scribner's, 1920). For a discussion, see Gossett, *Race*, chap. 15. As Gossett points out (397), Stoddard's book makes a brief appearance in F. Scott Fitzgerald's *The Great Gatsby* (1926; New York: Penguin, 1950), 18, disguised as *The Rise of the Colored Empires* by one "Goddard."

65. Patricia A. Turner, *I Heard It through the Grapevine: Rumor in African-American Culture* (Berkeley: University of California Press, 1993).

66. Nisbett and Ross, *Human Inference*.

67. James Baldwin, "Negroes Are Anti-Semitic Because They're Anti-White," *New York Times Magazine*, April 9, 1967, rpt. in Berman, *Blacks and Jews*, 31–41.

68. Sullivan, *Kant's Moral Theory,* app. I. But see Nancy Sherman, *Making a Necessity of Virtue: Aristotle and Kant on Virtue* (New York: Cambridge University Press, 1997), for the view that the traditional hyper-rationalist picture of Kantian ethics is misleading, and fails to appreciate the significance of his writings on moral psychology.

69. In his opinion in the 1978 Supreme Court case of *Regents of the University of California* v. *Bakke,* Justice Blackmun made the subsequently oft-quoted observation that "in order to get beyond racism, we must first take into account race."

70. Onora O'Neill, "Justice, Gender, and International Boundaries," in *The Quality of Life,* ed. Martha Nussbaum and Amartya Sen (Oxford: Clarendon, 1993), 303–23.

71. Rabbi Alan W. Miller, "Black Anti-Semitism—Jewish Racism," in Hentoff, *Black Anti-Semitism,* 101.

72. Nat Hentoff, Introduction to *Black Anti-Semitism,* xvii.

5. Revisionist Ontologies: Theorizing White Supremacy

1. Emmanuel Chukwudi Eze, ed., *Race and the Enlightenment: A Reader* (Cambridge, Mass.: Blackwell, 1997), represents an important start toward remedying this situation.

2. For a discussion, see, for example, Alison M. Jaggar, *Feminist Politics and Human Nature* (Totowa, N.J.: Rowman & Allanheld, 1983).

3. George M. Fredrickson, *White Supremacy: A Comparative Study in American and South African History* (New York: Oxford University Press, 1981); John W. Cell, *The Highest Stage of White Supremacy: The Origins of Segregation in South Africa and the American South* (New York: Cambridge University Press, 1982).

4. V. G. Kiernan, *The Lords of Human Kind: Black Man, Yellow Man, and White Man in an Age of Empire* (1969; New York: Columbia University Press, 1981); Edward W. Said, *Culture and Imperialism* (New York: Knopf, 1993).

5. Walter Rodney, "Black Power: A Basic Understanding" (1969), in *I Am Because We Are: Readings in Black Philosophy,* ed. Fred Lee Hord (Mzee Lasana Okpara) and Jonathan Scott Lee (Amherst: University of Massachusetts Press, 1995), 183.

6. For U.S. data, see, for example, Andrew Hacker, *Two Nations: Black and White, Separate, Hostile, Unequal* (New York: Scribner's, 1992).

7. Kimberlé Williams Crenshaw, "Race, Reform, and Retrenchment: Transformation and Legitimation in Antidiscrimination Law," *Harvard Law Review* 101 (1988), 1336.

8. Minority Rights Group, *No Longer Invisible: Afro-Latin Americans Today* (London, 1995); Frances Winddance Twine, *Racism in a Racial Democracy: The Maintenance of White Supremacy in Brazil* (New Brunswick: Rutgers University Press, 1998).

9. See, for example, Richard Delgado, ed., *Critical Race Theory: The Cutting Edge* (Philadelphia: Temple University Press, 1995); Kimberlé Crenshaw, Neil Gotanda, Gary Peller, and Kendall Thomas, eds., *Critical Race Theory: The Key Writings That Formed the Movement* (New York: New Press, 1995).

10. *Race Traitor: A Journal of the New Abolitionism;* for a collection of articles from it, see *Race Traitor,* ed. Noel Ignatiev and John Garvey (New York: Routledge, 1996).

11. David Roediger, *The Wages of Whiteness: Race and the Making of the American Working Class* (New York: Verso, 1991); Theodore W. Allen, *The Invention of the White Race,* vol. 1, *Racial Oppression and Social Control* (New York: Verso, 1994).

12. Immanuel Kant, *Groundwork of the Metaphysic of Morals,* trans. H. J. Paton (1948; New York: Harper & Row, 1964).

13. See, for example, Susan Moller Okin, *Women in Western Political Thought* (Princeton: Princeton University Press, 1979), and Lorenne Clark and Lynda Lange, eds., *The Sexism of Social and Political Theory: Women and Reproduction from Plato to Nietzsche* (Toronto: University of Toronto Press, 1979).

14. John Rawls, *A Theory of Justice* (Cambridge: Harvard University Press, 1971).

15. See, for example, Douglas S. Massey and Nancy A. Denton, *American Apartheid: Segregation and the Making of the Underclass* (Cambridge: Harvard University Press, 1993), for an account of the mechanisms by which de facto U.S. segregation continues to be maintained many years after the passage of the Fair Housing Act in 1968.

16. Rawls, *Theory of Justice.*

17. Susan Moller Okin, *Justice, Gender, and the Family* (New York: Basic Books, 1989), esp. chaps. 1 and 7.

18. In a more detailed treatment one would, of course, look at internal differentiations within the nonwhite population. My statement here is meant to be programmatic, drawing what I take to be the central line of conceptual demarcation.

19. Frantz Fanon, *Black Skin, White Masks,* trans. Charles Lam Markmann (1952; New York: Grove Press, 1967), 8.

20. Frantz Fanon, *The Wretched of the Earth,* trans. Constance Farrington (1961; New York: Grove Press, 1968), 38–42.

21. Cited in Fredrickson, *White Supremacy,* 155.

22. "*Dred Scott v. Sanford, 1857,*" in *Race, Class, and Gender in the United States: An Integrated Study,* ed. Paula S. Rothenberg, 3d ed. (New York: St. Martin's Press, 1995), 323.

23. Bill Lawson, "Moral Discourse and Slavery," in *Between Slavery and Freedom: Philosophy and American Slavery,* by Howard McGary and Bill E. Lawson (Bloomington: Indiana University Press, 1992), 72–76.

24. Richard Drinnon, *Facing West: The Metaphysics of Indian-Hating and Empire-Building* (New York: Meridian, 1980), xvii–xviii.

25. Richard Wright, "The Ethics of Living Jim Crow: An Autobiographical Sketch" (1937), in *Bearing Witness: Selections from African-American Autobiography in the Twentieth Century,* ed. Henry Louis Gates Jr. (New York: Pantheon, 1991), 39–51.

26. Bernard R. Boxill, "The Fight with Covey," in *Existence in Black: An Anthology of Black Existential Philosophy,* ed. Lewis R. Gordon (New York: Routledge, 1997), 276.

27. Winthrop D. Jordan, *White over Black: American Attitudes toward the Negro, 1550–1812* (1968; New York: Norton, 1977); Robert Berkhofer Jr., *The White Man's Indian: Images of the American Indian from Columbus to the Present* (New York: Knopf, 1978).

28. Gordon Lewis, *Main Currents in Caribbean Thought* (Kingston, Jamaica: Heinemann, 1983), 225.

29. Rex Nettleford, Introduction to Joseph Owens, *Dread: The Rastafarians of Jamaica* (Kingston, Jamaica: Sangster's, 1976), xiv–xv.

30. Lewis Hanke, *Aristotle and the American Indians: A Study in Race Prejudice in the Modern World* (Bloomington: Indiana University Press, 1959).

31. Robert Young, *White Mythologies: Writing History and the West* (London: Routledge, 1990); J. M. Blaut, *The Colonizer's Model of the World: Geographical Diffusionism and Eurocentric History* (New York: Guilford Press, 1993).

32. David E. Stannard, *American Holocaust: The Conquest of the New World* (New York: Oxford University Press, 1992), x.

33. Valentin Y. Mudimbe, *The Invention of Africa: Gnosis, Philosophy, and the Order of Knowledge* (Bloomington: Indiana University Press, 1988).

34. Horace Campbell, *Rasta and Resistance: From Marcus Garvey to Walter Rodney* (Trenton, N.J. Africa World Press, 1987).

35. Fanon, *Black Skin, White Masks*, 18.

36. Ngugi wa Thiong'o, *Decolonising the Mind: The Politics of Language in African Literature* (London: James Currey, 1986).

37. John Jacob Thomas, *The Theory and Practice of Creole Grammar* (1869).

38. Mervyn Alleyne, *Roots of Jamaican Culture* (London: Pluto Press, 1988), chap. 6.

39. Velma Pollard, *Dread Talk: The Language of Rastafari* (Kingston, Jamaica: Canoe Press, University of the West Indies, 1994).

40. Albert Murray, *The Omni-Americans: New Perspectives on Black Experience and American Culture* (New York: Outerbridge & Dienstfrey, 1970), cited in Shelley Fisher Fishkin, "Interrogating 'Whiteness,' Complicating 'Blackness': Remapping American Culture," *American Quarterly* 47 (1995), 428–66.

41. In "Interrogating 'Whiteness'" Fishkin provides a valuable overview of research on the remarkable degree of cultural interrelatedness.

42. Lucius Outlaw Jr., "Africology: Normative Theory," in Outlaw, *On Race and Philosophy* (New York: Routledge, 1996), 97–134.

43. Kathy Russell, Midge Wilson, and Ronald Hall, *The Color Complex: The Politics of Skin Color among African Americans* (New York: Harcourt Brace Jovanovich, 1992); Jan Nederveen Pieterse, *White on Black: Images of Africa and Blacks in Western Popular Culture* (New Haven: Yale University Press, 1992).

44. Kobena Mercer, "Black Hair/Style Politics" (1987), in Mercer, *Welcome to the Jungle: New Positions in Black Cultural Studies* (New York: Routledge, 1994), 97–128.

45. For example, Sebastian Clarke (drawing on Fanon) argues that in Jamaican rock steady, "the dancer could remain on his spot of earth, shake his shoulders, make pounding motions with his arms and hands (at an invisible enemy, an anonymous force), without recourse to or consciousness of a partner. The internal tension was demonstratively and explosively released": *Jah Music: The Evolution of the Popular Jamaican Song* (London: Heinemann, 1980), 81.

46. Lewis Gordon, *Bad Faith and Antiblack Racism* (Atlantic Highlands, N.J.: Humanities Press, 1995), 99.

47. See, for example, Joseph M. Murphy, *Working the Spirit: Ceremonies of the African Diaspora* (Boston: Beacon, 1994), and Paget Henry, "African and Afro-Caribbean Existential Philosophies," in Gordon, *Existence in Black*, 13–36.

48. Chandra Mohanty, Ann Russo, and Lourdes Torres, eds., *Third World Women and the Politics of Feminism* (Bloomington: Indiana University Press, 1991).

49. Fanon, *Black Skin, White Masks*.

50. Patricia Hill Collins, *Black Feminist Thought: Knowledge, Consciousness, and the Politics of Empowerment* (New York: Routledge, 1991); Joy Ann James, "Black Feminism: Liberation Limbos and Existence in Gray," in Gordon, *Existence in Black*, 215–24.

6. The Racial Polity

1. See, for example, the following works in, respectively, cultural studies, labor history, American literature, film theory, sociology, philosophy, history of science, gender studies, legal theory: Henry Louis Gates Jr., ed., *"Race," Writing, and Difference* (Chicago: University of Chicago Press, 1986); David R. Roediger, *The Wages of Whiteness: Race and the Making of the American Working Class* (New York: Verso, 1991) and *Towards the Abolition of Whiteness* (New York: Verso, 1994); Toni Morrison, *Playing in the Dark: Whiteness and the Literary Imagination* (Cambridge: Harvard University Press, 1992); Eric J. Sundquist, *To Wake the Nations: Race in the Making of American Literature* (Cambridge: Belknap/Harvard University Press, 1993); Daniel Bernardi, ed., *The Birth of Whiteness: Race and the Emergence of Cinema* (New Brunswick: Rutgers University Press, 1996); Michelle Fine, Lois Weis, Linda C. Powell, and L. Mun Wong, eds., *Off White: Readings on Race, Power, and Society* (New York: Routledge, 1997); David Theo Goldberg, *Racist Culture: Philosophy and the Politics of Meaning* (Cambridge, Mass.: Blackwell, 1993); Lewis R. Gordon, *Bad Faith and Antiblack Racism* (Atlantic Highlands, N.J.: Humanities Press, 1995); Lucius T. Outlaw Jr., *On Race and Philosophy* (New York: Routledge, 1996); Sandra Harding, ed., *The "Racial" Economy of Science: Toward a Democratic Future* (Bloomington: Indiana University Press, 1993); Ruth Frankenberg, *White Women, Race Matters: The Social Construction of Whiteness* (Minneapolis: University of Minnesota Press, 1993); Ian F. Haney López, *White by Law: The Legal Construction of Race* (New York: New York University Press, 1996); Richard Delgado, ed., *Critical Race Theory: The Cutting Edge* (Philadelphia: Temple University Press, 1995); Kimberlé Crenshaw, Neil Gotanda, Gary Peller, and Kendall Thomas, eds., *Critical Race Theory: The Key Writings That Formed the Movement* (New York: New Press, 1995).

2. But note that the same could be said about feminist theory. "Feminism, like most broad-based philosophical perspectives, accommodates several species under its genus": Rosemarie Tong, *Feminist Thought: A Comprehensive Introduction* (Boulder, Colo.: Westview, 1989), 1.

3. See Delgado, *Critical Race Theory*, and Crenshaw et al., *Critical Race Theory*. Some years ago, the African-American philosopher Lucius Outlaw Jr. called for a "critical theory" of race in "Toward a Critical Theory of 'Race,'" in *Anatomy of Racism*, ed. David Theo Goldberg (Minneapolis: University of Minnesota Press, 1990), 58–82. The "critical" in "critical race theory" has more than one meaning, signifying both the scare-quotes sense in which "race" is used and also (as in Outlaw) the general notion of a "critical theory" of society that seeks both to understand and transform it. "Critical white studies" can be seen as an offshoot of critical race theory that focuses specifically on whiteness.

4. Robert Blauner, *Racial Oppression in America* (New York: Harper & Row, 1972), 12–13.

5. Robert E. Goodin and Philip Pettit, eds., *A Companion to Contemporary Political Philosophy* (Cambridge: Basil Blackwell, 1993). In their Introduction (3), the editors state, "Nationalism—still less racism, sexism or ageism—does not figure [here], on the grounds that it hardly counts as a principled way of thinking about things." But the oppositional nationalism of subordinated groups and nations surely needs to be distinguished from the characteristically chauvinistic nationalism of hegemonic powers.

6. For some overviews and discussions, see Lorenne M. G. Clark and Lynda Lange, eds., *The Sexism of Social and Political Theory: Women and Reproduction from Plato to Nietzsche* (Toronto: University of Toronto Press, 1979); Susan Moller Okin, *Women in Western Political Thought* (Princeton: Princeton University Press, 1979); Alison Jaggar, *Feminist Politics and Human Nature* (Totowa, N.J.: Rowman & Allanheld, 1983); Diana H. Coole, *Women in Political Theory: From Ancient Misogyny to Contemporary Feminism* (Boulder, Colo.: Lynne Rienner, 1988); Susan Moller Okin, *Justice, Gender, and the Family* (New York: Basic Books, 1989).

7. Olympe de Gouges, "Declaration of the Rights of Woman and Citizen," in *European Women: A Documentary History, 1789–1945*, ed. Eleanor S. Riemer and John C. Font (New York: Schocken, 1980); Mary Wollstonecraft, *A Vindication of the Rights of Men; with A Vindication of the Rights of Woman and Hints*, ed. Sylvana Tomaselli (New York: Cambridge University Press, 1995); Simone de Beauvoir, *The Second Sex*, ed. and trans. H. M. Parshley (1949; New York: Knopf, 1953).

8. See, for example; Cornel West, "A Genealogy of Modern Racism," chap. 2 of *Prophesy Deliverance!: An Afro-American Revolutionary Christianity* (Philadelphia: Westminster Press, 1982), 47–65; Goldberg, *Racist Culture;* Lucius Outlaw Jr., "The Future of 'Philosophy' in America," chap. 8 of *On Race and Philosophy*, 183–204.

9. See, for example, Mary Briody Mahowald, ed., *Philosophy of Woman: An Anthology of Classic and Current Concepts*, 2d ed. (1978; Indianapolis: Hackett, 1983), and Linda Bell, *Visions of Women* (Clifton, N.J.: Humana Press, 1983). An important start has been made with Emmanuel Chukwudi Eze, ed., *Race and the Enlightenment: A Reader* (Cambridge, Mass.: Blackwell, 1997). Eze points out that "whereas feminist critics have extensively examined the gender-inflected nature of eighteenth-century science and philosophy, a similar critical engagement is lacking in the area of race" (8).

10. Jean Hampton, *Political Philosophy* (Boulder, Colo.: Westview, 1997), xiii–xv.

11. Jaggar, *Feminist Politics.*

12. Jane Mansbridge and Susan Moller Okin, "Feminism," in Goodin and Pettit, *Companion to Contemporary Political Philosophy*, 269.

13. Coole, *Women in Political Theory*, 259.

14. Okin, *Women in Western Political Thought*, 10.

15. Martin Delany, 1852 writings, quoted in Imanuel Geiss, *The Pan-African Movement: A History of Pan-Africanism in America, Europe, and Africa*, trans. Ann Keep (1968; New York: Africana, 1974), 164.

16. W. E. B. Du Bois, "To the Nations of the World," in *W. E. B. Du Bois: A Reader*, ed. David Levering Lewis (New York: Henry Holt, 1995), 639.

17. Frantz Fanon, *The Wretched of the Earth*, trans. Constance Farrington (1961; New York: Grove Press, 1968), 40.

18. C. L. R. James, *The Black Jacobins: Toussaint L'Ouverture and the San Domingo Revolution* (1938; New York: Vintage, 1963), 283.

19. Gary Y. Okihiro, *Margins and Mainstreams: Asians in American History and Culture* (Seattle: University of Washington Press, 1994), 129–33; Paul Gilroy, *The Black Atlantic: Modernity and Double Consciousness* (Cambridge: Harvard University Press, 1993), ix, 17, 27.

20. W. E. B. Du Bois, "The Souls of White Folk," in Lewis, *W. E. B. Du Bois,* 454.

21. Eric Williams, *Capitalism and Slavery* (1944; New York: Capricorn, 1966); E. L. Jones, *The European Miracle* (New York: Cambridge University Press, 1981). For a defense of this "Third Worldist" perspective, see J. M. Blaut et al., *1492: The Debate on Colonialism, Eurocentrism, and History* (Trenton, N.J.: Africa World Press, 1992) and *The Colonizer's Model of the World: Geographical Diffusionism and Eurocentric History* (New York: Guilford, 1993).

22. Blaut, *Colonizer's Model,* 59.

23. David Hume, footnote added in the 1753–54 edition of his essay "Of National Characters," first published in 1748; cited in Eze, *Race and the Enlightenment,* 33.

24. It is through Martin Bernal's *Black Athena: The Afroasiatic Roots of Classical Civilization,* vol. 1, *The Fabrication of Ancient Greece, 1785–1985* (New Brunswick: Rutgers University Press, 1987) that the challenge to conventional histories of Greek civilization first became known to a mass white readership. But the claim is much older in the oppositional ("vindicationist") black tradition, going back, in fact, to the nineteenth century. See, for example, Cheikh Anta Diop, *The African Origin of Civilization: Myth or Reality,* ed. and trans. Mercer Cook (1955, 1967; Westport, Conn.: Lawrence Hill, 1974).

25. James, *Black Jacobins,* 47.

26. Edward W. Said, *Culture and Imperialism* (New York: Knopf, 1993), 53–59.

27. Gilroy, *Black Atlantic,* 49, 9, 7.

28. For an expansion of this argument, see Charles W. Mills, *The Racial Contract* (Ithaca: Cornell University Press, 1997). Cf. James Tully, *Strange Multiplicity: Constitutionalism in an Age of Diversity* (New York: Cambridge University Press, 1995), chap. 3.

29. Tully, *Strange Multiplicity,* 64–65, 78–79.

30. George M. Fredrickson, *White Supremacy: A Comparative Study in American and South African History* (New York: Oxford University Press, 1981).

31. For critiques of mainstream sociology, see, for example, Blauner, *Racial Oppression in America;* David T. Wellman, *Portraits of White Racism,* 2d ed. (New York: Cambridge University Press, 1993); Stephen Steinberg, *Turning Back: The Retreat from Racial Justice in American Thought and Policy* (Boston: Beacon, 1995).

32. Wellman, *Portraits of White Racism,* 39.

33. W. E. B. Du Bois, *Black Reconstruction in America, 1860–1880* (1935; New York: Atheneum, 1992); St. Clair Drake and Horace R. Cayton, *Black Metropolis: A Study of Negro Life in a Northern City* (1945; Chicago: University of Chicago Press, 1993).

34. Michael C. Dawson and Ernest J. Wilson III, "Paradigms and Paradoxes: Political Science and African-American Politics," in *Political Science: Looking to the Future*, vol. 1, *The Theory and Practice of Political Science*, ed. William Crotty (Evanston, Ill.: Northwestern University Press, 1991), 189.

35. Rogers M. Smith, "Beyond Tocqueville, Myrdal, and Hartz: The Multiple Traditions in America," *American Political Science Review* 87 (1993), 549, 557.

36. John Rawls, *A Theory of Justice* (Cambridge: Harvard University Press, 1971); Robert Nozick, *Anarchy, State, and Utopia* (New York: Basic Books, 1974).

37. Nozick, *Anarchy, State, and Utopia*, chap. 7, n. 2.

38. Louis Hartz (with contributions by others), *The Founding of New Societies: Studies in the History of the United States, Latin America, South Africa, Canada, and Australia* (New York: Harcourt, Brace & World, 1964). Hartz speaks of "the fragments of Europe" in the New World.

39. Francis Jennings, *The Invasion of America: Indians, Colonialism, and the Cant of Conquest* (New York: Norton, 1976); Theodore W. Allen, *The Invention of the White Race*, vol. 1, *Racial Oppression and Social Control* (New York: Verso, 1994); Pierre L. van den Berghe, *Race and Racism: A Comparative Perspective*, 2d ed. (New York: Wiley, 1978); Alexander Saxton, *The Rise and Fall of the White Republic* (New York: Verso, 1990); Roediger, *Wages of Whiteness* (the phrase originally comes from Du Bois's *Black Reconstruction*); Donald R. Kinder and Lynn M. Sanders, *Divided by Color: Racial Politics and Democratic Ideals* (Chicago: University of Chicago Press, 1996); Andrew Hacker, *Two Nations: Black and White, Separate, Hostile, Unequal* (New York: Scribner's, 1992); Cheryl I. Harris, "Whiteness as Property," *Harvard Law Review* 106 (1993), 1709–91.

40. See Jennifer L. Hochschild, *The New American Dilemma: Liberal Democracy and School Desegregation* (New Haven: Yale University Press, 1984), chap. 1.

41. See, for example, Stokely Carmichael and Charles V. Hamilton, *Black Power: The Politics of Liberation in America* (New York: Vintage, 1967).

42. Jennings, *Invasion of America*.

43. George M. Fredrickson, *Black Liberation: A Comparative History of Black Ideologies in the United States and South Africa* (New York: Oxford University Press, 1995), 15.

44. Delgado, Introduction to *Critical Race Theory*, xiv.

45. Herbert Blumer, "Race Prejudice as a Sense of Group Position," *Pacific Sociological Review* 1, no. 1 (Spring 1958), 3–4. See also van den Berghe, *Race and Racism*.

46. Allen, *Invention of the White Race*.

47. Ian F. Haney López, "The Social Construction of Race," in Delgado, *Critical Race Theory*, 191–203.

48. The fact that it is (perceived) group rather than individual interests that are the main determinant of white and black attitudes is one of the central and most important findings of Kinder and Sanders's *Divided by Color*.

49. Ian F. Haney López, "White by Law," in Delgado, *Critical Race Theory*, 547.

50. Ian F. Haney López, *White by Law: The Legal Construction of Race* (New York: New York University Press, 1996).

51. Noel Ignatiev, *How the Irish Became White* (New York: Routledge, 1995); Elaine K. Ginsberg, ed., *Passing and the Fictions of Identity* (Durham, N.C.: Duke University Press, 1996), esp. Adrian Piper, "Passing for White, Passing for Black," 234–69.

52. Du Bois, *Black Reconstruction.*

53. Derrick Bell, "Property Rights in Whiteness: Their Legal Legacy, Their Economic Costs" (1988), in Delgado, *Critical Race Theory,* 75–83; Harris, "Whiteness as Property"; George Lipsitz, "The Possessive Investment in Whiteness: Racialized Social Democracy and the 'White' Problem in American Studies," *American Quarterly* 47 (1995), 369–87.

54. For details, see, for example, Melvin L. Oliver and Thomas M. Shapiro, *Black Wealth/White Wealth: A New Perspective on Racial Inequality* (New York: Routledge, 1995); Douglas S. Massey and Nancy A. Denton, *American Apartheid: Segregation and the Making of the Underclass* (Cambridge: Harvard University Press, 1993); Hacker, *Two Nations.*

55. Oliver and Shapiro, *Black Wealth/White Wealth,* 51.

56. Henry Louis Taylor Jr., "The Hidden Face of Racism," *American Quarterly* 47 (1995), 397.

57. Obviously, there is a greatly differentiated class and gender benefit. A full treatment, which is beyond the scope of this book, would require the analysis of these differentials within the white population and the possible opening they offer for progressive social change.

58. Oliver and Shapiro, *Black Wealth/White Wealth,* 18.

59. Mary Frances Berry, *Black Resistance, White Law: A History of Constitutional Racism in America* (1971; New York: Allen Lane, 1994); Desmond King, *Separate and Unequal: Black Americans and the U.S. Federal Government* (Oxford: Clarendon, 1995).

60. Massey and Denton, *American Apartheid;* Hacker, *Two Nations;* Steinberg, *Turning Back;* Kinder and Sanders, *Divided by Color.* The quoted words are from *Divided by Color,* 34, 252, 287.

7. White Right: The Idea of a *Herrenvolk* Ethics

1. See, for example, Alvin I. Goldman, "Ethics and Cognitive Science," *Ethics* 103 (1993), 337–60, and Larry May, Marilyn Friedman, and Andy Clark, eds., *Mind and Morals: Essays on Cognitive Science and Ethics* (Cambridge: MIT Press, 1996). This issue should not be confused with the older debate on naturalism or nonnaturalism about the metaphysics of value, for example, whether the good should be identified with pleasure or a transcendental Platonic Form. "Naturalization" here has to do with cognition and justification. As May, Friedman, and Clark summarize the new program in their Introduction, "Contemporary moral naturalism is largely meta-ethical naturalism" (3).

2. See, for example, Hilary Kornblith, ed., *Naturalizing Epistemology,* 2d ed. (Cambridge: MIT Press, 1994).

3. Philip Kitcher, "The Naturalists Return," *Philosophical Review* 101 (1992), 53–114.

4. Ibid., 58–59, 64–65.

5. The terms originally come from cognitive psychology, from the work of such theorists as Leon Festinger and Amos Tversky.

6. There is no room to defend this thesis here, but Marx can illuminatingly be seen (*avant la lettre*) as a conservative "naturalized epistemologist." Most postmodernists, by contrast, are methodologically radical in that they characteristically repudiate or deny the possibility of objectivism.

7. Kitcher, "Naturalists Return," 82–83.

8. Owen Flanagan, "Ethics Naturalized: Ethics as Human Ecology," in May et al., *Mind and Morals,* 30, 39.

9. See, for example, George M. Fredrickson, *White Supremacy: A Comparative Study in American and South African History* (New York: Oxford University Press, 1981).

10. bell hooks, "Overcoming White Supremacy: A Comment," in hooks, *Talking Back: Thinking Feminist, Thinking Black* (Boston: South End Press, 1989), 112–19.

11. Frances Lee Ansley, "Stirring the Ashes: Race, Class, and the Future of Civil Rights Scholarship," *Cornell Law Review* 74 (1989), 1024n.

12. For critiques of the "racism is dead" view, see, for example, Douglas S. Massey and Nancy A. Denton, *American Apartheid: Segregation and the Making of the Underclass* (Cambridge: Harvard University Press, 1993); Stephen Steinberg, *Turning Back: The Retreat from Racial Justice in American Thought and Policy* (Boston: Beacon, 1995); Donald R. Kinder and Lynn M. Sanders, *Divided by Color: Racial Politics and Democratic Ideals* (Chicago: University of Chicago Press, 1996).

13. General Social Survey, University of Chicago.

14. Fredrickson, *White Supremacy,* xi–xiii.

15. Kinder and Sanders, *Divided by Color,* 6–7.

16. Ibid.

17. Gunnar Myrdal, *An American Dilemma: The Negro Problem and Modern Democracy* (1944; New York: Harper & Row, 1969).

18. As I explained in Chapter 3, I am taking for granted throughout the standard left "constructionist" view of race. Generalizations about "whites" are then to be read not as essentialist biological assertions but as shorthand for a more cumbersome locution— "those individuals whose phenotype/genealogy entitles them to be socially categorized as 'white' within a system of white/nonwhite racial hierarchy."

19. Jennifer L. Hochschild, *The New American Dilemma: Liberal Democracy and School Desegregation* (New Haven: Yale University Press, 1984), 1.

20. Ibid., chap. 1.

21. Derrick Bell, *Faces at the Bottom of the Well: The Permanence of Racism* (New York: Basic Books, 1992); Andrew Hacker, *Two Nations: Black and White, Separate, Hostile, Unequal* (New York: Scribner's, 1992).

22. Rogers M. Smith, "Beyond Tocqueville, Myrdal, and Hartz: The Multiple Traditions in America," *American Political Science Review* 87 (1993), 549–66. See also the follow-up discussion, "Beyond Tocqueville, Please!": comment by Jacqueline Stevens, reply by Rogers Smith, ibid. 89 (1995), 987–95.

23. Virginia Held, "Whose Agenda? Ethics versus Cognitive Science," in May et al., *Mind and Morals,* 69.

24. May et al., Introduction to *Mind and Morals*, 7. Cf. here my points in Chapter 2 on the usefulness for radicals of "naturalizing" epistemology.

25. Lewis Gordon gives a detailed and valuable analysis of racism as bad faith in his *Bad Faith and Antiblack Racism* (Atlantic Highlands, N.J.: Humanities Press, 1995). I would certainly not deny the role of such "hot" cognitive factors. My point is rather that explanation in "cold" terms is also possible. In many cases, presumably, both factors will be at work, so that one should see these two explanation-schemas as complementary rather than competing.

26. Goldman, "Ethics and Cognitive Science," 337–38.

27. Mark Johnson, "How Moral Psychology Changes Moral Theory," in May et al., *Mind and Morals*, 49.

28. See Paul M. Churchland, "The Neural Representation of the Social World," ibid., 100–105, and Andy Clark, "Connectionism, Moral Cognition, and Collaborative Problem Solving," ibid., 110–14.

29. James Oakes, *The Ruling Race: A History of American Slaveholders* (New York: Vintage, 1983), 30.

30. Jean-Paul Sartre, Preface to Frantz Fanon, *The Wretched of the Earth*, trans. Constance Farrington (1961; New York: Grove Press, 1968), 26.

31. Norman Daniels, Preface to *Reading Rawls: Critical Studies on Rawls' "A Theory of Justice"* (1975; Stanford: Stanford University Press, 1989).

32. Cheryl I. Harris, "Whiteness as Property," *Harvard Law Review* 106 (1993), 1709–91.

33. David T. Wellman, *Portraits of White Racism*, 2d ed. (1977; New York: Cambridge University Press, 1993), 53.

34. Kinder and Sanders, *Divided by Color*, 92.

35. Joe R. Feagin and Melvin P. Sikes, *Living with Racism: The Black Middle-Class Experience* (Boston: Beacon, 1994), 1.

36. Gregory Howard Williams, *Life on the Color Line: The True Story of a White Boy Who Discovered He Was Black* (New York: Dutton, 1995).

37. David Roediger cites John Bukowczyk on the category of the "not-yet-white" European ethnic: *Towards the Abolition of Whiteness* (New York: Verso, 1994), 181–98. See also Noel Ignatiev, *How the Irish Became White* (New York: Routledge, 1995).

38. Goldman, "Ethics and Cognitive Science." See also Robert M. Gordon, "Sympathy, Simulation, and the Impartial Spectator," in May et al., *Mind and Morals*, pp. 165–80.

39. Lillian Smith, *Killers of the Dream* (1949; New York: Norton, 1994), 69, 84, 27–29.

40. W. E. B. Du Bois, "The Concept of Race" (1940), in *I Am Because We Are: Readings in Black Philosophy*, ed. Fred Lee Hord (Mzee Lasana Okpara) and Jonathan Scott Lee (Amherst: University of Massachusetts Press, 1995), 259.

41. C. L. R. James, *The Black Jacobins: Toussaint L'Ouverture and the San Domingo Revolution* (1938; New York: Vintage, 1963), 33–34.

42. Bell, *Faces*, epigraph, v.

43. David R. Roediger, *The Wages of Whiteness: Race and the Making of the American Working Class* (New York: Verso, 1991), 49.

44. Edmund S. Morgan, *American Slavery, American Freedom: The Ordeal of Colonial Virginia* (New York: Norton, 1975), 4; Roediger, *Wages of Whiteness*, 20.

45. Samuel Clemens, *Adventures of Huckleberry Finn*, Norton Critical Edition, ed. Sculley Bradley et al., 2d ed. (New York: Norton, 1977), 168–70. For a discussion, see Jonathan Bennett, "The Conscience of Huckleberry Finn," *Philosophy* 49 (1974), 123–43.

46. Francis Jennings, *The Invasion of America: Indians, Colonialism, and the Cant of Conquest* (New York: Norton, 1976), 15, 71.

47. John Locke, *Two Treatises of Government*, ed. Peter Laslett (1960; New York: Cambridge University Press, 1988), *First Treatise*, para. 67.

48. Jennifer Welchman, "Locke on Slavery and Inalienable Rights," *Canadian Journal of Philosophy* 25 (1995), 67–81.

49. Locke, *Second Treatise*, para. 124.

50. Michael C. Dawson, *Behind the Mule: Race and Class in African-American Politics* (Princeton: Princeton University Press, 1994), 51–53.

51. Harris, "Whiteness as Property."

52. Ibid., 1713, 1753.

53. Goldman, "Ethics and Cognitive Science," 349.

54. Cited in Joe R. Feagin and Hernán Vera, *White Racism: The Basics* (New York: Routledge, 1995), 145.

55. Kinder and Sanders, *Divided by Color*, 264. They cite the work of Samuel Stouffer and W. G. Runciman.

8. Whose Fourth of July? Frederick Douglass and "Original Intent"

1. "The Meaning of July Fourth for the Negro," in *The Life and Writings of Frederick Douglass*, ed. Philip S. Foner, 5 vols. (New York: International Publishers, 1950–75), 2:181–204 (henceforth cited as *Douglass*). (In William L. Andrews, ed., *The Oxford Frederick Douglass Reader* [New York: Oxford University Press, 1996], the speech is anthologized under the title "What to the Slave Is the Fourth of July?") It was published later the same year in pamphlet form as *Oration, Delivered in Corinthian Hall, Rochester, July 5th, 1852*.

2. Andrews, *Douglass Reader*, 108.

3. See, for example, Bernard Boxill, "Two Traditions in African American Political Philosophy," in *African-American Perspectives and Philosophical Traditions*, ed. John Pittman (New York: Routledge, 1996), 119–35.

4. Andrew Hacker, *Two Nations: Black and White, Separate, Hostile, Unequal* (New York: Scribner's, 1992); Donald R. Kinder and Lynn M. Sanders, *Divided By Color: Racial Politics and Democratic Ideals* (Chicago: University of Chicago Press, 1996). Hacker's title comes, of course, from the famous judgment of the Kerner Commission appointed by President Lyndon Johnson to investigate the causes of the 1960s race riots: the warning that the United States was "moving toward two societies, one black, one white—separate and unequal." One might quarrel with a characterization that suggested by implication a (mythical) unified and equal past, but at any rate there is no doubt that this warning has been largely vindicated.

"In neighborhoods across the country, blacks and whites are separated more completely now than they were at the turn of the century.... To a remarkable extent, white and black Americans live physically separate lives.... In the extreme, blacks and whites look upon the social and political world in fundamentally different and mutually unintelligible ways": Kinder and Sanders, *Divided by Color,* 286–88.

5. All quotations are from *Douglass,* 2:181–204.

6. See Steven Butterfield, *Black Autobiography in America* (Amherst: University of Massachusetts Press, 1977), 32, 47–64, cited in Rafia Zahar, "Franklinian Douglass: The Afro-American as Representative Man," in *Frederick Douglass: New Literary and Historical Essays,* ed. Eric J. Sundquist (New York: Cambridge University Press, 1990), 116 n.

7. Shelley Fisher Fishkin and Carla L. Peterson, " 'We Hold These Truths to Be Self-Evident': The Rhetoric of Frederick Douglass's Journalism," in Sundquist, *Frederick Douglass,* 189–204.

8. For this reason, John Hope Franklin gets Douglass wrong when he says that, in the July 5 speech, Douglass "found no consolation even in the words of the Declaration of Independence": "Race and the Constitution in the Nineteenth Century," in *African Americans and the Living Constitution,* ed. John Hope Franklin and Genna Rae McNeil (Washington, D.C.: Smithsonian Institution Press, 1995), 26.

9. See Boxill, "Two Traditions."

10. Waldo E. Martin Jr., "Images of Frederick Douglass in the Afro-American Mind: The Recent Black Freedom Struggle," in Sundquist, *Frederick Douglass,* 276–78.

11. Waldo E. Martin Jr., *The Mind of Frederick Douglass* (Chapel Hill: University of North Carolina Press, 1984).

12. For an overview of different positions, see, for example, the readings collected in August Meier, Elliot Rudwick, and Francis L. Broderick, eds., *Black Protest Thought in the Twentieth Century,* 2d ed. (New York: Macmillan, 1971).

13. Martin, "Images of Frederick Douglass," 280–83; Wilson J. Moses, "Writing Freely? Frederick Douglass and the Constraints of Racialized Writing," in Sundquist, *Frederick Douglass,* 78–81.

14. Thurgood Marshall, "Racial Justice and the Constitution: A View from the Bench," in Franklin and McNeil, *Living Constitution,* 317.

15. Kenneth Clark, "Black Power Is a Sour Grapes Phenomenon," 1967 address to the convention of the Association for the Study of Negro Life and History, in Meier et al., *Black Protest Thought,* 610–21.

16. Kenneth B. Clark, "Racial Progress and Retreat: A Personal Memoir," in *Race in America: The Struggle for Equality,* ed. Herbert Hill and James E. Jones Jr. (Madison: University of Wisconsin Press, 1993), 18.

17. See Elizabeth Mensch, "The History of Mainstream Legal Thought," in *The Politics of Law: A Progressive Critique,* ed. David Kairys, 2d ed. (New York: Pantheon, 1990), 13–37.

18. A. P. d'Entrèves, *Natural Law: An Introduction to Legal Philosophy,* 2d ed. (London: Hutchinson, 1970).

19. Ibid., 79, 110.

20. Cicero, *De republica,* III, xxii, 33, cited ibid., 25.

21. D'Entreves, *Natural Law,* 26.

22. See, for an introductory discussion, Jeffrie G. Murphy and Jules L. Coleman, *Philosophy of Law: An Introduction to Jurisprudence* (Boulder, Colo.: Westview, 1990), chap. 1.

23. D'Entrèves, *Natural Law,* 79.

24. Allan C. Hutchinson, ed., *Critical Legal Studies* (Totowa, N.J.: Rowman & Littlefield, 1989); Richard Delgado, ed., *Critical Race Theory: The Cutting Edge* (Philadelphia: Temple University Press, 1995); Kimberlé Crenshaw, Neil Gotanda, Gary Peller, and Kendall Thomas, eds., *Critical Race Theory: The Key Writings That Formed the Movement* (New York: New Press, 1995).

25. Meese called for a return to original intent as part of the Reagan administration's rollback of civil rights progress in the 1980s; see Julius L. Chambers, "Afterword: Racial Equality and Full Citizenship, the Unfinished Agenda," in Franklin and McNeil, *Living Constitution,* 319–35. In fact, Meese actually cited Douglass approvingly in a speech at Dickinson College in 1985; see Harry V. Jaffa, "Attorney General Meese, the Declaration, and the Constitution," in *Original Intent and the Framers of the Constitution: A Disputed Question,* ed. Harry V. Jaffa (Washington, D.C.: Regnery Gateway, 1994), 55–73.

26. My account here and below follows Gregory Bassham, *Original Intent and the Constitution: A Philosophical Study* (Lanham, Md.: Rowman & Littlefield, 1992).

27. Ibid., 2.

28. Bruce Ledewitz, "Judicial Conscience and Natural Rights: A Reply to Professor Jaffa," in Jaffa, *Original Intent,* 110.

29. Bassham, *Original Intent,* 29, 34–35. The quotes are not exact but my synopsis of his position.

30. Cass R. Sunstein, *The Partial Constitution* (Cambridge: Harvard University Press, 1993), 93.

31. Cited in Bertell Ollman and Jonathan Birnbaum, eds., *The United States Constitution: 200 Years of Anti-Federalist, Abolitionist, Feminist, Muckraking, Progressive, and Especially Socialist Criticism* (New York: New York University Press, 1990), 96.

32. "Letter to Gerrit Smith," in *Douglass,* 2:149–50.

33. George W. Crockett Jr., "Remembering Litigation, Protest, and Politics in Mississippi during the Civil Rights Movement," in Franklin and McNeil, *Living Constitution,* 93.

34. Marshall, "Racial Justice," 317.

35. "Change of Opinion Announced," in *Douglass,* 2:155.

36. "The Meaning of July Fourth for the Negro," in *Douglass,* 2:202.

37. "The Claims of Our Common Cause," in *Douglass,* 2:261.

38. "The Kansas-Nebraska Bill," in *Douglass,* 2:317. Cf. "The Reproach and Shame of the American Government," in *Douglass,* 5:401–2.

39. "The True Ground upon Which to Meet Slavery," in *Douglass,* 2:368.

40. "The *Dred Scott* Decision," in *Douglass,* 2:418–20.

41. "Essay #3 by Brutus," in Ollman and Birnbaum, *United States Constitution,* 85.

42. William M. Wiecek, *The Sources of Antislavery Constitutionalism in America, 1760–1848* (Ithaca: Cornell University Press, 1977), 75–76.

43. Ibid., 62–63.

44. Kinder and Sanders, *Divided by Color,* chaps. 8–9.

45. A. Leon Higginbotham Jr., *In the Matter of Color: Race and the American Legal Process: The Colonial Period* (New York: Oxford University Press, 1978).

46. Ian F. Haney López, *White by Law: The Legal Construction of Race* (New York: New York University Press, 1996). Though it was modified in various ways over the years, this act was not fully repealed until 1952.

47. "The Constitution and Slavery," in *Douglass,* 1:361–67.

48. See, for example, Houston A. Baker Jr., *Modernism and the Harlem Renaissance* (Chicago: University of Chicago Press, 1987).

49. Paul Laurence Dunbar, "We Wear the Mask," cited in Baker, *Modernism,* 39.

50. See chap. 2, "Abolitionism: The Travail of a 'Great Life's Work,' " in Martin, *Mind of Frederick Douglass.*

51. Jennifer L. Hochschild, *The New American Dilemma: Liberal Democracy and School Desegregation* (New Haven: Yale University Press, 1984), chap. 1.

52. Cited in Higginbotham, *Matter of Color,* 377, 380.

53. Gunnar Myrdal, *An American Dilemma: The Negro Problem and Modern Democracy* (New York: Harper, 1944), lxix–lxxi.

54. For an excerpt of the crucial passages of the decision, see, for example, "*Dred Scott* v. *Sanford,* 1857," in *Race, Class, and Gender in the United States: An Integrated Study,* ed. Paula S. Rothenberg, 3d ed. (New York: St. Martin's Press, 1995), 322–25, and for the definitive discussion, Don E. Fehrenbacher, *The Dred Scott Case: Its Significance in American Law and Politics* (New York: Oxford University Press, 1978). The defendant, John Sanford, had his name misspelled as "Sandford" in the official report, and the spelling has varied ever since.

55. "*Dred Scott,*" in Rothenberg, *Race, Class, and Gender,* 323–24.

56. "The *Dred Scott* Decision," in *Douglass,* 2:411.

57. "Position of the Government toward Slavery," in *Douglass,* 3:105.

58. Jaffa, *Original Intent.*

59. Jaffa, "Original Intent and Justice Rehnquist," ibid., 103.

60. Jaffa, "Are These Truths Now, or Have They Ever Been, Self-Evident?" ibid., p. 78.

61. "[T]he idea that each person matters equally is at the heart of all plausible [modern] political theories": Will Kymlicka, *Contemporary Political Philosophy: An Introduction* (Oxford: Clarendon, 1990), 5.

62. See, for example, Susan Moller Okin, *Women in Western Political Thought* (Princeton: Princeton University Press, 1979); Ellen Kennedy and Susan Mendus, eds., *Women in Western Political Philosophy: Kant to Nietzsche* (New York: St. Martin's Press, 1987); Diana H. Coole, *Women in Political Theory: From Ancient Misogyny to Contemporary Feminism* (Boulder, Colo.: Lynne Rienner, 1988).

63. Aristotle, *Politics,* trans. T. A. Sinclair, rev. Trevor J. Saunders (1962; Harmondsworth: Penguin, 1981); Anthony Pagden, *Lords of All the World: Ideologies of Empire in Spain, Britain, and France, c. 1500–c. 1800* (New Haven: Yale University Press, 1995), chap. 1.

64. Thomas Hobbes, *Leviathan,* ed. Richard Tuck (New York: Cambridge University Press, 1991), chap. 13.

65. John Locke, *Two Treatises of Government,* ed. Peter Laslett (1960; New York: Cambridge University Press, 1988), *Second Treatise,* chap. 5.

66. Emmanuel Eze, "The Color of Reason: The Idea of 'Race' in Kant's Anthropology," in *Anthropology and the German Enlightenment: Perspectives on Humanity,* ed. Katherine M. Faull (Lewisburg, Pa.: Bucknell University Press, 1995), 196–237.

67. See, for example, "Emer de Vattel on the Occupation of Territory," in *Imperialism,* ed. Philip D. Curtin (New York: Walker, 1971), 42–45.

68. There is no space here to explore the interesting idea of Douglass as a politically divided "tragic mulatto," both resenting his rejection by his white father and seeking the consolatory embrace of the white Founding Fathers. But such an analysis would go some way to explaining Douglass's own ambivalences and conflicted divisions. As more than one commentator has pointed out, Douglass was a black leader who sometimes resented being classified as a black man; an opponent of racism who occasionally made disparaging remarks about Mexicans, Indians, and his fellow blacks; a critic of white America's treatment of its native population who nevertheless accepted the legitimacy of the settler project, and insisted that blacks (more like Europeans than Native Americans, in his opinion) have equal rights within it. See Moses, "Writing Freely?" and Martin, *Mind of Frederick Douglass,* chap. 8.

69. See, for example, Ronald Dworkin, *Taking Rights Seriously* (Cambridge: Harvard University Press, 1977) and *Law's Empire* (Cambridge: Harvard University Press, 1986).

70. Donald E. Lively, *The Constitution and Race* (New York: Praeger, 1992), 34, 33.

71. Fehrenbacher, *Dred Scott Case,* 5.

72. Unlike Douglass, contemporary black scholars have long perceived the underlying truth in Taney's decision. John Hope Franklin comments: "There is no evidence … to contradict [Taney's] reading of the status of free blacks at the time of the Declaration of Independence and the framing of the Constitution": "Race and the Constitution," 28. Derrick Bell observes that Taney's conclusion was "a view rather clearly reflecting the prevailing belief in his time as among the Founding Fathers": "The Real Costs of Racial Discrimination," in Franklin and McNeil, *Living Constitution,* 187.

73. George M. Fredrickson, *The Black Image in the White Mind: The Debate on Afro-American Character and Destiny, 1817–1914* (1971; Hanover, N.H.: Wesleyan University Press, 1987), Preface, chaps. 1–2. For a critique of the generally restrictive stipulations of Fredrickson and other like-minded American historians about the appropriateness of the use of the concept "racism," see David E. Stannard, *American Holocaust: The Conquest of the New World* (New York: Oxford University Press, 1992), 269–78.

74. For the crucial excerpts, see Emmanuel Chukwudi Eze, ed., *Race and the Enlightenment: A Reader* (Cambridge, Mass.: Blackwell, 1997), 95–103.

75. Fredrickson, *Black Image,* 1.

76. Higginbotham, *Matter of Color.*

77. Reginald Horsman, *Race and Manifest Destiny: The Origins of American Racial Anglo-Saxonism* (Cambridge: Harvard University Press, 1981).

78. Ronald Takaki, *Iron Cages: Race and Culture in 19th-Century America* (New York: Oxford University Press, 1990), chap. 1.

79. George Fredrickson, *White Supremacy: A Comparative Study in American and South African History* (New York: Oxford University Press, 1981), 145.

80. Fredrickson, *Black Image*, chap. 11.

81. Ibid., 320.

82. Alexander Saxton, *The Rise and Fall of the White Republic: Class Politics and Mass Culture in Nineteenth- Century America* (New York: Verso, 1990); Pierre van den Berghe, *Race and Racism,* 2d ed. (New York: Wiley, 1978); Myrdal, *American Dilemma;* Fredrickson, *White Supremacy.* I have included Myrdal's idea of a caste society even though Myrdal is *the* twentieth-century "anomaly" theorist. My justification is the useful point made by Stephen Steinberg: that Myrdal's framing of race primarily as a moral dilemma is flagrantly contradicted by the data in his own massive 1,000 + -page book, which make it abundantly clear that race is a matter of political economy. "Myrdal's conceptual framework placed a gloss over the raw facts.... He took facts that were potentially explosive, and he defused them by cramming them into insulated conceptual boxes," writes Steinberg in *Turning Back: The Retreat from Racial Justice in American Thought and Policy* (Boston: Beacon, 1995), 40.

83. Hochschild, *New American Dilemma*, chap. 1.

84. I do not mean that the definition of "America" cannot change; obviously it has changed considerably since the nation's founding. I mean rather that on the traditional understanding, America *is* essentially a white nation. Nor am I denying the obvious historical truth that many morally praiseworthy white Americans have opposed white racism and white supremacy, and have done so precisely in the name of national ideals. My point is simply that they have not been the majority.

85. Crenshaw et al., Introduction to *Critical Race Theory,* xxvi.

86. Gary Peller, "Race-Consciousness," ibid., 127–58.

87. "West [Indian] Emancipation," in *Douglass,* 2:437.

88. Similarly, one of the key ideas of Myrdal's *American Dilemma* is that once blacks begin to rise into the ranks of the middle class, racism will vanish, since what is keeping it alive is a naive empiricist extrapolation from the current racial division of labor. That a century and a half after Douglass's speech and half a century after Myrdal's book race is still so firmly embedded in the national white psyche that even middle-class and professional blacks continue to receive differential treatment shows the fundamental mistakenness of this analysis and its rooting in the "anomaly" view of racism. See, for example, Ellis Cose, *The Rage of a Privileged Class* (New York: HarperCollins, 1993), and Joe R. Feagin and Melvin P. Sikes, *Living with Racism: The Black Middle-Class Experience* (Boston: Beacon, 1994).

89. Fredrickson, *Black Liberation: A Comparative History of Black Ideologies in the United States and South Africa* (New York: Oxford University Press, 1995), 27–28.

90. "At Home Again," in *Douglass,* 2:126.

91. "Prejudice against Color," in *Douglass,* 2:128–29.

92. W. E. B. Du Bois, *Black Reconstruction in America, 1860–1880* (1935; New York: Atheneum, 1992).

93. See my "White Supremacy," in *A Companion to African-American Philosophy,* ed. John Pittman and Tommy Lott, (Cambridge, Mass.: Blackwell, forthcoming).

94. As previous chapters have emphasized, the findings of Kinder and Sanders's *Divided by Color* are that racial *group* interests, not individual interests, matter most to whites.

95. Reynolds Farley, "The Common Destiny of Blacks and Whites: Observations about the Social and Economic Status of the Races," in Hill and Jones, *Race in America,* 228. In the passage quoted, Farley cites Frances Fitzgerald, *Cities on a Hill: A Journey through Contemporary American Cultures* (New York: Simon & Schuster, 1986); James R. Kluegel, "If There Isn't a Problem, You Don't Need a Solution," *American Behavioral Scientist* 28 (1985), 761–85; and James R. Kluegel and Eliot R. Smith, "White Beliefs about Blacks' Opportunity," *American Sociological Review* 47 (1982), 518–32.

96. Thomas Ross, "Innocence and Affirmative Action," in Delgado, *Critical Race Theory,* 551–63.

97. See Benjamin DeMott, *The Trouble with Friendship: Why Americans Can't Think Straight about Race* (New York: Atlantic Monthly Press, 1995).

98. See, for example, Ernest Q. Campbell, "Moral Discomfort and Racial Segregation: An Examination of the Myrdal Hypothesis," *Social Forces* 39, no. 2 (December 1960), 228–34; and Frank R. Westie, "The American Dilemma: An Empirical Test," *American Sociological Review* 30 (1965), 527–38. For a discussion, see Steinberg, *Turning Back,* 61–67.

99. Stanford M. Lyman, "Race Relations as Social Process: Sociology's Resistance to a Civil Rights Orientation," in Hill and Jones, *Race in America,* 390.

100. Cheryl I. Harris, "Whiteness as Property," *Harvard Law Review* 106 (1993), 1709–91; abridged in Crenshaw et al., *Critical Race Theory,* 276–91.

101. *Griggs* is standardly seen as a juridical high point in a realistic analysis of systemic racial discrimination, because it took what Alan Freeman calls the "victim" rather than the "perpetrator" perspective, focusing on discriminatory effects rather than conscious intent. See Alan David Freeman, "Legitimizing Racial Discrimination through Antidiscrimination Law: A Critical Review of Supreme Court Doctrine," in Crenshaw et al., *Critical Race Theory,* 29–46. In the years since 1971, *Griggs* has been eviscerated.

102. Chambers, "Afterword," in Franklin and McNeil, *Living Constitution,* 325.

103. Derrick A. Bell Jr., "*Brown* v. *Board of Education* and the Interest Convergence Dilemma," abridged in Crenshaw et al., *Critical Race Theory,* 20–29.

104. Mary L. Dudziak, "Desegregation as a Cold War Imperative," *Stanford Law Review* 41 (1988), 61–120, abridged in Delgado, *Critical Race Theory,* 110–21.

105. Sunstein, *Partial Constitution.*

106. Lively, *Constitution and Race,* 174.

107. However, William Julius Wilson's *When Work Disappears: The World of the New Urban Poor* (New York: Knopf, 1996) shows that there is little reason to expect such a shortage. For inner-city blacks, higher unemployment is a more likely development.

108. See, for example, Jennifer Welchman, "Locke on Slavery and Inalienable Rights," *Canadian Journal of Philosophy* 25 (1995), 67–81.

Index